PETER KING

FOREWORD BY BILL WALSH

SIMON & SCHUSTER
NEW YORK   LONDON   TORONTO
SYDNEY   TOKYO   SINGAPORE

Inside the Helmet

A PLAYER'S-EYE VIEW OF THE NFL

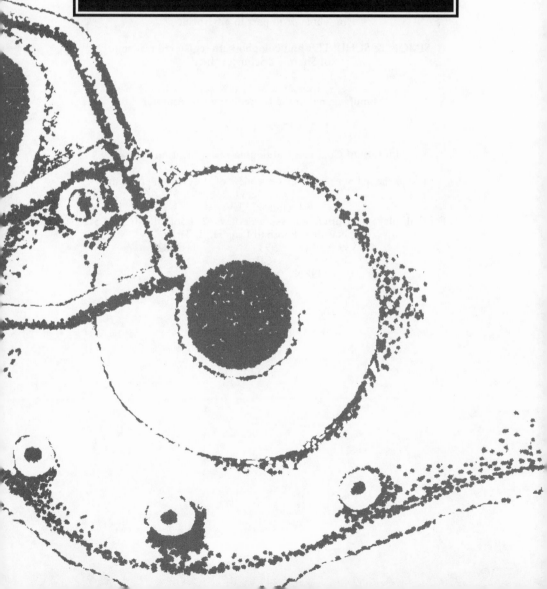

SIMON & SCHUSTER
Simon & Schuster Building
Rockefeller Center
1230 Avenue of the Americas
New York, New York 10020

Designed by H.J. Kim
Manufactured in the United States of America

1 3 5 7 9 10 8 6 4 2

Library of Congress Cataloging-in-Publication Data
King, Peter, date.
Inside the helmet : a player's-eye view of the NFL / Peter King.
p.   cm.
Includes Index.
1. Football players—United States—Interviews 2. Football—United States.
3. National Football League. I. Title.
GV939.A1K48   1993   93-25827
CIP
ISBN 0-671-74704-5

For Ann, my best friend

Acknowlegments

Foremost, I'd like to thank Boomer Esiason, Jimmy Johnson, Bruce Smith, Haywood Jeffires, Rod Woodson, Ernest Givins, Barry Sanders, Johnny Holland, Steve Tasker, Sean Landeta, Reyna Thompson, Dante Scarnecchia, Mel Gray, Sam Anno, and Rohn Stark for being excellent and cooperative subjects.

In addition, the following people helped me enormously: Steve Sabol and his crew at NFL Films, Cheryl Esiason, Sam Wyche, Rich Dalrymple, Michael Irvin, Albert Lewis, Dave Wannstedt, Chris Palmer, Kevin Gilbride, Chip Namias, Bill Keenist, Mike Murray, Dan Henning, Darryl Talley, Scott Berchtold, Pat Hanlon, Bill Johnston, Craig Kelley, Bill Walsh, Sid Gillman, Charles Barkley, Dave Levy, Floyd Peters, Ed Bouchette, Mike Silver, Ricky Watters, and John Teerlinck.

My wife, Ann, and daughters, Laura and Mary Beth, were saints for giving me the time and support to do this.

My editor at Simon & Schuster, Jeff Neuman, was a saint for being so patient with me, and brilliant in giving the book the direction it needed.

And, finally, my book agent, David Black, should take a bow, or some brickbats. Without him, I'd never be writing books.

Contents

Foreword

Football is detail work. It's teaching. People in baseball may disagree, but I think football is the real thinking person's game, and I think that's what you'll see in this book. Coaches and players know that today, but that's not how it used to be. I'd like to think that my coaching successes have had some effect in changing the image.

Intelligence was never something I thought much about until I started getting passed up for head coaching jobs in the seventies. The Bengals passed me over when Paul Brown retired, and I lost out when the Rams changed coaches too. After missing out on some of these jobs, I became alerted to an overriding thought around the league about me: I would be good in the laboratory, but I'd never be enough of a taskmaster to be a good head coach. Owners wanted someone who'd yell and scream and whip their players into submission, but I don't believe that's how to coach. I think you have to treat players intelligently. Sometimes you have to threaten players, and discipline them, and yell at them. But my approach is to teach, because players need to be prepared mentally to play the sophisticated football of the nineties.

If there's one thing that frustrates me a little bit about fans and the media, it's that they really don't—and they can't—grasp the mind-boggling and painstaking detail that goes into a football game. When things go wrong, they lash out. That's their right, certainly. But I wish they could step back sometimes and look at a play that's gone awry and say, "Why didn't that work?" They need to understand the detail.

I remember going down to San Diego to play a preseason game when I was coaching the running backs for the Raiders in 1966. Before leaving the hotel, I was sitting in my room flipping around the TV dial and I stopped to watch Sid Gillman, the Chargers' coach, on his show, running his game films. He was teaching the game to the viewers at home.

It may sound funny, but it was fascinating watching something as simple as the slant pattern that day. Sid, whom I regarded as a brilliant coach in every phase, went into the minute details of the slant pattern, how it had to be coached and how it had to be run by the receiver. Then you watched the Chargers and discovered how well they ran it, and you knew it had to have been coached brilliantly for them to run it that well. Details. That's when I knew how important every single detail was in football.

That was a revelation to me. And the longer you're in the game, the more you see how significant the details and the teaching and education are. Everyone knows that the quarterback is the brain center of a football team, but few people know what that means and what it entails. Here, one of the game's smartest quarterbacks, Boomer Esiason, brings you into his football life for a week and shows you. I don't know that a quarterback has ever laid open his life, in battle and in study, the way Esiason does here. The same is true about the other positions covered in this book.

As a coach, I know I have to start with smart players. It might not have been so important in past eras, but today we're asking players to do so much and to know so many schemes. Without basic intelligence, they simply can't play. And if they're not just plain smart, they're not going to be able to do the things a sophisticated coach is going to ask. With the speed on the field today, their technique and knowledge of what they have to do has to be keen or they'll get buried. A player like Bill Ring of the 49ers, who wasn't physically gifted, was a great contributor, despite his lack of speed and size and quickness, because he was a tremendous student of the game.

Foreword

As you'll see in this book, intelligent players have an infinitely better chance to succeed. On offense, they have to cope more and more with things like the no-huddle and quick snaps. In a few years, who knows? Maybe there won't be huddles. On defense, they have to cope with different schemes and all the substitution. When I look for players now, even at Stanford, I can rule out a lot of people fast. They have to have above-average intelligence combined with the ability to function under stress.

Peter King is one of the few writers I know who can put football, the real thinking person's game, into worthy words. In *Inside the Helmet,* he's managed to take the complexities of the game and the best players in the game and show how rich a sport it is, for the mind as well as the body. You will come away from the book knowing what football is really about.

Bill Walsh
Palo Alto, California

Introduction

Football is simple in about one in a hundred plays. A left tackle slips and falls, and the quarterback gets sacked. A cornerback gets decked at the line of scrimmage, and the wide receiver beats him for a long touchdown pass.

Football is hard the rest of the time. The maddening thing for me, as a football writer, is how simplistic many people make the game out to be. Boomer Esiason had a dreadful year in 1992; he's thirty-two now, his mechanics are messed up, and he's not throwing the deep ball like he used to. Ergo, he's finished. Jerry Rice beats Charles Dimry for four or five touchdowns one Sunday in Atlanta. Ergo, Dimry's a worthless corner who ought to be pumping gas somewhere. Well, I don't think it's that simple.

Esaison might be washed up, but how can we know for sure when his offensive line has been in tatters for two years, his top receiver, Eddie Brown, misses 1992 with a neck injury, and his coaching staff can't decide on an offensive philosophy? And Dimry might stink as a man-to-man corner because he's not fast enough to play it, but in zone and nickel situations isn't he a disciplined player with an instinctive nose for the ball? So don't go telling me Esiason and Dimry are done. I don't buy it. Tell me what the scouts and the coaches and the teammates say, and show me the film, and then let me draw my own conclusions.

The same is true with big plays in a game. A team loses, and the fans want to know: Whose fault was it? Well, there are probably six or twelve or fourteen people at fault—players, coaches, pushy agents. A team goes down the tubes and watch, the fans and the press and the pundits will finger one guy. The Jets in 1992? Bruce Coslet, the coach, screwed up the season. The Bills in the last couple of Super Bowls? Jim Kelly, the quarterback, took the pipe. He's the goat.

I've thought for some time that in these attempts to simplify the game we do football a disservice. Football is the real thinking person's sport in America, not baseball. I'm a Rotisserie nerd, and I love baseball. But if I read one more treatise on how much thought it takes Tony LaRussa and Dave Duncan to figure how to pitch Wade Boggs, I'm going to puke. It takes two or three days of film study and arguing in coaches' meetings for Dave Wannstedt to figure out how he's going to defend Barry Sanders. The essence of baseball is one on one. The essence of football is eleven on eleven. "You're talking basic math compared to physics when you talk baseball compared to football," my friend Billy Ard, the former Giants guard, says. "I'm surprised nobody's ever tried to make the complexity of football understandable."

That's why I set out to write this book. How does a quarterback really prepare for a game? How does a running back know which hole to pick? How does a coach get his team ready? What strange language do these guys speak that keeps all the rest of us on the other side of some football-knowledge line of demarcation? I wrote this book to translate, in human and literate terms, football in the nineties into a voice real people can understand, and to give the game a depth it deserves. I wrote this book to take you inside the helmet.

To do this book, I needed players and a coach to be free with their thoughts and their time. They couldn't be just any people. They had to be cornerstone-of-the-game people. Jimmy Johnson said yes. Bruce Smith said yes. Barry Sanders said yes, and Haywood Jeffires, as did Rod Woodson, Boomer Esiason, Steve Tasker, and the league's best special-teams players. I had to see the 185 pages of game plan and preparation that Esiason sees every week, beginning Tuesday night when the fax machine in his house starts spitting it out; he let me. I had to hear Johnson give the Cowboys his set-the-tone-for-the-week speech; he let me. I had to watch Sanders run on videotape and listen to his stream of consciousness on what he sees when he runs; he let me.

To those men I'm appreciative, because I feel educated about football today. And I hope you are, because they're giving you a slice of the real thinking person's game.

The Quarterback

IN THE EYE OF THE STORM

It's another pleasant valley off-day for Boomer Esiason, the quarterback of the Cincinnati Bengals. He's deep in the heart of his northern Kentucky backyard, at his built-in brick grill, turning the chicken. Life is good here; there's a lake, deep and blue, down at the end of the property, and a long built-in pool with lots of twists and turns, and the prettiest yard north of the Augusta National Golf Club.

It is where a quarterback should live, this place: the best. The Quarterback House. (And it's where he'll live in the off-season now anyway, even after his March 1993 trade from the Bengals to the New York Jets.) A twenty-three-room wood-frame house, with sixteen skylights, four beers on tap, and a 35-inch color TV in the bedroom. In the new family room, still under construction, Esiason will have one of those digital green sports tickers high on one wall, the kind sports bars use to give the latest scores around the clock.

Esiason tends to the chicken. He's talking baseball. In high school, back on Long Island, he went 15–0 as a varsity pitcher, and he often wonders what might have been if he didn't take the football scholarship to Maryland. He wants to go down to Riverfront Stadium one day and get on the mound during batting practice. He wants to face the Reds. He'd love to be sixty feet, six inches away from Barry Larkin, to stare in at him and fire.

"I'd try to outsmart him," Esiason says. "He'd be expecting

fastballs. He'd be thinking I'd want to prove how hard I could throw, and he'd be looking fastball all the way."

"Right," I say, "so here's what you'd do: First pitch, straight change. About seventy-two miles an hour. And there's no way he'd be ready for that. Strike one."

"Nope," Esiason says. His eyes are steely. "I'd buzz him. First pitch, I'd throw it right at his head. That'd get him thinking, wouldn't it?"

The food is ready and we sit down, me and Esiason and his wife, Cheryl. He finishes describing how he'd strike out Larkin and turns his attention to the question of the evening: What makes an NFL quarterback? "There's something that you have to have," he says, searching for the right words, "something . . . something competitive . . ." and his voice trails off.

But he's already answered the question. You have to have the confidence to buzz Barry Larkin and the certainty to know you'll strike him out even if you haven't pitched since high school. That's what you have to have.

There are people who love power and authority: politicians, police chiefs, coaches, CEOs, drill sergeants. Quarterbacks are as powerful and commanding as any of them; the good ones, anyway. They don't show it much off the field, but they ooze it once they step onto it. Esiason is one of the boldest. In a 1991 preseason game against Green Bay, the offense was struggling, and Esiason laid into his teammates in the huddle. "What the hell are you guys doing?! You're making these guys look like Ray Nitschke and Willie Wood out here!" *In a preseason game.*

He is a striking figure, even here in The Quarterback House. Born Norman Julius Esiason in East Islip, New York, in 1961 to parents of Scandinavian descent, he's grown to be a formidable six-foot-four, 218 pounds, with bright blond, almost white, hair, combed back on his large head. The name Boomer comes from his punting his late mom in the womb during the pregnancy; he was intense even then. Today he has bright eyes that focus on you and don't let go. You notice their intensity even during simple things. He'll be driving, or playing Ping-Pong, and then his eyes will narrow for a split second before he slams the ball down your throat. Whatever he's doing, he takes command.

On Sunday at 1:00, he is the focus of an entire city, and often a state and region. For three or four hours, he can control people's emotions and affect their lives. It's more power than even a great pitcher has, because there are so many more baseball games in a season. A football game is a much bigger event, happening only once a week and only in the fall. When a city looks to a football team for mental relief in the wake of bad economic times, like Pittsburgh in the seventies or Buffalo in the nineties, a quarterback has a tremendous amount of power, and if he doesn't accept it or get used to it, it will destroy him. "It almost scares me, the effect we have on how people feel in Pittsburgh on Mondays in the fall," Steelers president Dan Rooney said. "I'm telling you, you can go into downtown Pittsburgh on Monday and tell from the people whether we've won or lost the previous day."

A mayor doesn't have that kind of power, not with any consistency. Nor, for that matter, does a president, not very often anyway. But a football team does. Its quarterback does.

"Quarterback is the hardest position in American sports," Esiason says. "But it's what everybody wants to be, you know what I'm saying? There's so much power in it. You control everybody out there. You're the focus of so many people's lives, different from any other position in any other sport. And there's only twenty-eight of 'em starting in the NFL. To be one of the top seven or eight, it's a head rush, ain't it?

"It's the greatest job anybody could ever want. All the pressure, the excitement, the power, the fun, the struggle—it's all rolled up into one. It's the highest of highs. The challenge of a pro or college or high school football game is taking your offense and taking what you've learned and applying it to a defense that is just trying to kick your ass. I mean, there is nothing as straining and ferocious and volatile as one play in one football game.

"Quarterback isn't the only tough position. If you're a cornerback, you're one-on-one, running backward against some of the finest athletes in the world. If you're an offensive lineman, you're on the defensive against the Bruce Smiths, the Reggie

Whites, big, heavy guys. But the quarterback has to be able to just sit in there, not only on the field but off the field and take everything that comes with it. Everything. You have to just roll with the sacks and the touchdowns and the wins and the losses, and you have to stay on an even keel, you know what I'm saying? Because the game is always changing around you and the defenses are always changing what they try to do to you.

"The even keel is so important, because I think my team takes on my personality. If I'm down, they're down. If I'm up and laughing in the locker room, I think they see it's okay to laugh. If they see me joke around when the head coach is talking, they know it's okay to be loose. That's some serious stuff. But you know that's the way I like it to be. I'm under the microscope, and I wouldn't want it any other way."

"If you had another job in the NFL," I ask in the kitchen of The Quarterback House, "would you be happy?"

"I'd hate it," he says.

"He has to be the general, you know," Cheryl says. "Stormin' Norman, that's him."

"Patton's my main man," Esiason says.

Of course, the field general. Gary Danielson, the former Detroit and Cleveland quarterback, now a TV analyst, is one of the best at talking about this aspect of the job. "Playing quarterback," he says, "is like conducting a symphony orchestra while playing an instrument. No one understands. No one can understand. But the great ones have a trait I don't think I ever had. Boomer has it some, I think. The great quarterbacks never think they played bad. They believe in themselves so much, and it's so dog-eat-dog to get to that level. They have to believe they're great. Even the ones that don't express it outwardly, they feel it."

This commanding presence under pressure is a factor, but there are other, more important, factors too. They haven't changed very much over the years, at least according to the leading quarterbacking doctor of yesterday, the legendary Sid Gillman, and one of today, Green Bay coach Mike Holmgren.

Gillman is eighty-one. He has designed offenses for seven teams in the American, National, and United States Football

Leagues. He is still employed by five NFL teams as an offensive consultant. They send him game tapes, he sends back his opinions; ask him for an opinion and you'll always get one.

Holmgren is forty-five. In 1992, he fell off the Bill Walsh tree into the northern Wisconsin tundra, along with GM Ron Wolf, to salvage the Packers. A thoughtful, quiet man, Holmgren knows the passing game as well as anyone in the NFL right now.

Gillman believes in a downfield passing style, like the Raiders play. Holmgren likes the controlled passing game. But they look for the same things in a quarterback.

Gillman's list:

1. *Arm strength.* "I want him to be able to throw the ball long and throw it short with touch, but he has to be able to drill the goddamn ball."
2. *Consistent accuracy.*
3. *Football intelligence and anticipation.* "Defenses are so complicated with so many players now that coaches walk up and down the sidelines with six situation subs trailing them. A quarterback has to read coverages and know exactly when and where to throw the ball, now more than ever before."
4. *Mobility.* "You don't have to move like Steve Young. Norm Van Brocklin was one of the greatest quarterbacks ever, and I could beat him in a sprint. You just have to be able to move when those big horses are chasing you."
5. *Guts.* "Mentally and physically, you've got to be ready to take it. You set up seven yards behind a line, and if there are missed blocks, you're a sitting target. You've got people trying to kill you. You've got to be able to make split-second decisions under the threat of getting killed."

Holmgren's list:

1. *An accurate arm.* "I used to think it was arm strength, but the quarterbacks I had at San Francisco—Montana, Young, Bono—were obviously very good without having exceptional arm strength."

2. *Reasonable arm strength.* "You can't play in the NFL without it. If he has reasonable arm strength today, a quarterback can be exceptional."

3. *Football intelligence.* "Not a 4.0 student. I'm talking about being football smart, about looking at a play and knowing why and how it happened, about being able to stand at the line and know what to call with the whole world screaming at you."

4. *Mobility.* "You have to be able to run for first downs today with so many breakdowns due to the increased pass rush we're seeing."

5. *Courage.* "The great guys—Montana, Marino, Esiason—might say they don't think about getting hit, but that's BS. They think about it all the time. But they can block it out. They can make important, pressurized decisions knowing they could get seriously hurt on any play."

Asked to expand on what it takes to be an NFL quarterback, Holmgren has definite thoughts. "First of all, it's an incredible athletic feat. There's so much happening around you, and you have to throw the ball through and over very big people to an exact target that might be thirty or forty yards away. And you have about 1.5 seconds to make your final decision and make your throw, every time you choose to pass. There's more to it. It's not just a decision anybody can make. It's a decision you have to study for and practice for, day after day after day. You have to know exactly what every player on your team is supposed to do on every play, so you don't run into somebody or some receiver doesn't run the wrong way.

"And the thought process of making a decision is so involved. Say you want to learn Chinese. You go to a class and learn it over a period of years, and you practice speaking it, and pretty soon, after a few years, you can speak Chinese fairly well. Imagine trying to learn something as difficult, an entire system of plays, and taking the knowledge and making decisions on what to call and where to throw, all within split seconds, and doing it with people running at you trying to knock your ass off. I don't think there's any comparison except in auto racing, where drivers have to make split-second decisions that could cost them their lives.

"You've got to be so strong mentally to make it. As soon as the ball is snapped, the violence and the sheer noise—I'm not talking about crowd noise, because players get immune to that; I'm talking about the noise of pads and bodies hitting each other—make it so hard to make an intelligent, quick decision."

Gillman loves Esiason, calling him the most nearly perfect quarterback technically in the game. "The way he steps back in the pocket, exactly the number of steps he should, not stutter-stepping so he's in a different spot every time, makes it easy to build an offense around him. You know where he'll be. His mechanics of throwing are good. He makes good decisions. He's the type of quarterback I wish I could have coached sometime."

Quarterbacks are always front and center, even when they don't want to be. It's the nature of the job. In 1988, the Bengals, behind NFL Most Valuable Player Esiason, went to the Super Bowl and nearly beat the dynastic 49ers. On the other side, in 1987 Esiason, the club's player representative, had to lead his players in a strike he never thought was the right thing. "I had to represent the will of the players," he said. So he played labor leader like he plays quarterback. He loaned money to teammates who never paid him back, and he got hit in the head by a quarter thrown during a strike rally. "In 1987," he said, "I was called a scumbag, and worse. In 1988, those same people are cheering for me. Funny business."

Quarterbacks have to be able to take the crap and take the nice things and come out the next day and want to be a great player, no matter what winds buffet their personal or professional life.

"I think a lot of it has to do with how competitive a person you are," Esiason said. "If you're not a competitive person, you're not going to be in this game very long, because it's such a nasty game."

"When," Esiason was asked, "did you realize how competitive you were?"

"Early," he said. "When I was six."

When little Boomer was six, growing up on Long Island, his dad took him to a Rangers game at Madison Square Garden. They had great seats—in the corner, front row—and wide-eyed Boomer had his face pressed up against the glass all night. During the game, there was a fight in front of him, and he started banging the Plexiglas and screaming as loud as he could for blood and havoc and for the Rangers to beat up the other guys.

Jim Kelly and Phil Simms and Dan Marino can tell stories like this. Quarterbacks might be the pretty boys, but look at them closely and you'll see the scars. They fought, most of them anyway, to get where they are. Quarterbacks are not grown in Suburbia USA, with no hardship. There's got to be a hard edge to the early life of a quarterback.

"I believe that, totally," Esiason said. "For a long time, I've said that a lot has to do with the way you're brought up and the systems you play. I'll never forget in high school when my coach, Sal Ciampi, made us all do the Who Wants It drill. The Who Wants It drill is you and an offensive lineman against a defensive lineman and a linebacker or safety. And you've got to get around the block and then it's you against the guy tackling you. What a balls-out drill. That was the big thing at East Islip High School. Forget the game. How'd you do in the Who Wants It drill? The next day in school, you could go back and say, 'Hey, I kicked ass in the Who Wants It drill.' Because in that drill, you have to fight past the blockers at the line and fight the defensive guy who's trying to kill you."

Fighting. That's another Esiason thing. It happened most weekends of his East Islip adolescence. Once, when he was sixteen, Esiason had to set the broken nose of a friend, Eddie Yankus. "I cupped my hands around his nose and *crack!* I snapped it back in there. Then we went back out and partied the rest of the night," he said.

What is it about good quarterbacks that makes them so much different?

"This is going to sound corny, but it's desire. You've got to have the attitude like, 'I'm the friggin' best at what I do, and I don't give a damn what anybody says to me or does to me, because it's not going to shake that. I'm going to achieve and I'm going to be the best quarterback.' Probably the greatest thing that ever happened to me was not being born with a silver spoon in my mouth."

The most important element of a quarterback, Esiason believes, is mental toughness. Assume, of course, you can throw a football first. "You've got to be able to handle all the things that go along with the job. I don't just mean the bad things. I mean the MVP awards, the good things when your team's on a roll. You've got to be able to handle that, too. One thing about football: It's a very unforgiving sport. It can ruin you, all in one day. When you make it, season after season, and build up a reputation, you still feel like it can be gone in a day. It's that fragile. So you have to be able to mentally handle the good and bad, especially at this position because there isn't one in professional sports where you're under the microscope as much.

"The second ingredient, I think, is this: You have to hate losing. It's got to tear you up. I can't sleep well Sunday night or Monday night after a loss. I can't watch the Monday night game and go to sleep like a lot of players do because . . . well, I just can't. Losing has to eat at you inside, make you sick to your stomach, feel like somebody's just died. A baseball player, he can lose fifty times a year and still be on the team with the best record. I don't think I could handle losing fifty times. You've just got to hate to lose. And you've got to set the example for the rest of the team, I think. I guess you've got to realize where you fit into your ball club. Usually a quarterback is one of the leaders. He should be. Everywhere I've been, whether it's in high school, college, or here in Cincinnati, it's been the same way. I've set the example. If I set the example after a loss that it's okay to come in the next week and nothing's wrong, everything's okay, then everybody will follow that."

To enter the life of a quarterback, imagine this: You are walking down the main street of your town, and everything—the hardware store, the 7-Eleven, the realtor, the supermarket—is the same as you've always imagined, and then, as you cross the block, suddenly Main Street turns into Mainstrasse. The bakery looks like a bakery except you can't read the writing on the storefront because it's in a foreign language, and everybody inside the bakery speaks that foreign language. You recognize the bread and the smell and the people. You just can't understand them.

Every autumn Monday, Wednesday, Thursday, Friday, and Saturday morning about 8:00, Boomer Esiason drinks some orange juice, scans the local paper and *USA Today* to dig up the latest printable dirt, kisses Cheryl and the two babies, puts some Huey Lewis or Mariah Carey in the CD player of his Jeep Cherokee, and drives eighteen minutes to this different world. For the last nine years, he could find this world on Cincinnati's dingy and smelly near west side, under a viaduct, hard by railroad tracks that carry coal from the south and cars from the north. (As a NY Jet, the destination will change, but the routine will be the same.) The oasis in the midst of this grimy infrastructure is called Spinney Field, and the Cincinnati Bengals train here. There are fields of AstroTurf and grass for practice, ringed by evergreen trees planted some years ago to make the place look a little nicer. In fact, it doesn't look very nice at all. "It's everything that pro football shouldn't be," Esiason said. "It's in a grimy part of town with terrible air, with really mediocre facilities for a pro football team. But I love it down here. You're with the fellas, and you're literally a man's man down here." It is where the Bengals practice every day, trying to win their first NFL championship ever.

Adjacent to the fields is what looks like a giant metal Sears shed. The Bengals meet and plot strategy, dress and lift weights in here. It's in here that you start to realize you're in one of the twenty-eight foreign lands of the National Football League.

It's funny to listen to the transformation in Esiason from the outside world to the footballspeak world. On a September Wednesday in 1991, he drove into the parking lot at 8:20 A.M., talking about his father, who raised Boomer as a single parent; Boomer's mom died when he was nine.

Walking from the Jeep to the front door of the office shed, Esiason said, "Not having a mother, not having that parental direction, can really screw you up. Somehow I turned out all right. I think I did because I shared a lot of things with my dad. He was pretty cool, my dad. Hey, I screwed up, and he'd discipline me not with the whip or a smack or a hit, but mentally. You know, he'd say, 'You really let me down.' That had more effect on me."

Once in the front door, the footballspeak began. Wafting out of the third office on the left, offensive line coach Jim McNally was already telling one of his guys, "On the 19 call, we said Anthony would take a big split if it was a key fumble-type deal, to see if he could get this guy to lighten himself . . ."

The Bengals' inner world looks normal enough. The people are friendly, particularly the coaching secretary, Sandy Schick, in the second office to the left, and McNally. But most people in the building speak that weird footballspeak, and it is soon easy to see why people out there in the real world can't understand much of what really happens in a football game. That sounds pompous, but you have to hear the voices, and see the days, to know what a different world this is.

At 8:30, Esiason goes into a quarterback meeting in the head coach's office with his two backups, Donald Hollas and Erik Wilhelm—both blond, both six-four, both looking like Esiason wannabes—head coach Sam Wyche, and quarterback coach Dana Bible. (When Wyche was dismissed as Cincinnati coach after the '91 season, David Shula replaced him, but the same schedule, routine, and terminology were maintained for the quarterbacks.)

On Tuesday evening, the coaches had faxed Esiason that week's game plan so he could study it and come into this meeting prepared. The pace is quick. The three quarterbacks sit in chairs with pull-over desktops; Wyche, who is standing, moves quickly around a board, marking plays with Magic Markers, making additions and adjustments to the game plan.

"Let's go to the updates," Wyche said. "Add 84 and 85 comeback, and maybe even better in some ways is the 76 single and tag and X or Z. You're still going to get your look down the middle, you're going to get your jolly down the shooter, and you kind of play for the comeback, looking down the middle after you hit the . . . Well, you're looking to see which safety is doing the reaction comeback to the inside. At least you get an option. The thing about the 84 and 85 is you get more protection, but

I'm not sure we don't just clog things up, since we don't do it as a steady diet. You get an extra guy in there, but he gets stuck in your way. The only other option there, Boomer, is that rather than call the 84 and 85 comeback is to tell one of the backs—or a true comeback—to say 84 Come Babe. And then turn around and throw JB flat. You know: CHECK! YOU'VE GOT 84! CHECK THE BACKER! And get out there and control that corner. You've still got to have the middle read. You're giving up the jolly in the middle, so you're not going to have that control, but you're going to control to the comeback side. As I've just talked through that . . . let's see . . . yeah, that's probably the best of all worlds there. Either to the single—did I say double?—I meant to say single . . ."

"No, you said single," Esiason said.

Wyche: "Or, come off the 84 and 85 Come-Babe, but tell the back to the side you think you're going there. Just say screw it and go back. Splat. Or off of your single or pick one of the other guys and tag him. You drop the 18 or 19 nothing from triple hook and . . ."

Esiason: "Ah, this is the 77 part we're talking about."

Wyche: "That's right, 76 from this list. It says 76 or 7, but only 76 dover . . . Okay, we have this on the board. Gringo. In between series, we're sitting on the bench. We'll say all right, we're going to set alert pro. Set alert pro or strong set alert. Let's say we go to pro set alert. Right? They're going to come up and if you say 'Right, right, right, flip it, flip it,' they're going to pro right flip."

Esiason: " 'Cause you can run all of these with the flip."

Wyche: "Correct. And if you come to the line, you can say, 'Right, right, right, Tom, Tom, Tom, Kenny Anderson, Kenny Anderson, Kenny Anderson.' "

A little bit later.

Wyche: "Okay, we're going to go through an adjustment here and make sure we're square on it. The boss back. All right, a little wrinkle here. Drug slat jolly single. Those are probably our three best passes anyway, so we're in good shape there. This one is run from triple flip, where we can run it from strong flip half-back cheats. JB knows that. Always slips, so you'd be a right,

right, right, flip, flip, flip, Yogi yard. You know it's so easy for us to go right foot, right foot, JB, triple, triple, triple. Correct?"

Esiason: "No problem. You want to run this?"

Wyche: "Cheater, triple. The double he just cheats up. He's going to be in the trips."

This is just nuts, I tell Esiason later. It's Russian with no interpreter. He laughed. "Give me a play," I said. "Take me into your mind on a play, from start to finish."

"All right," he said. "Second and seven at the Washington 25. And the formation is signaled in from the sidelines: Strong, flip, check. What I'm being told is to put the backs 'strong' toward the tight end; 'flip' puts both wide receivers opposite the tight end in a slot formation; 'change' means James Brooks lines up right behind me as a running back, with Eric Ball, the fullback, behind the tight end. I get up to the line of scrimmage and see the Redskins are playing a 45 defense. That's four defensive linemen, one each over each guard and tackle, no one over the center, with two linebackers in the middle and the outside strong linebacker lined up right over the tight end. They've got a 45 defense, and I've got a run check on. Meaning we have a strong right formation on and do we want to run strong side, over the tight end, against their defense, or do we want to audible? The defense they have, we want to run weak side against, because they're heavy against our tight end."

"So it's your decision whether to run strong or weak side?" I said.

"Right," he said. "So I yell out at the line: 'Strong right foot, strong right foot, run check, run check, move it, move it.' So they move it. When I say move it, they move it to their formation. And I'll give them a snap count, 200, meaning the ball gets snapped on two. So now I get up there to see what we have, and I call the play right there. I'll say, 'Dallas auto switch, Dallas auto switch.' Dallas meaning left—L, the L sound, meaning left—auto switch meaning it's a counter play back to the weak side. Auto means weak side counter, switch tells the guard that's pulling, and the back is running up inside. So I'm yelling 'Strong right flip, strong right flip, run check, run check, 200, 200, move

it, move it, Dallas auto switch, Dallas auto switch.' "

I'm starting to understand this. But Esiason starts smiling now, because this is too easy. Something is happening on defense.

"The Redskins like to shift, and from the 45, they go right into the 46 look, the old Bear defense. And the forty-five-second clock is ticking down, and I don't have much time to get the play off, and we're inside the red zone [their 30-yard line and in], second and seven, and I'm thinking all of a sudden, 'This is their blitz down. They're coming.' So I've got to think of my blitz audibles. I'm in flip formation, I'm in strong backs, they're running eight men up to the line of scrimmage, they're coming.

"I go, in a hurry, '2-80, 2 zulu, 2-80, 2 zulu, check 95, check 95, green, green, green! Everybody got it?!' They got it. What we're going to try to do is hit James Brooks on a wide flare to the strong side, thinking Rodney Holman, the tight end, can get out and kind of wall off the inside linebacker who's man to man on James Brooks.

"All of what I just told you has to get done in forty seconds. Max."

He went on. "Sam used to tell us that the most important time in a football game is the seven seconds between the time you call the play and the time you get to the line of scrimmage. He'd tell us to rehearse in our own minds what we were going to do on the play. It's much like a shortstop. He's supposed to say to himself, 'Okay, first and third, one out, if the ball's hit to me, what do I do with it?' But now, because we call so many plays at the line of scrimmage, that's been taken away. We might have that much time to think about the play sometimes, and sometimes we don't. Sometimes it's a lot quicker than that.

"And sometimes, when their defense changes, you don't have the right people in the game to make the right audible call. Maybe there's a whole new crew of players on their way in, and we don't have a flanker in there, we have a tight end. And the right blitz audible to call is '3-76, 3-76,' and the other tight end doesn't know how to run that particular route. I don't have the flanker in there, but I really need the flanker. And the clock's going down, and I've got to get the play off in a few seconds, and I

32

still don't have the right people to run the audible I've called. So I call, in a hurry, '3-76, 2-78,' and I turn around to scream over the crowd noise to the fullback: 'Eric, move up! Run a hitch!' "

"My head's spinning," I said.

"That's why you have to know every play, every audible, every code word, every single nuance of the game plan, because 60,000 people will be screaming, with three or four million more watching on TV, with every eye on you, and coaches, officials, players all waiting for you, and you hardly being able to hear anything, and the clock ticking down second by second. I have to get every player in the exact right position with all these things going on around me. The one with the coolest head survives. The one with the coolest head wins. He's cool-headed because he prepares, is what I believe. I mean, you just can't walk up to the line and start yelling out, 'Strong, right, zipper, cowboy, trigger, bush, bo, bo, bo, bo, bo, move it, check. Uh-oh! Check pirate, check pirate, check pirate, check Andy cal, no motion, no motion, Ralph it, Ralph it, Ralph it!' You've got to know what you're doing. It takes years to master it. It took me two and a half years to feel totally comfortable in this stuff.

"Now, I love it."

The meeting went on for about forty-five minutes, each sentence as strange and unintelligible as the one before it. At 9:30, the entire team met, and Esiason joined the other fifty or so players in the team meeting room in the middle of the complex. Since the Bengals have just opened their season with three straight losses, Wyche was somber in his three-minute tone-setting speech. "I still believe in this team," he said. "We're working our butts off, and everyone in this room knows it. Don't ever accept losing. Just so you know: I personally think—and the staff thinks too—that we can win this ball game. To do that, nobody cuts a corner. Nobody throw in the towel. We all work together, and we win. Now let's go."

At last, somebody speaks some English. Football cliché English, but English nonetheless.

That's it for a while, though. More footballspeak follows. Each position group went into meetings with individual coaches.

In the room next door to Wyche's, offensive linemen are meeting with McNally. They're watching film of that week's opposition, the Redskins, and game-planning.

"If you see triple single, tell Boomer in the huddle, just tell him to keep coming to this thing right here," says McNally. "There's nobody else. The next guy to come is a free safety. The back's got a crease. Now, we've got 38 counter switch, right. This is the defensive tackle. The technique he's going to use on him is cross-flip. See the head across the bottom? That's an Ozzie call. If you get it, Vern, great. Remember, Ozzie means the big man's outside, and we're going to turn you loose on the outside guy. Now here's the most important thing. If he comes upfield, we can't trap him, we've got to hold or adjust him.

"Okay, we've got a 19 call," McNally continued. "Anthony will take a big split if it's a T-bubble type deal. Remember, Anth, versus this kind of a look, if you have to tighten down to Vern, okay. This is a good look at a rake. When in doubt, drop-step."

After the meeting broke up, I asked McNally to translate that last little piece of footballspeak. Here goes: The 19 call is a running play the Bengals would use against Washington's base defense. Anthony is Cincinnati left tackle Anthony Munoz. McNally wants Munoz to take a big split—to line up a foot or so farther away from left guard Bruce (Vern) Reimers than he normally would—if he has a linebacker across the line from him in a T-bubble, which is the Bengals' term for the linebacker playing the tackle soft, or a couple of yards off the line. The play the Bengals are watching on tape, however, shows the linebacker across from Munoz but close to the line of scrimmage, in which case, McNally tells Munoz, he can cut the gap between himself and Reimers. The rake is a blocking technique in which Munoz tries to knock Reimers's man off balance before taking on his own man. When Munoz drop-steps, he moves his right foot back, to better position himself for a rake block.

"Got that?" McNally said. "Test tomorrow. And tomorrow, you'd better know what a Gilligan means."

"Huh?" I said.

"That's our term for putting linemen out on an island," McNally said.

Every one of these terms had some real-world meaning. There's a pass route called "Moochie," and it's named after Mike "Moochie" Martin, a former Cincinnati receiver who used to run it well. Just this week, Wyche was looking for a name for a running play with the number sixty-one in it. He settled on Mantle. Esiason told him, "Hey, Mantle never hit sixty-one home runs. That was Roger Maris. Let's call it Maris." Esiason was right, but Wyche figured his players had a better chance of remembering Mantle than Maris, so he kept the Mantle tag.

It's not exactly rocket science, as they say. It is, however, a whole new language, which brings to mind something Steve Tasker, the superb special teams player for Buffalo, is fond of pointing out. "The average career span of an NFL player is 3.4 years," Tasker told me once. "The average career span of an NFL player with a college degree is five years."

The meetings reminded Esiason of another way a quarterback must set an example. The week before the 1991 season began, with Bible running an offensive meeting, Esiason said aloud, "How much longer are we meeting?"

Bible shrugged off the question, but he got in Esiason's face later. "Do you realize what you did?" he said to Esiason angrily.

"Do you realize we've been meeting today for four hours with only a fifteen-minute break? Come on!" Esiason said.

"You let everybody off the hook in the room!" Bible told him. "Everybody heard you say that. They completely turned their heads off and said, 'We've met enough.' You can't do that."

Weeks later, Esiason recalled the story word for word. "It's just one more way you can see what a quarterback means," Esiason said. "If a coach tells you that, you know he's seeing it and feeling it too."

Morning meetings over, the players hit the field for a walk-through. Most teams do this in today's NFL. Some time before practice starts in earnest at 1:30 or so in the afternoon, the players walk out onto the practice field in civvies and walk through the new plays called for in the game plan. For the Bengals, it happens before lunch, to get them rejuvenated after sitting in meeting rooms for the whole morning.

During lunch, Esiason dealt with another part of his job: interviews. Usually he meets with local writers and sportscasters after practice in the defensive meeting room just off the team meeting room, but somebody always catches him for a few questions at lunch when the locker room opens to the press. With the team 0-3, Esiason's message was very upbeat. He plans what to say each week, depending on the mood and record of the team and can rarely be coaxed into saying something he doesn't want to.

Quarterbacks have to be very good at this part of the job. It's absolutely essential, almost a sixth factor in Mike Holmgren's prescription for quarterbacks. "Dealing with the press," Cleveland quarterback Bernie Kosar says, "is almost like the fifth quarter on Sunday. You have to set the tone for the week ahead. All the players and the staff are going to be reading the papers and watching TV, and it's important that after a great win or a bad loss you put it in perspective. You always have to look forward to the next week, and you always have to measure what you say."

What Randall Cunningham really wants to say after getting sacked six times and losing to Washington is, "If I had any offensive linemen, I wouldn't be running for my life all the time, and we would have kicked their ass today." But what he says—after thirty minutes of cooling off, showering, dressing, and thinking about his remarks—is something like, "We just made some mistakes today that we'll have to correct. We've still got a fine team, and everybody's trying their hardest." From reading quarterbacks' quotes on Sunday, you'd think all these guys went to Boredom School together. Put Jim Kelly or Warren Moon or Dan Marino or Joe Montana in front of a camera, and it sounds like they're reading from a teleprompter.

"You know why?" one marquee quarterback told me. "Because we're scared of what's going to come out. I like writers. But I've been burned so many times with what were harmless quotes that now all I do is say the programmed stuff."

Consequently insight into the real game is hard to find now. Put yourself in their position, though. Would you be forthcoming? Imagine being in Jim Kelly's shoes. In the fifth game of 1989, left tackle Howard Ballard missed a block on Colts defensive end Jon Hand, allowing Hand to sack Kelly and separate Kelly's left shoulder. In pain after the game, Kelly let slip his true feelings—that the offensive line was pretty solid except for left tackle. Inside the locker room, the players rallied around Ballard and spurned Kelly, who'd broken a major rule in team etiquette: He'd publicly singled out a teammate for criticism. Later that season, running back Thurman Thomas retaliated, saying the team had one weakness—Kelly. He really didn't mean it. But coach Marv Levy made Thomas and Kelly apologize publicly for their statements. Still, the chasm between Kelly and the team was a palpable one that many players would discuss off the record. In 1990, Kelly threw a party after every home game at his spacious suburban home, trying to make everything all right again. At the same time, he turned into one of the game's most scripted interviews.

Esiason is just as calculating, but he is more spontaneous and more available than most quarterbacks. He is universally thought to be one of the league's best interviews, which is good and bad. Good, because he knows the press has a job to do and he knows that part of his salary is for public relations; he's the most recognizable and valuable pro sports face in town. Bad, because he's in demand all the time and can't just have a normal, anonymous day at the office. Bill Walsh, Sam Wyche's old mentor with the 49ers, was asked about Esiason's patience and willingness to meet the press daily during the season and stay until the last question has been asked. Walsh said he thought Esiason was overdoing it. "In my opinion, I don't think Boomer ought to be the sole team spokesman there. He takes on so much responsibility with the media."

"Who else is there?" Esiason countered. "Nobody. Who else stands up on this team and takes charge? Nobody. I feel it's part of my job, part of the job description. Sometimes, you even need to talk to the guys on your own team about things. A couple weeks ago, after we played Houston, the defense gave up over 400 yards total offense, and [safety] Rickey Dixon said, 'Well, we thought we did our part. If the offense could have just counter-punched . . .' What did I have to do, since my offensive teammates were pissed? I pulled him into a room a couple days later and said, 'Rickey, let me explain something to you. I know you, and I know you didn't mean what you said. I'm sure you just stated it wrongly. But this is what was written, and hopefully you didn't mean it this way.' He told me, no, he wouldn't have ever said that. That's just a part of my job on this team."

At noon, one of the local writers asked him what's wrong with the team. "It's like a virus affecting the team," Esiason said. "It's not like the other teams are taking things away from us. It's like I take my turn screwing things up, then Eddie Brown does, then Rodney Holman does, then James Brooks does. We just have to fight through this."

"Is Sam taking his turn screwing things up?" some other writer wondered.

Red flag. A cardinal rule of quote-giving: Don't openly question the coach, because writers will have a field day with it, especially in a newspaper-warring town. "No, Sam's fine," Esiason said. "Sam's been taking a lot of the heat for this, and he doesn't deserve to. He's been our shield. I really appreciate what Sam's done for the team and for me. He taught me to flourish in this offense. For me not to appreciate him would be ridiculous and selfish on my part."

Then he went into one of the building's quiet rooms, film man Al Davis's office, to talk to the Washington writers. First rule of talking to out-of-town writers: Praise the opposition. "It truly is a great challenge to go up against such a great team," Esiason said. He also used the virus line again, and he said there were no divisions on the team, and that the team would fight through this adversity. "Some way, somehow, we'll get things turned around," he said. "Everyone else can afford to be pessimistic. The quarterback can't afford to be pessimistic. Everybody looks at the quarterback."

When he got through with the Washington writers, he was asked how he really felt about dealing with the media.

"Well," he said, "it's always going to be there. They've got a job to do. I think in the long run it's something that can really be positive. If you care to do it, you can cultivate an image with the way you act around the press and treat the press. Because that's how you're going to get known in the outside world.

Think about it. If there's no TV, if there's no radio, if there's no newspapers covering us, I'm probably making $500 a week, not what I make now. [Which, in 1991, was $176,470.58 a week.] The media presents all kinds of opportunities, and I can't believe more guys don't take advantage of it."

At practice that day, the Bengals practiced "Set Alert," a series Esiason had been longing to run all season. Back at training camp, Esiason had asked Wyche if he could put in a series of plays that didn't force him to call a long series of names and numbers at the line of scrimmage. Instead, Esiason would match a formation and motion sequence with one code word and the exact play with another code word, so he could get to the line of scrimmage and say something like "Jack Flip!" and bang, take the snap before the defense had a chance to catch its breath or adjust to what it thought the offense was doing. Wyche liked the idea, so they practiced it and got it ready for the Redskins. If the opportunity presented itself, they'd run the sequence Sunday.

Actually, Esiason quite often chips in ideas, even during the heat of battle. In the Bengals' 41-14 playoff win over Houston in 1990, the Bengals came into halftime comfortably ahead, but Esiason was itching to put in a new play. Wyche handed him the chalk, and Esiason went to the board, in front of the offensive players and coaches, and told everybody how the Oilers were selling out to stop the Bengals' right-end sweeps. Why not run a play from their Grace Right series, with Esiason faking a hand-off to a right-end-sweeping Eric Ball, and then putting the ball on his own hip and, with every one of the Bengals going right, Esiason just loping around left end? Wyche thought about it, and said, "Okay. If we get inside their ten, we can do it."

"Bitchin'. Cool. Let's do it," Esiason said.

Sure enough, midway through the third quarter, the Bengals had the ball at the Houston ten, and Esiason called Grace Right Keeper, and it worked perfectly, and Esiason scored. So the coaching staff had faith that Esiason knew the landscape out there, and he'd know when something would work and when it wouldn't.

Actually, Esiason had become surprisingly comfortable with

the offensive staff. He started out under Wyche as a rookie in 1984, a second-round draft choice from Maryland, an offensive sponge dying to learn everything right here, right now. The Bengals were then led by veteran quarterback Ken Anderson, who was in his twilight, and Esiason was the heir. But it would take time with Wyche's coaching hieroglyphics for Esiason to learn everything. Although he started four games as a rookie, he had to wear a wristband that contained all the plays, so he'd have a reference guide in case he got confused as the game wore on. He beat Cleveland 12-9 in his first start. But even though he won the starting job in 1985, it took until about mid-1986 for him to feel like the job was second nature, to stop fighting some of the plays and schemes the staff imposed on him. He grew to respect Wyche's contributions, although everyone in Cincinnati thought he disliked Wyche because they'd clashed so openly during the 1987 strike. While Esiason thought the Bengals should be a passing-dominated team and that Wyche should be tougher with the players—especially the defensive players, whom he thought got away with more than they should have—he did respect him as an offensive mind.

"When you're a young player, you tend to think you know it all. It's like the old adage, when you're between twelve and eighteen, you think you know it all. And all of a sudden, you hit age twenty-two, and you realize how smart your father really is," Esiason said. "The point is, would I like to throw more? Yes, I would like to throw more. Every quarterback would. As much as I disagree, as much as I would never coach this way, if he feels like running the ball is going to give us our best chance to win, then I'm with him. And I'm going to tell you, more often than not, the coach is right. He's right, and it's from years of experience."

Wyche has an advantage most coaches can't have: He was an NFL quarterback. "Coaches think [quarterbacks] can see so much more than we really can," says Gary Danielson. "But what really happens is that, you'll be at the line, and you'll get a feel and an instinct that something should be there you can capitalize on. The play starts, and it's never black and white. It actually is all a blur out there, and you just react to the situation you see."

And so Esiason, in the eight years he played under Wyche, has never faced much of a grilling when he came off the field after throwing an interception. Wyche understood.

After practice, Esiason settled into an empty office—McNally's—and watched some Washington defensive film. He wanted to see for himself why the staff put in certain plays against certain Washington defenses. Then he sat in the defensive meeting room to meet the local writers for his daily session with them, twenty minutes of mostly friendly sparring about how badly the Bengals were playing and what they could expect against the Redskins. In the midst of this, a TV cameraman not familiar with the daily routine began setting up to shoot Esiason talking with the press. "Hey," Esiason said, "I'll do TV when I get out of the shower, okay?" All told, Esiason spent over an hour and a half talking with the media this day.

"That enough?" he said to the writers, rising from his chair at the end.

"Until tomorrow," the *Cincinnati Enquirer*'s Jack Brennan told him.

He showered and got the TV stuff out of the way—"Nobody's played so well that they're immune to the heat, and we've all made mistakes," Esiason told three local minicams—and then he's back in his footballspeak world.

He ducked into a darkened room with the receivers—Eddie Brown and Tim McGee are his main targets—and backup quarterbacks, a Dallas–Washington film on the screen. Esiason took control of the tape machine. This was his weekly meeting with his receivers to get their input on what will work and against whom in the Washington secondary; the next day, he'll take this input in with him to his 8:30 meeting with the head coach, and he'll lobby for certain favorite plays.

The group watched how Washington's secondary covered a pass play, then Esiason or somebody chipped in with a comment about what the Bengals could do that would work against the Redskins. Right away, the Bengals noticed the huge gap between Washington's right cornerback, Martin Mayhew, and the receivers he covers.

"Hey, Timmy," Esiason called out. "Look at the hole right

here in the middle of the field. We can run the donut here."

A minute later, he said: "See, Eddie? Triple right flip 76 pastry! We'll have time to throw the ball."

"Look at the coverage now," Esiason said later. "Too soft."

"Look at Mayhew," McGee said. "He looks like he's trying to run a route, not cover."

Brown saw something he liked and said, "How about 85 Z cross?"

"I'll put that in," Esiason said. "Good idea—85 Z cross. You know, I don't think I've ever seen the middle of the field look so open in my entire life."

When it ended, I told Esiason the whole concept of film-watching is probably the least understood aspect of football. I had just seen one of the best passing teams in football over the past few seasons look at one of the best defenses in football, not having played them for three seasons, and watched how the quarterback and receivers figured how to best beat this defense.

"You saw Mayhew playing really soft, and you saw the safeties playing you with a lot of cushion, and I can see what you're thinking," I tell him. "You see a hole there where you can do comeback routes and intermediate routes."

"Teams will never do the same thing week in and week out," he replied. "But at least you can get individual techniques down, and you can get some ideas about what might work. I mean, if we can't complete some stuff over the middle this game, we might as well just quit football. When we used to play the Browns, with Frank Minnifield and Hanford Dixon at the corners, we had such a tip on them. When I could see the stripe on their helmet, it was a dead giveaway they were playing zone. When I couldn't see the stripe, I knew they were playing man. And so if I had to audible, I knew exactly what to audible to, based on whether it was man or zone coverage."

"I don't get it," I said.

"If they're standing a little bit sideways, their bodies pointed toward me, I can see the stripe on their helmet, because the stripe goes directly from the front of their helmet to the back. But if I couldn't see the stripe on their helmet, meaning that their bodies would be straight on the receiver and I couldn't see the front of their helmet, then I knew they were playing man.

"You look for tips like that. I try to see who's directing traffic out there. This week, it's Brad Edwards, their safety. I try to see who I can fool, who'll be tough to contend with, who stays on his best in coverage. Does it always work every week? No. Am I prepared every week? Yes. I'm not like Chris Spielman [the film-obsessed Detroit Lion linebacker], locking myself in a room for four hours a night without the outside world coming in. I'd drive myself crazy. But I get what I need out of it. I'm not surprised very much by anything anybody does to us."

It was 5:30, and Esiason had been here nine hours. One more thing to do. Esiason spent twenty minutes taping a public service announcement for a local charity. Esiason likes to play the community-minded leader. The minicam ran, and Esiason smiled easily and said, "We all have to make our community a better place in which to live. It means a lot to all of us." A couple of takes more, with a few more United Way-type lines, and it was done. Esiason's day was done.

Wednesdays are massage days for Esiason. When he gets home, he eats, and then his masseuse gives him one of his twice-weekly massages. He started massage therapy in 1988, and he doesn't know how he ever got along without it. During the season, things start to hurt, and they get more hurt during practice, and there's no chance to get healthy until the off-season; Esiason thinks massage therapy staves off more severe injury and speeds the healing process.

Then he studies for forty minutes. "If you sit down for four hours every night and try to read everything, it all becomes garbled," Esiason said. "But if you separate things and take them in chunks and say to yourself, 'Okay, this week we have eighty-two passes, the most we've had to prepare all season. Let me study the eighty-two pass plays, let me look at the film, let me look at their formations, let me understand what we do against certain defenses.' At night, before I go to bed, I spend at least forty minutes going over this thing. I start when the game plan gets faxed to me on Tuesday night, then I do a little bit every night."

Wednesday (at least in Cincinnati) is Esiason's only nonsocial day. On Thursday, he takes his linemen out for dinner at The

Boat House, a yuppie fish-and-steak place on the Ohio River just east of downtown, then has his weekly night out with the boys—a card game at one of the linemen's homes. ("Neat. A real card game, with chips on the table, cigars in the mouths and stories in the air.") Friday night is pizza night with the family; they'll order in or go out for it. On Saturdays before home games, the Esiasons have in family and friends from Long Island (his) and Maryland (hers), up to twenty people a weekend.

Thursday, Friday, and Saturday mornings are spent practicing, refining, and coordinating. In their Thursday morning session, Wyche told Esiason the Redskins have middle-of-the-league defensive backs. "We face guys like this every week," Wyche said. "They're winning because their defensive line really comes off of the ball. And their offense controls the ball so well you've got to make the most of all your chances."

Before home games, Esiason will do as little as possible on Saturday afternoons. On this particular Saturday, he played Scrabble with some friends from the Island and then watched some college football. The basement rec room of The Quarterback House has six or eight Esiason buddies slumped into naugahyde couches watching Auburn–Texas, while a few others shot around at the pool table. Everyone's vegging out, waiting for Sunday, 1:00, to come. In the fireplace, a warm fire roared. "I enjoy these days and these sixteen weeks more than any other time of the year," Esiason said, breaking from the college game for a while. "There's nothing like sitting in a room like this on a Saturday when it's forty degrees out and blustery. You've got a big fire going, the ball game's on, you've got a big game the next day. It's the most exciting time of all." Upstairs, Cheryl supervised the cooking of her husband's traditional night-before-game dinner: spaghetti with her homemade tomato sauce. Esiason eats at 7:00 and leaves the full house.

By 8:30, Esiason had his game plan binder open to the next day's plays in room 830 of the Cincinnatian, a European-style hotel at Sixth and Vine in downtown Cincinnati. He'd passed his weekly test with Wyche that morning, a test of all the things they'd possibly use that week. At the front of Wyche's office,

Wyche stood as he'd stand on Sunday, on the sidelines, and gave Esiason signals. The conversation, rapid-fire, went like this:

Wyche: "I give you this signal."
Esiason: "Seventy-two right right flank."
Wyche: "And that?"
Esiason: "Slot."
Wyche: "Right. And if I just do this?"
Esiason: "Seventy-six halfback green."
Wyche: "Okay. This."
Esiason: "Seventy-six single."
Wyche: "Okay. If I do this?"
Esiason: "That's your 76 dover."
Wyche: "Okay, I do this?"
Esiason: "That's your 81 double."
Wyche: "Okay, this?"
Esiason: "That's your 82 bingo."
Wyche: "Okay, this?"
Esiason: "Eighty-two grid."
Wyche: "Okay, this?"
Esiason: "Three-78 Sanders."
Wyche: "All right, we're on the five-yard line, lane change,
    I give you this."
Esiason: "Doctor death."
Wyche: "And this?"
Esiason: "Eighty-four bandit."
And so on.

As a final check that night, before going to bed, Esiason had me quiz him on his plays again, as Wyche did that morning. Nine of the first fifteen offensive plays of the game for the Bengals will be passes, and this made Esiason very happy. "I love this game plan. If we execute it well, we win. I don't care what they do.

"I never remember a Saturday night where it wasn't like this," he said.

"Like what?" I said.

"Like I knew we'd win the game the next day."

He watched CNN Headline News for a few minutes, and just before 11:00, the lights were off.

The front desk woke him at 7:30. In the shower, Esiason thought about defenses, Redskins defenses. "I picture their red pants and their white jerseys and their red helmets. Or burgundy, whatever color it is. I try to picture exactly what they're going to do to us. I try to picture what Matt Millen's going to look like with that big heavy face mask with spit hanging all over his mustache and coming off his helmet and him yelling and screaming. I try to prepare myself for that. I try to picture Wilber Marshall and Darrell Green and wonder how they'll play. Green's five-eight but he plays like he's six-ten, he's so athletic. I've never seen Brad Edwards or Martin Mayhew, but I try to visualize how they'll play, just from watching their first three games of the season on film.

"My coach in college, Jerry Claiborne, gave all of us a book, *Psycho Cybernetics,* on the power of positive thinking. It talked about visualizing yourself getting the job done. When he gave it to me, I was very skeptical. But I came to realize how much your mind can help you in football. That's why, now, the fact that they're 3-0 and we're 0-3 has absolutely no bearing on this game whatsoever for me. The other thing is, I always feel like I have an angel with me. I'm not a very religious person, but the angel is like my mother watching out for me. She was with me when I won the MVP. She was with me through all the adversity I've ever had. I always feel she's there with me."

Room service came with the orange juice, fruit, and pot of coffee, and then Esiason was gone in his Jeep, six blocks down to Riverfront Stadium. Before the game, he told everyone he saw on the ball club, "Just go out and have some fun today, baby."

The Bengals did have some fun. They rallied from a 27-10 deficit to tie the game at 27, only to lose 34-27 on a Gerald Riggs seven-yard run with just over two minutes to play. The Bengals should have won. Esiason was medium sharp, completing eighteen of thirty-seven passes under a heavy rush all game. Eight of the incompletions were catchble balls dropped by his

46

receivers. Esiason got whacked a few times in the game, once on a clean shot from the side by defensive end Charles Mann while he was throwing. He threw one interception, a poorly thrown ball intended for Brown that landed right in Brad Edwards's stomach, stunting the first Cincinnati drive of the day.

Esiason's frustration with his day, his week, his entire season was summed up perfectly on one play. The Bengals were down 24-10, having spent their first half starting and sputtering and dropping and stopping, with the defense giving the Redskins seven yards every time they lined up for an offensive play. On second-and-thirteen from the Cincinnati 26, Esiason sent Brown and McGee deep, to opposite sides of the field. Rodney Holman, after making a quick block at the line of scrimmage, beat the linebacker covering him and was galloping free over the middle. Esiason, with little pressure, arched a perfect spiral right down the middle of the field. Holman's eyes took in the ball, very slightly behind him, and he reached back for it, alone. In front of him was plastic pasture. This would be a thirty-yard gain minimum, a forty-yarder if he could break a tackle or two.

The near-perfect pass hit Holman in the hands, bounced off his stomach, and fell to the ground. Incomplete.

Later in the quarter, the Bengals rebounded. Esiason paced up and down the sidelines with the Cincinnati defense back on the field. When he'd see a defensive player, he'd say, "Get us the ball! We've got it going!" The defense forced the Redskins to punt from their 12, and the Bengals began from the Washington 46, with 3:30 left in the third quarter.

Here's the next series of downs as seen through Esiason's eyes:

First and ten, Washington 46.

"I love playing football at times like this. We'd been down 27-10, out of it almost, and we scored to make it 27-17, and our defense holds, and we're back in it. The crowd's in it, the players are in it. You can feel it. The game can change right here, right now."

As Esiason runs onto the field, Wyche yells, "Remember your keys! Remember your audibles!" Esiason nods. Plain advice, but

47

good advice. He would need to remember them on this series.

Tight ends Jim Riggs and Rodney Holman are on the field, with one back, Harold Green, and wideouts Brown and McGee. In the huddle, Esiason says, "Thirty-eight-39 counter-switch, check with me, bullet, trips right." It's a running play, where Riggs goes in motion from right to left and the line flows left, but Green, running toward left guard, takes the handoff and runs counter to the blocking—to the right. The check-with-me comes in at the line of scrimmage, where Esiason will holler a coded series of words that could change the direction in which Green runs.

"Bullet, bullet, bullet!" Esiason yells, under center. "Viking, Viking, Viking! Forty-five, forty-five! HutHUT!"

The ball is snapped, and everything is going well, even the nudge left tackle Anthony Munoz successfully gives a Washington defensive tackle, knocking him a millimeter off his path and giving Green the gap in the line he needs. Everything is going well, until right guard Paul Jetton, who pulls to the left to escort Green through the line, somehow misses his man. Jetton flat out misses linebacker Andre Collins, who creams Green. Gain of three.

Second and seven, Washington 43.

The Bengals now want some sure yards, and they will go to their Pro Bowl tight end, Rodney Holman, to try to get them. Holman has played poorly this season like so many Bengals, but Esiason still loves to throw him the underneath stuff over the middle and watch him get eight or ten yards. This time he calls Yogi Angle, where the tight end runs out about eight yards and, at his option, runs inside or outside depending on the coverage he gets.

"This is a down and distance I know they tend to blitz, so I'm looking for that approaching the line. But I see they're not going to blitz here. I can see it in Matt Millen's eyes—he's looking around everywhere to make sure who he's going to pick up and looking to see who the outside rushers are going to pick up—but I can't figure out quite what coverage they're going to be in. But this is a staple play that we hit eighty, eighty-five percent of the time. I'm feeling good about it."

Disaster number one: Linebacker Monte Coleman does something Esiason's never seen on film—he runs from his left outside linebacker slot to double-cover Eddie Brown. Great. Now one of the best cornerbacks in football, Darrell Green, and a quick linebacker, Coleman, are smothering Esiason's second option on the play.

Disaster number two: "What the hell is Millen doing covering Rodney!" Esiason thinks. Millen, the middle linebacker, isn't keying on Harold Green coming out of the backfield, as he should have been, according to the films Esiason has watched. Instead, he is covering Holman. This throws Esiason off.

Disaster number three: Holman runs a crummy pass route. He should have sprinted out about five yards, chucked whoever's covering him, and turned to look for the ball. Instead, he misses Millen, and Millen cuts in front of Holman, and Millen looks right at Esiason, daring him to try to get the ball to his favorite tight end.

Disaster number four: Somebody forgets to block Wilber Marshall, who's coming in clean from Esiason's right.

Esiason takes in all this in about a half a second. And then there's a millisecond here where Esiason thinks to himself: "SHITTTT!"

"They kind of caught me here. I never expected Millen to be covering Rodney, and I never expected Coleman to be running out like this at the wideout. I want to go to Rodney here, but Millen really screwed me. See, I can't throw that ball there, with Millen in front of Rodney like that. You can tell Millen really did his homework. He knew what Rodney was going to do on that particular play. Plus, Rodney doesn't run a good route. Rodney needs to make contact with his man and bang him off the play and give me something to throw at. But he lets Millen take him out of the play."

The millisecond fades. Esiason can't throw to Holman and he can't really throw to Brown, but what choice does he have, with the hot breath of Marshall almost fresh on his shoulder pads?

His body turns and he quickshoots a pass through a needle's eye—away from Coleman, in front of Darrel Green the corner, with some mustard on it—for Brown.

Now for disaster number five, which Esiason—just as he's pancaked to the turf—never sees: The ball hits Brown right in the chest, but he drops it.

(Esiason on pain: "Hell yes, you feel the pain. You can feel the hit coming. You can almost hear it coming. There's a sound that comes up on you, like the sound a dog hears and nobody else can hear. It's like when you're on the edge of sleep in your bed at home, and you can just tell somebody else is in the room with you. Even if you don't see it coming, you know it's coming. Remember the quote from Jack Lambert, about how quarterbacks should wear skirts? Come on. You know how difficult it is for a quarterback to deliver an accurate pass knowing he's about to get his ass kicked? Pretty damn difficult, let me tell you. But you do it. When you're exposed, and you're hit, you feel it right in the chest, in pain and in shortness of breath. It hurts. But you don't enter a game saying to yourself, 'Oh no, I hope nobody hits me today.' It's such a part of the game, every game, that you know it's coming, and you think, hey, it's no fun, but I've got to take it. And if the pass is complete, it's kind of a good pain. It's hard to explain, but you feel so good you were able to hang in there, get absolutely clobbered—usually in an area where you aren't padded—and still complete the pass.")

Esiason picks himself up and looks around. He sees Holman.

"Jesus Christ, Rodney!" Esiason says. "That was a bullshit route out there."

"Sorry," Holman says.

Third and seven, Washington 43.

"We have to make a first down. I'm not coming off this field without a first down. We can't afford to come off the field and let the momentum die. I know they're going to be in a nickel defense, and in the back of my mind I'm thinking I might be able to run for it if they're playing man coverage, because then they'd probably leave me uncovered except for the rushers. When I look over the defense coming to the line here, I know I'll be able to run if I have to. The next thing I do is look to the first-down marker. I plant it in my mind where I have to get to for the first down. In this case, it's the 35. I focus on the 35, and I just know that somehow we have to get there on this play."

The play is a legal pick play, where Holman and Brown are supposed to come from opposite sides in a crisscross over the middle and run their men into the confusion of the middle. But Holman, uncharacteristically, gets knocked off his route just off the line of scrimmage by a Washington linebacker—this is obviously not his day—and Brown can't get out of traffic before the rush gets to Esiason, and Tim McGee is well covered down the left sideline.

"Fuck it," Esiason thinks, and then, in his best gallop, he starts to sprint for the 35, staring at the four-inch-wide 35-yard-line stripe.

Around the 37, he goes into his slide, two Redskins converging on him, and he lands in a pile at the 34. First down.

The crowd goes nuts. No jubilation from Esiason, though.

"RODNEY!" he yells at his tight end. "What kind of shit is that? You can't get manhandled like that! Jesus Christ!"

First and 10, Washington 34.

The Redskins have seen Esiason screaming at Holman. The Bengals wouldn't go to him now, at such a critical juncture of the game, would they?

They would.

"Tell you why," Esiason says. "He's a great player. He's in the Pro Bowl almost every year. He's like everybody else—he's going to have days where he's not at the top of his game. I might be mad at him, but I know eventually he'll end up making a play to help us."

Like this one, Esiason hopes: 76 Bandit. While Brown clears the middle by running a deep post pattern and McGee runs a quick out pattern toward the sidelines, Holman, starting from the right side, will wriggle free at the line and run across the middle on a shallow crossing pattern.

It all works as planned, and a well-protected Esiason spies Holman for what will be a nice eight- or ten-yard gain. The pass is a little high, right about face-mask level. Holman puts his hands up to catch it, turning his head to look the ball into his hands.

Kerplunk. Another drop.

Can't anybody here play this game?

Second and 10, Washington 34.

"I'm churning inside. I'm frustrated. But we're doing this to ourselves. If we make the plays and the reads, we'll score."

Run the frickin' ball, Wyche decides. And so he sends in a standard running play, a counter, a play designed for running back Craig Taylor to start left and everyone to block to the left, and then for Taylor to find a crease and head right. Remember your keys, Wyche had told Esiason. And so, at the line, Esiason sees the corners, Darrell Green and Martin Mayhew, lining up straight-up, in man coverage, on wideouts Brown and McGee. The encyclopedic playbook study now comes in: *Corners playing man. Outside rushers looking blitz. The middle's going to be linebacker-free.*

Audible. Esiason picks a play where Taylor sprints over center with the handoff, then cuts back right, toward the cone of the end zone. Esiason figures if the wideouts take the corners out of the play and the linebackers blitz, Taylor will be one-on-one with safety Brad Edwards and have a fifty-fifty chance to break a big play.

"Two Cowboy Trigger Riggs Spine!" Esiason yells left. To the right, he yells: "Two Cowboy Trigger Riggs Spine!" Turning back to Taylor, he yells: "Two Cowboy Trigger Riggs Spine!"

Taylor is a second-year player, and he doesn't play much.

"You got it?" Esiason hollers back at him.

"I got it!" Taylor answers.

Tick, tick, tick. The forty-five-second clock's down to about eight.

Esiason pauses to make sure the corners are playing man. That's the look Green and Mayhew are giving.

"HutHUT!"

The play takes exactly seven seconds from snap to finish. Esiason takes the handoff and whirls to his right, 180 degrees, while stepping backward. Simultaneously, Taylor surges forward and every offensive lineman takes the inside shoulder of the man on him and plows him to the right. There's a gap over the center, as Esiason had thought there would be. Just as the gap widens, the ball held out by Esiason slams into Taylor's gut. He grips it and surges into the hole. If not for a crushing block by Bruce Reimers on Wilber Marshall, Taylor would have gained a yard and been crushed by Marshall. Two other Redskins lunge and miss, and Taylor is gone, one-on-one suddenly with Edwards, racing toward the right cone.

Esiason looks for yellow flags. He knows Taylor will beat Edwards, and he wants to make sure there is no penalty. No flags. He whoops. Taylor scores. It's 27-24, the Bengals are alive, and the place is going crazy.

Esiason runs off the field. "I got 'em!" he yells to Wyche, who slaps his helmet in glee.

Later, Esiason says, "A play like that, it's better than sex. Really. I mean, how long does an orgasm last, three or four seconds? This play, it lasts seven or eight seconds, and when it works, you're in ecstasy."

Emotion is such a big part of this game. It is not something that has lessened with the times, not something that all the money in the world, which these guys have, affects very much. When you win, you exult. When you lose, you hurt.

Forty-five minutes after that touchdown, Esiason goes from orgasmic to quasisuicidal as Washington wins, 34-27. Walking off the field after the game, Esiason is disconsolate. He needs a few minutes to compose himself after bad losses like this. "The guys don't do it on purpose," he says of the dropped balls.

He walks into the tunnel toward the Bengals' locker room. He keeps his head down.

"You must feel sick," I say.

"Sick? I'm dying. That's what happens in this job."

Esiason's game died through miserable 1991 and 1992 seasons, and the Bengals, with wunderkind quarterback David Klingler in reserve, dealt Esiason to the Jets six months before the 1993 season.

The day after the trade, Esiason stood in his new camp head-quarters, coach Bruce Coslet's office at the Jets' training facility on Long Island—half an hour from his hometown—and talked about being reborn. His 1991 season stunk, and 1992 smelled even worse before David Shula benched him in favor of the kid Klingler. But now here he was, practicing golf swings in Coslet's big corner office, waiting to salvage his career. "You'll be spending a lot of time in here," Coslet said. "Get used to it."

"I love it," Esiason said. "I couldn't be happier."

Later, he said, "Everybody thinks my arm's hurt. It isn't. But how can you tell people? You keep saying it over and over again, and then you're saying it so much that people start to think, 'Hey, his arm must be hurt or else he wouldn't be talking about it so much.' And everybody thinks I'm through. I wish you would come and watch films of what my last couple of seasons have been like. Running for my life, guys running the wrong patterns, guys not open . . . Hey, I'll take my share of the blame. I deserve some. But don't say I'm finished. I've got another Super Bowl in me. I'm sure of that.

"We'll just see how I do. But you know what? At quarterback, if you don't love being in pressure situations, forget it. You'll never make it."

The Pass-Rusher

THE ONE-MAN GANG

A Monday night in the fall of 1992, and detoxing doesn't get much better than this. Bruce Smith was in Shogun, a Japanese hibachi place just east of Buffalo, eating and talking and parrying with his best friend, Bills linebacker Darryl Talley. They love nights like this, when they can gossip about the league and their games and their team. They can unwind, relax, breathe deeply.

They can start to put themselves back together for another war.

Heaven knows the six-foot-four, 275-pound Smith can use it. The way he folded himself into his chair—lowering his wide rear end slowly, favoring his back, and keeping his left leg out to the side and flexing it—told how Smith was feeling. That, plus the "Uhhhhhhhhhh!" that came out of his mouth every time he moved significantly. Tall and sculpted, with a dark, distinctive face, Smith would be hard to miss in most crowds. But in a Japanese place, in Buffalo, on a slow night? He was the man. If it's possible to gawk politely, that's what people were doing.

Through the hibachi shrimp appetizer, Smith kept rotating his neck. "Damn," he said. "My neck's killing me."

A few minutes later, during the hibachi chicken, Smith kept flexing his left leg. "My thigh," he said, wincing. "Took a helmet there."

Working on the Japanese noodles with his chopsticks, Smith

stopped and started twisting his back and shoulders. "Aaaaagh," he moaned, breathing raggedly for a minute. He winced. "Took a shot in my upper back yesterday."

During these two hours away from their professional battle-field, Smith also massaged a shoulder, flexed a hand, and wiggled an ankle. Talley, not to be outdone, moved very slowly each time he had to get in and out of his chair. Each week for three weeks, he'd been tearing an abdominal muscle more and more. "Yeah, it's one of those four-to-six-week jobs," he said, stretching out after dinner. "Thing is, I don't have four to six weeks to give right now."

I asked Bruce Smith what hurt.

"What doesn't?" he said. "That's the question. You think I'm kidding? I'm not. You touch any spot on my body and I wince."

"We're in Indianapolis yesterday," Talley chipped in, "and it was a typical day in the life of Bruce Smith. He was sliced and diced like a Veg-a-Matic. The tight end blocks him on the titty, the tackle's boxing him out with shoves and punches. Sometimes the guard dives in on him. He's got to get away from this on every play."

Talley took his dinner fork. "This is Bruce," he said. Then he bent his fork, slowly, until tines pressed against handle. "This is what they try to do to him. This isn't one week or one day. A great pass-rusher in the NFL is going to feel like this every week during the season, and worse. He's getting whammed on sixty-five times in three hours, sixteen times a year."

Talley turned to Smith. "Tell him about Mattes yesterday," he said.

"You know Mattes?" Smith said to me.

"Ron Mattes, the offensive tackle?" I said.

"Yeah," Smith said. "He's one of the guys I have no respect for in this game, because he's always trying to hurt you. Well, I've been waiting to get back at him because he tried to cheapshot me so bad a long time ago. So I throw him down yesterday . . ."

Talley took it up. "And Bruce says to Mattes, 'You're the motherfucker who tried to end my career six years ago!' Mattes is on the ground, flopping around like a fish out of water. It was great. I went over to Mattes and said, 'You must have done something to make Bruce very mad. If I were you, I wouldn't do that again.' "

The play that spurred Smith's anger happened in Seattle in 1988, when Mattes was a Seahawks tackle and Smith was already a star defensive end for the Bills. As Smith rushed the passer, he eluded the Seattle guard and headed like a freight train for Seattle quarterback Dave Kreig. Mattes said he spied Smith steaming toward the quarterback and dove at him, trying to stop him, while the guard also made a lunging attempt to block Smith. The guard hit Smith high, and Mattes hit him low, around the knees. Smith to this day claims Mattes was diving for his knees, deliberately trying to hurt him. Mattes said: "I have to say that on film the play looked bad. But I guarantee you I had no intentions of hurting Bruce. The way the play developed, I thought I was going to have the only chance to knock Bruce away from hitting the quarterback, and the guard recovered in time to block him too. I just threw my body at him. It turned out that I hit him low and the guard hit him high and Bruce thought we were trying to set him up to hurt him. We weren't."

Pass-rushing is the most violent part of the every-down game. Rushing the passer also can be one of the most artful. I met with Smith, one of the very few dominant pass-rushers in football, seven times over a two-year period, and there wasn't a single time when we didn't talk about the violence and the pain and the brutality of the game. I watched game film of him and of future opponents with him, and the double-teaming of two 300-pound players, slamming and punching and grabbing and battering the pass-rusher, even one in full equipment, is stunning when watched in isolation on a big screen. You think, Hey, the guy's got big shoulder pads and a helmet, but what's there to protect his ribs and his guts and his lower back and his thighs and his hamstrings and his ankles and his feet. I charted the Buffalo defensive plays in their November 1992 game with Miami, and on twenty-one of the fifty-five snaps, the sole responsibility of two Dolphin offensive linemen was to block Smith. That doesn't count the times he had the open hand of a receiver slap him to try to get him off his course before a tackle or guard blocked him man-to-man, or the times he got lost in the middle of a pile on a running play. There were probably about twenty plays in the game when Smith was purely single-blocked. But the wedge-blocks, especially by 305-pound guard Keith Sims and 302-pound tackle Richmond Webb, were stunning in their finality and brutality. Imagine John Goodman blocking jockey Eddie Delahoussaye. Not a pretty sight. Neither was 607 pounds of Webb and Sims blocking 270 pounds of Smith—unless, of course, Smith could outsprint them to the far outside, turn the corner, and get to chase quarterback Dan Marino.

One night in 1991, I asked Talley for a half-hour of his time to talk about Smith. No one in the game knows him better. It's possible that no one in life knows him better. They're roommates in training camp and on the road during the season. They play next to each other and behind each other. They grouse about flaws in game plans, invent little line games to pull on the spur of the moment during games. Though Smith is the quiet one and Talley the get-in-your-face mother hen of the Bills' locker room, they're tied together like no other Bills' mates. It's like they need each other to complete their football identities, Smith's greatness and Talley's doggedness making for a perfect right side of a defensive front seven, Smith's quiet presence and Talley's insightful realism giving them a good grip of the game. What an important person Talley is to Smith and to the rest of the me-first Bills—a classic team guy who's a throwback to the days when all that mattered was winning, not incentive clauses. But, of course, incentive clauses being as important as they are these days, it's crucial to have a Talley in the locker room to remind everyone of the importance of winning.

The half-hour stretched into three hours. I asked him why the NFL seems to place nearly the same premium on the pass-rusher as it does on the passer.

"Here's what rushing the passer is," Talley said. "You're telling somebody to line up and run twenty-yard wind sprints every down, with a 300-pound man grabbing him and blocking him and often times some other guy hitting him, and you're asking him to run that wind sprint at a quarterback who's getting the ball off in a few seconds. The great ones can be quick and get around the corner, or they can run over the blocking or slice through the blocking. Some way, you've got to get to the quarterback, and that's all that matters."

The pass-rusher's job, though, is in such flux. Speed is so crucial because formations are spread all over the field. The two-way defensive end—stuff the runner, rush the passer—who really can rush like a lithe linebacker is a true rarity: Bruce Smith, Reggie White, Clyde Simmons, Neil Smith. That might be it, folks.

"That's right," Talley said. "The game's changed since Bruce and I came into the league. It's almost like playing basketball, with everyone spread out and the fast guys ruling the game. See, although the sack is an exciting part of the game, the people who rule the game really don't want to see it. No matter how great a 7-3 game is, people who make the rules think the fans say, 'That was a boring game.' But if it's a high-scoring game, no matter if it really was any good, people will say, 'Boy, that was an exciting game!'

"But down on the field, playing in the games, I find that fans love great defense and special teams, because they know a low-scoring, close game can turn on any snap. Which is why Bruce is so important to us. He can explode out of his stance on any play and make a difference."

Once, I asked Smith if he considered what he did, rushing the passer, an art.

"It's an art," he said. "It's also a car accident."

You are looking live at Joe Robbie Stadium, where, tonight, there will be many car accidents.

It is November 1992. After nine games, the Bills and Dolphins are tied for the division lead at 7-2. Smith, the pre-eminent pass-rusher, is in a big game against his biggest annual quarry, Miami quarterback Dan Marino, who Smith thinks is just about the greatest athlete in any sport he's ever seen. Smith and Talley are motormouths whenever the subject of Marino comes up, as it did in the days before this game in Buffalo.

Smith: "He's a pass-rusher's nightmare. He's got good protection, which is bad enough. But he never holds onto the ball long enough to let you get your hands on him. And if he does . . . pfffft! He gets rid of it when he senses you coming."

Talley: "Should have been a pitcher. What a release. What a fastball. Throws strikes, too. Perfect strikes."

Smith: "The guy throws the fastest pitch in football."

Talley: "Just flicks it. Sidearmed, overhand, whatever he needs to do."

Smith: "That's right. Whatever it takes. He just threads the needle."

Talley: "Yeah, a seamstress. Should have been a seamstress. I'm covering Tony Paige, their fullback, out of the backfield once, and I'm right on him. Walt Corey [Buffalo's defensive coordinator] says the hand is quicker than the eye. He tells us, 'Don't look back at the quarterback. Keep your eye on the receiver.' For one split second, I turn back to look for the ball. I mean a split second. And I turn back and boom! The ball's landing right in Paige's hands. Never saw it. Amazing."

Smith: "Last thing you want to see: Last minute against Miami, we're up by four, he's got the ball and three timeouts. I guarantee you he'll put on a show. You get that feeling in your gut like he's gonna do something."

Talley: "In that situation, he throws darts. Just throws darts. It's unfair."

Smith: "That's right, unfair. Why can't somebody else play him twice a year, every year?"

Talley: "Yeah. You know how they say familiarity breeds contempt? Well, we can't get familiar with him. We can't read him. Maybe in our case familiarity breeds respect."

Smith: "Can't get used to him because he's a student of the game. Instinctive. Smart. Hard to read. Knows exactly what throw to make and when."

Talley: "I just wanna know one thing: Is he psychic?"

Ba-da-bing.

In Miami, the operative sentence around the offensive line the week before the game was, "Look for Bruce." Offensive line coach John Sandusky told his group: "If you're blocking air, look for Bruce. Slide over and help on him."

"I've heard that about ten times," said center Bert Weidner.

"Every time we play the Bills, we hear that," Sims said.

On the field about ninety minutes before the game, Smith and Marino found themselves on the Buffalo bench, sitting together, talking pleasantly. How's the wife? Marino wanted to know. The knee? Smith loves Marino, but this is creepy, like Marino was softening him up before the kill. Without being unpleasant, Smith excused himself to go get a mad-on.

If history told the Dolphins anything entering the game, it was that Smith would be the responsibility of Webb and Sims, and probably both pretty often. "Because Bruce can overpower you physically," Sims said, "you go into a game with him concentrating on the little things, like technique. Stay low, keep your leverage, keep your feet moving. If you use your best technique, you can block anyone. And you always remember what side you're getting help from, if there's a chance it's coming. If Bruce is trying to beat me to the inside and I've got help from Richmond, I can overplay him on my right and let Richmond handle the left. You'd like to have help every time on Bruce. In Seattle, I had to block Cortez Kennedy a lot one-on-one, and what a job that is. In a different way, that's what it's like to block Bruce."

If someone on the other team says something to Smith before a game on the field, he'll speak to them. If the Bills are playing the 49ers or Jets, teams he thinks play dirty and try to block his knees, he'll say something like, "Let's keep it clean today." But tonight, he'll say nothing to Webb, the Pro Bowl tackle across the line from him. Webb doesn't talk to him. He doesn't talk to Webb. Webb has gotten much attention for holding Smith sackless in their previous five meetings, and while Smith doesn't hold the attention against Webb, he doesn't want to be pals with him over it, either. It's a pride thing. "There's respect there, real respect," Smith said. "But not a lot of words. We just want to go out there and play."

The Dolphins win the toss. On a breezy, sixtyish night, a windbreaker night, Smith digs in on the right side of the Buffalo defensive line, across from Webb. He is thinking: *Get a sack. Early. Get to Marino. Get in the backfield.* Talley is over his right shoulder. Marino lines up under Weidner, the inexperienced center (regular Jeff Uhlenhake is hurt), takes the snap and spins to hand off to running back Mark Higgs.

Bam. Biff. Ooof. Sims blocks Smith's left rib cage. Webb explodes out and tries to powerpush Smith backward. Smith, wedgeblocked, is powerless. Higgs gains eleven.

Second play: Smith tries to snake through the gap between Sims and Webb on a quick Marino three-step-drop strike to Mark Duper, but they weren't born yesterday. They wedge him and neutralize him.

Third and fourth plays: Two more Higgs runs. Talley and Smith play line games on these, with Smith darting inside at the guard, Sims, while Talley occupies the tackle, Webb. The hope? That in a one-on-one blocking situation, Smith will break into the backfield and get the ballcarrier or Marino for a loss. Sims neutralizes him both times, keeping Smith out of the backfield and away from the play both times. "At a time like that, inside, you're thrilled," Sims said later. "You've watched him devastate people all week on film, and to be truthful, you've got some nervousness before the game because he's done so much to so many good people. Right here, at this point of the game, I'm thinking: 'I've blocked him on four plays. I've got sixty to go. He can beat me on any one of the sixty.'"

The Dolphins have a perfect plan tonight, though. Marino doesn't take a deep drop in the first two series. "You don't want to take many of those against Buffalo," he'd say later, in deference to Smith. Miami keeps throwing the high-stepping Higgs into the teeth of the Bills' run defense, which has never been very good, and he keeps coming away with five- and eight-yard chunks. After nineteen Dolphins plays, Smith has one tackle, Marino's ten for ten, the Dolphins lead 14-3, and Smith is pacing on the sidelines. The Bills decide to abandon their defense of choice for the night, 42 Fish (designed to show a different rushing look to the Dolphins, to try to free some pass-rusher to find Marino), because on three different occasions the wrong guy blitzed at the wrong time, leaving a hole for Higgs to run through or a gap for Marino to pass through. "I just think everybody was too pumped up to think about 42 Fish," Talley says. "It was new, and we had guys so excited about the game that they missed some calls that hurt us."

The worst thing is, Smith appears almost uninterested. He says later it wasn't that. "Here we were in a new defensive front, something we'd never tried before, and they're rolling all over us. Emotion and momentum go hand in hand, and right then we didn't have either. You can't stay excited play after play when you're getting whipped."

"We definitely noticed it," Sims says. "We slowed him down. To do that, you've got to run the football, so he can't get that consistently good start at the quarterback; he has to wait a split-second to see if we'll run. We're effective when we can run it because it frustrates Bruce. He can't feed off it and get excited. We're noticing that in the huddle."

It gets worse. Three plays later, Smith is overcoming Webb in a man-to-man situation, motoring around the corner toward Marino on a pass play when . . . BOOM! This Bart Weidner guy from Kent State comes in and levels the unsuspecting Smith. On the next Dolphin snap, guard Harry Galbreath helps out Webb, and Galbreath knocks Smith to the ground.

This knocks some vitriol into Smith. "It was getting ridiculous out there," he says later. "I had to make some plays."

Three minutes left in the half now, the Bills creeping back in it at 14-13, and here comes Smith, out of the huddle, shuffling up the line to the hole over center, moving nose tackle Jeff Wright over Sims and Talley over Webb. Smith will do this four or five times a game, just to give the opposition a different look on a passing down; sometimes it's a planned call by Walt Corey from the sidelines, sometimes a gut feeling by Smith. Here it's Corey's call, just to shake things up.

(Don't think of this as an exact science. Once, in 1991 against Indianapolis, Smith forgot the Bills were in a regular defensive front; he thought there were two extra defensive backs in the game, and he thought he was supposed to shift to left end, with Talley playing right end. Talley saw Smith jogging to the left and yelled, "Hey! Bruce! Where the fuck you goin'?! Get back over here!" Too late. The Colts steamrolled Talley on a running play and gained a chunk of yards. In the huddle, all faces stared at Talley and Smith as they fought. Smith said, finally, "All right, shut up! You act like you ain't never fucked up!")

Smith shifts over center. "I noticed right away," Weidner says. "The biggest thing I've noticed centers doing is they lose their composure when Bruce is over them. I just got down into my stance and told myself, 'Remember the fundamentals.' Which are, move your feet well, get back off the ball into the pass-blocking set, stay low, and get leverage."

Nice theory. But it would have taken wide-receiver quickness to stop Smith. He makes a slashing move, busting past Weidner, hitting the gap to Weidner's left and then sprinting and diving, clawing at Marino's ankles as he releases a pass.

Next play: Smith and Webb, man-to-man.

"Pass-rushing is really a chess game a lot of times," Smith says. "You have to set up the guy you're playing against. Maybe you do something a certain way five times and then, the sixth time, you do it a little bit different."

"With Bruce," Webb says, "you usually look for the inside rush first because he does it so well."

But Smith has been going outside, straight ahead, outside, outside through the first half. And now, when he breaks at Webb's right shoulder with a quick, jutting inside move, Webb is slow in reacting. Smith smashes into Marino a half a step after Marino's incomplete release. That was Marino's second incompletion of the half.

Smith is into it now. He's energized. But he's not the only impact guy out there. On the next play, he lines up over Weidner's head again, a disquieting sight for Marino. The game is turning right here and if Smith can explode out of his stance and get past Weidner again . . .

"Seven! Eighty-five!" Marino calls. "Seven! Eighty-five! SetHUTHUT!"

The weird cadence brings Smith shooting across the line. Encroachment. Five yards.

Same thing, believe it or not, on the next snap.

Four real plays later, at the Buffalo eight, Weidner remembers his line coach's week-long mantra. "Look for Bruce," wafts

John Sandusky's voice through his head. "If you're not blocking anybody, look for Bruce." Marino fades back on a five-step drop, looking, looking, looking, and Weidner, blocking no one, turns left to help Webb block Smith. Just as Weidner turns to help on Smith, Buffalo linebacker Cornelius Bennett bursts through Weidner's crevice, and the specter of Bennett bearing in makes Marino rush, and Marino's arm hits Bennett's arm on his follow-through, and the ball flops to the ground.

Advantage Bills. The Dolphins kick a field goal and go up 17-13, but without the double-team on Smith, and without Bennett's hustle, it could well have been 21-13.

Smith is angry in the halftime locker room. "I can't believe that!" he hollers. "Two offside penalties in a row! Ridiculous!" He turns to his defensive mates and says, "Some way, somehow, I'm going to make this up to you."

Marv Levy, the Bills' coach, isn't exactly a father figure to his team. But at halftime, a Levyism pops into Smith's head. "Visualize what you intend to do. See it. Dwell on it. Do it. It'll happen. You can make it happen," Levy preaches.

Of course, Marino calls a play-action pass on the first play of the second half. Smith, his adrenaline high, isn't thinking of what Webb is going to do to him. He's thinking about what he's going to do to Webb. Smith figures: If I take a hard step inside, because of how I beat him on the inside earlier, I can force him inside; then, I sprint to the outside, hope Marino takes at least a five-step drop, and try to make a play. In the meantime, Talley can occupy the blocking back on an inside blitz. Voila. For the first time in five years, Smith sacks Marino, speed-rushing around right end, enveloping him before he could clearly see his targets, and dropping him for a seven-yard loss.

"You said you'd do it, boss!" Talley yells at Smith, quaking and jiggling his arms to the crowd.

Immediately, walking back to the huddle, seeing the downcast face of Webb, Smith thinks: Turning point of the game.

Marino says nothing. "Dan's pretty good about those things," Webb says. "I'm just thinking: Settle down. Go back to the things you do well."

It's the first play of the second half, and Marino feels the pocket closing already. Smith, envigorated, shakes his shoulders at the next snap and leaves Webb in his dust on an outside rush. As Smith is tackling Higgs, Webb tackles Smith. Holding, Dolphins, and two plays later Miami punts from its end zone. The Bills score quickly. They lead 20-17.

They win 26-20. The game turned, just as Bruce Smith thought, on that first play of the second half. A great play by a great pass rusher.

Before the 1986 draft of college players, San Francisco coach/ draft czar Bill Walsh faced a sizable defensive rebuilding job. The 49ers especially needed defensive ends and pass-rushers, since their two most formidable quarterback terrorists of the decade's first half, Fred Dean and Dwaine Board, now averaged thirty-two years of age.

He knew the way the game was going. "By the mid-eighties," Walsh said, "the passing games around the NFL were becoming so sophisticated and the quarterbacks so well-schooled that we knew we needed more quality pass-rushers. We weren't the only ones. Everybody was looking for them." He also knew the colleges weren't producing many obvious pure pass-rushers, the six-five, 265-pound power-forward types with great power and speed. Walsh figured he'd have to invent some.

Everybody was desperately seeking supermen, actually. In his final five years as the coach of the Giants, Bill Parcells went on only one campus scouting trip—to see a pass-rushing linebacker from Georgia Tech named Pat Swilling, in 1986. One of his big regrets to this day is not taking Swilling—voted the 1991 NFL defensive player of the year by the Associated Press—before the Saints did in the third round. In 1988, the Buffalo Bills scouted or interviewed Pierce Holt, a bullish pass-rusher from Angelo State in Texas, nine times, hoping they'd have a chance to take him with their second-round pick. The 49ers chose Holt one pick before Buffalo would have. The Bills had to settle for Thurman Thomas. "These days," Buffalo director of college scouting John Butler said in 1992, "you'll be out on the road in some hotel after a day of scouting, and you'll run into a scout from another team, and one of the first things that'll come up is, 'Hey, you seen anybody who can rush the passer?'"

And so Walsh, several weeks before the '86 draft, took a scouting list of every draft-eligible player with pass-rushing skills in the country, and he handed it to an eager young scout on the 49er staff, Mike Lombardi. "Break all these guys down," Walsh said. That's footballspeak for: Find game films, watch game films, rate the players, get reports on these guys from the area scouts, separate the wheat from the chaff, and then get back to me. How soon? Yesterday. Lombardi ordered the film and watched it and read the reports and did his job, and he found a gem. His name was Charles Haley. He played at James Madison University in Harrisonburg, Virginia, and no one knew much about him. He sure didn't have the numbers to merit pro consideration. At smallish James Madison, he had but seventeen quarterback sacks in four seasons. Great pros have seventeen in a season, against great players. But the 49ers found out that Haley was a career inside linebacker at James Madison, switching outside only for the last four games of his senior year. Inside linebackers aren't sackers; outside guys are. And so Lombardi got a film from one of Haley's final four games that senior season, against Georgia Southern, and he watched the game.

Soon he saw something he knew Walsh would like.

He took the film into Walsh's office at the 49er complex south of San Francisco. Walsh was there with some coaches and staffers, talking about prospective 49ers, and they all watched the film for a while, until Lombardi got to the play he wanted to show Walsh. Envision this: Georgia Southern plays an option offense. When the quarterback rolls out, a running back trails him, so that if the play gets bogged down, the quarterback can pitch to the running back.

"Here's the play you'll want to see," Lombardi told Walsh, the film running in the darkened room. Haley was playing right outside linebacker. The quarterback sprinted to his right, away from Haley, with a running back trailing the play. Haley gained and gained and gained, running down the quarterback from behind. From the film, it appeared for a microsecond as if the quarterback could see Haley lunging for him, the tackler's arms spreading out to envelop the quarterback's waist. And suddenly the quarterback flicked the ball from his right wrist to the running back's breadbasket, and somehow Haley righted himself in a flash and took four sprinting steps to the running back and leaped at the back. He fell in a heap, under Haley, for a loss of four yards. The quarterback stared at the pile. He seemed stunned. Maybe he was wondering, who was that masked man? Lawrence Taylor, maybe? Reggie White? How did he make that play?

"That's what we're looking for, guys," Walsh said, sitting up in his chair, clicking off the projector. "That's what we need."

This kind of split-second judgment ticked off the scouting department, because they all were schooled not to make split-second judgments. But this is how Walsh did his geniuslike thing. "I always figured if I saw a player do it once, we could coach him to do it over and over again," Walsh said.

Walsh sent a scout and an assistant coach to Harrisonburg, and they came away impressed with everything but the guy's breadth. He spread 225 pounds over a 6-5 frame, and it looked like the first hard whack from a 300-pound left tackle or 255-pound blocking back would snap him in two. But he was so fluid, and he was so strong in the shoulders, and he could slice through holes so well and speed-rush the way an NFL pass-rusher had to. Walsh asked the defensive line coach at the time, Bill McPherson, where he'd pick Haley.

"Eighth or ninth round, I guess," McPherson said.

"Geez," Walsh said. "If you like him so much, let's pick him and find a way to use him."

Which is exactly what they did. They picked him in the fourth round, found him to be adept at disrupting the passing game, and they put him in position to do just that. They created the Elephant Defense, Haley being the elephant. (Why elephant? Because of the old pachydermian joke: Where does an elephant sit? Anywhere he wants to. Where does Haley play? Anywhere he wants to.) On probable running downs, Haley was dispatched to the strong side of the formation, where he played a standup outside linebacker. On probable passing downs, Haley lined up on the weak side of the formation and went, he hoped, one-on-one with an offensive tackle, trying to get to the quarterback.

The 49ers bulked Haley up a few pounds, then played him whichever way they thought he could best beat a path to the quarterback. It worked: Over his first five seasons, during which the 49ers made the playoffs every year and won the Super Bowl twice, Haley averaged .74 sacks per game. In his illustrious career, Lawrence Taylor averaged .81 sacks per game.

A couple of postscripts: Haley wasn't alone in rebuilding the 49er pass rush. Six picks after Haley in that 1986 draft, Walsh tabbed Kevin Fagan, who was in the process of rehabilitating a major knee injury at the time of the draft. During rehab, the right kneecap shattered, and doctors had to graft bone from Fagan's pelvis to put the kneecap back together. Three operations and sixteen months later, Fagan took the field for the 49ers. In 1988, Fagan and new draftee Pierce Holt joined Haley to form the guts of a pass rush that helped the 49ers to two Super Bowl wins in a row and a heartbreaking NFC championship game loss in 1990.

One moral here is that the best guys aren't always the top picks. Haley got taken number ninety-six and Fagan 102 in 1986, and Holt was picked thirty-ninth in 1988. You've got to find them and coach them and put them in the position to succeed. The other moral is, you've absolutely got to have a pass rush in today's NFL to win.

Excepting the 1990 Giants, who won the Super Bowl with guile, a relentless running game, and superb special teams, every Super Bowl champion from 1983 to 1992 was in the top dozen in the league in sacks. And consider what probably are the three great defensive seasons of the last decade:

Year	Club	W-L	Sacks	NFL Rank
1985	Chicago	18-1	64	3
1986	NY Giants	17-2	59	4
1991	Philadelphia	10-6	55	1

The Bears and Giants dominated the league, both winning the Super Bowl. The Eagles were the scariest team to miss the playoffs in years. "See what a pass rush will do for you?" the Eagles' defensive coordinator, Bud Carson, said in 1991. "When you get rushers in the face of the offense like we do, the offense doesn't have time to think. That's what great defense is all about; you make the offense do something it doesn't want to do. If you rush the quarterback and chase the quarterback and drive the quarterback nuts . . . well, that's the easiest way to win a football game."

Look at those three teams, the Bears and Giants and Eagles. Who will make the Hall of Fame from them? From that Chicago team, running back Walter Payton and linebacker Mike Singletary will go, with linebacker Wilber Marshall, defensive end Richard Dent, and defensive tackle Steve McMichael possible. From the Giants, Lawrence Taylor's a lock and linebacker Harry Carson possible. From the Eagles, defensive end Reggie White will go; perhaps linebacker Seth Joyner, defensive end Clyde Simmons, and quarterback Randall Cunningham, but their careers are still too young to tell. Payton's the only offensive lock from those three imposing teams. Most of the great players on three of the very good teams from the TV era are front-seven players, players whose jobs rest on disrupting quarterbacks.

"I don't know a team that's won a Super Bowl without an imposing pass rush," said Lombardi, now the Browns' director of pro personnel. "You don't bring pressure, you don't win in the NFL. You have to find a way to disrupt an offense and turn the ball over. It's just a fact of life."

Over the last decade or so, since Lawrence Taylor began putting his imprint on the sport, the position of pass-rusher—whether the player be an outside linebacker or defensive end or some hybrid elephant like Haley—has only grown in importance and stature. A look at the decade, and how much the pass-rusher has grown in importance:

The Lawrence Taylor Awakening, 1981–1983
In his first intrasquad scrimmage in training camp in 1981 with the Giants, Lawrence Taylor sacked the quarterback four times in a forty-five-minute period. He didn't know what the plays were or his exact assignments, but it didn't matter. He could get to the quarterback. And the Giants turned him loose to do that and to chase down rushers from behind and to make offensive coordinators leaguewide stay up nights trying to fig-

ure out how to stop this new plague. "I was shocked how easy it was at first," Taylor says now. "I couldn't figure out why people were making such a big deal of it. All I was doing was beating the blocker into the backfield." The league started keeping sacks as an individual statistic in 1982, right about the time Taylor pushed pass-rushing into the fore.

Looking at the period by the numbers, the average NFL team's sacks-per-game rose from 2.28 in 1981 to 2.71 by 1983. By then, the seeds of the next pass-rushing trend were firmly planted.

The 46, 1984–1985

The Bears taught the league about mismatches here, placing eight quick and strong defensive players on the line of scrimmage and daring the offense to block them. The design: Throw all kinds of defensive chaos at the quarterback, and the passer will never have the requisite time to consider all his options. Some teams tried to copy, but the quickness and speed and brute force of the Bear players made everyone else flooding the line look like a bunch of cheap imitators. "My career was winding down [in 1984 in Minnesota] when I played against that team," said quarterback Archie Manning, "and I just remember how scared a feeling it was being in the offensive backfield. They sacked us eleven times. I thought it was the most incredible, unstoppable defense I'd ever seen."

With the impetus of the Bears' league-record seventy-two sacks, the 1984 league average was 2.93 sacks per team per game, another record that still stands.

Looking for Mr. Goodrush, 1986–1991

Give me a pass-rusher, any pass-rusher. While only the very lucky teams at the top of drafts—Buffalo with Bruce Smith in 1985, Kansas City with Neil Smith in 1988, for instance—seemed to have much luck finding franchise pass-rushers, the draft crapshoot forced teams to be innovative. The 49ers took the small-college 225-pounder Haley and made him into a pass-rusher. Seattle relied on a 227-pound special-teamer, Rufus Porter, to fill their void.

It's a misconception to think that teams weren't getting to the quarterback. They were. Bill Parcells used to stand on the sidelines at Giants games and scream at his offensive linemen, "I don't want my quarterback getting touched!" He'd walk through the locker room on Monday morning after a decisive win and scornfully say something to his linemen like, "Simms got hit eight times yesterday. You guys stink." But coaches like Parcells put such an emphasis on protecting the quarterback that it was hard for defenses to penetrate their fortresses with any consistency.

By 1988, there were a bunch of LT wannabes out there sacking the quarterback. Phoenix had Freddie Joe Nunn, Green Bay had Tim Harris, Detroit had Mike Cofer. Reggie White was an impact player in the late eighties for Philadelphia, maybe the best run- and pass-playing end the game had ever seen. But there just weren't enough of them to go around.

"If you knew you couldn't get the real superstar type of rusher," said Butler of the Bills, "then you just looked up and down the lists for guys with one or more of the tools, and you brought them in and tried to develop them." What a ridiculous, inexact science this was. In 1986, the top two pass-rushers drafted were Jon Hand, by Indianapolis, and Anthony Bell, by the Cardinals. They were picked fourth and fifth in the draft overall. History chortles at them. The two best pass-rushers chosen were Pat Swilling, in the third round by New Orleans, and Clyde Simmons, in the ninth by Philadelphia. "You tell me why things like that happen, and you can have my job," Butler said.

Here's why, in part. By the mid-eighties, teams were so enamored with size and speed and how well players worked out for them in the postseason combine workouts that they often forgot to look at how they played. The stat sheets that come out each spring list each prospect's athletic ability and weightlifting ability and intelligence and every other mental and physical test, and are positively numbing. Why does Buffalo go back and study Pierce Holt nine times instead of taking another game film out and seeing if he's for them? Teams started drafting attributes instead of players. Strange business.

The sack numbers fell in this period, down to 2.38 per team per game, while completion percentage stayed the same. And, as Butler said earlier, every scout in every Ramada Inn every fall was looking for a pass-rusher like he'd look for a lost wallet: with desperation.

The Offensive Adjustment Era, 1991–present

The league's emphasis on size and speed and violence—and on a bunch of imaginative formations that left the quarterback more vulnerable than ever—was killing quarterbacks. In 1991, a league study found that 702 players of the approximately 1,540 employed missed at least one game with an injury. That included eighteen of the twenty-eight quarterbacks who started the season. And in 1992, the count was up to twenty of twenty-eight.

Under such fire, how did NFL quarterbacks record their highest-ever completion percentage, 57.5 percent, as a group? By throwing short. By dumping the ball off like never before. By telling receivers like Haywood Jeffires to cut off his routes earlier and look for shorter passes. Jeffires led the AFC in 1992 with ninety catches. He averaged 10.1 yards per catch, almost two yards less than in any previous season. This wasn't happening just in Houston; the average yards per pass attempt, leaguewide, was at its lowest point, 5.76, in over a decade.

"What's happening," Tampa Bay defensive coordinator Floyd Peters said as the 1992 passing numbers declined, "is that three-step drops by the quarterback are in vogue now. More people are doing what the 49ers are doing than I ever remember—throwing to the backs and dumping the ball short to the sure-handed wideouts. I call it controlled throwing. It's like some teams used to believe you could move the ball so reliably on the ground and only on the ground. The 49ers have changed that. Now teams think they can play a possession game by throwing. But in order to keep the heat off the quarterback, everything has to be quick, in rhythm. The defense has to be quicker than ever to counteract that. Most teams can't."

One team that did in 1992, Dallas, did it only after acquiring Charles Haley early in the season. "I think he might be the final

73

piece to our puzzle," a quietly exultant Jimmy Johnson said the morning of the trade. "I firmly believe that if you don't have the big-time pass-rusher today, you don't win." Dallas went from seventeenth to first in NFL defensive rankings with Haley aboard.

It's almost impossible today to play classic football, with the seven-step drop and the deep pass routes, and keep your quarterback intact. "There are a few teams out there who can put the incredible pressure on you with the pass rush, and if you come up against them, I think you're killing your quarterback, if you expect him to do what he used to," Peters said. "Those days are over. And if you don't have your quarterback, you don't have hope."

There's such an emphasis on protecting the quarterback now that the vogue is for two things: big blocking backs who can run (Barry Word, Jarrod Bunch, and Daryl Johnston, to name three), and the 49er playbook. Short stuff, quick stuff, Bruce Smith-proof stuff. The Dolphins blew that Miami–Buffalo game described above because they got greedy in the second half, going away from the three-step drops when they should have been patient and controlled, as they were in the first half. Give that game to them again and you can bet they'd have Marino playing more risk-free in the second half.

"No matter what offense you play today," said Phil Simms, the veteran quarterback, "I think the quarterback's a ticking time bomb who's bound to go down. It's just luck if he doesn't. If I was coaching a team now, I'd almost have to sit down my starting quarterback a week or two during the year. I've just come to think this way. You have no idea how good it feels after that bye week we have now. You give me that bye week and one more week during the season, and I think a lot of quarterbacks would be playing better and feeling incredibly better at the end of each season. Teams are finding ways to get to the quarterback, either with the great pass-rushers or with the secondary blitzes or whatever. They're going to keep doing it."

Here's how Floyd Peters, a five-decade veteran of the NFL as a player and coach, sees the nineties: "For offenses, more of the short drops and quick throws and one back," he said. "For defenses, well, if you want to get to the quarterback, you'd better get some corner who can cover, you'd better blitz on first down, and you'd better find yourself a couple of Reggie Whites or Bruce Smiths."

Then he laughed. Loudly.

So many people treat pass-rushers like they're unstoppable, that at some crucial point of the game, the great ones are going to find a way to disrupt something you're doing. That's true, most of the time.

There is one man, though, who is more schooled at stopping the great ones than anyone. Not that he stops them consistently. He just has had the most practice. He is Joe Bugel, the former coach of the Phoenix Cardinals, and he has prepared to play Lawrence Taylor and Reggie White a total of thirty-six times.

"What a great job I have, huh?" Bugel said one fall 1992 day in Phoenix, leaning back in his office and guffawing a time or two.

He went to his video machine to put on a game tape, his favorite one of 1992, a 27-24 win over Washington, his former team. Bugel coached the Redskins' offensive line for nine years, long enough to cut his teeth on every great pass-rusher in the NFC East in that era. In 1990, he took the Phoenix job, and though he wasn't successful, he had some great days with a terribly young and mediocre offensive line.

That's why he wanted to turn on the tape of this conquest of the Redskins so badly. His office, done in a Southwestern wood motif, had a video screen the size of one of those minicinema screens, and the images of the football tape fit it perfectly. He'd been waiting to show this moment. With 3:48 to go in the game, the defending Super Bowl champs led 24-20, and Phoenix took the ball, with backup quarterback Chris Chandler under center, at the Card 15.

The screen was frozen, and before running the tape, Bugel gave his fifty-words-or-less philosophy. If you know Bugel, you know nothing with him is ever fifty words or less.

"Look, anytime you go up against a Lawrence Taylor or a Reggie White or a situation here with Charles Mann and Wilber

Marshall, your job is to do the best you can in trying to stop them from taking control of the game. There are probably five or six guys in the game right now—Taylor, White, Smith, Derrick Thomas, Junior Seau, Cortez Kennedy, and maybe the New Orleans guys, Swilling and Jackson—who I feel can take over a game. You've got to set up your protection with those guys in mind. It limits your formations, but it's just something you accept.

"Right from the start, we had to stay up late at night preparing for Taylor. It used to be we thought we had to build the huge tackles for the running game, but now we don't necessarily need the 300-pound tackles; we need the tackle who can move, because he's going to be blocking a tackle who can move. We had some very good success early. We kind of owned 'em. Then Taylor started taking over. You know how we'd prepare for Taylor? It was really interesting. The first thing we'd do is get a reel of all of Taylor's moves—outside move, inside move, bull move, stunts, whatever—and get five or six of each of those. Then we'd show that reel to our defensive people who were going to imitate Taylor. I'd get Charles Mann up there to practice the club technique—you know, Taylor would club you with a forearm on his pass-rush to try to knock you goofy. And then we'd take our fastest guys, Darrell Green and Gary Clark, guys like that, and we'd get them out there, ready for the scout team. We'd have fifteen minutes, in full pads, of Mann and Joe Jacoby, our left tackle, going at it. I'm telling you, it was World War III out there. Brutal. Then, we'd get Jacoby ready for Taylor's speed by lining up Green or Clark across from him and having them simulate Taylor's speed. Now, they were faster, of course, but we'd keep on Jacoby to remember his technique and his footwork and resist the urge to just run after the guys because when he got into the same situation with Taylor he'd have to keep his footwork right. When he played Taylor, I guarantee you he was ready. You know, things like that, I think, are what made The Hogs.

"The other thing we did was the wedgeblock. Not very hard to figure out. But when Taylor was really at his peak, we'd get two huge bodies—Donnie Warren and Jacoby—and they'd combine to block him, one huge monster from one side and the other huge monster from the other side. You scheme to block one guy with whatever it takes, then you figure out how to block the others. We call the other guys on the line Gilligan when we had to play the Giants, because they're usually on an island.

"So that's what we did. I think you have to double-team block the Smiths and the Whites now, because the great pass-rushers are better than the great offensive linemen. It's a fact of life."

Lesson over. He breathed.

Movie time. Bugel put his pride and joy into motion. The film showed, over and over again on this eighty-five-yard drive, that you can stop anybody you want to if you devote enough people to doing it. Play in point: First and ten from the Washington 34, and Marshall steams in from Chandler's left and Mann from his right. Chandler looks both ways quickly to eye his protection. And what protection it was. To his right, a motion man, wide receiver Ricky Proehl, has turned upfield just in the time and space that Mann is trying to get to Chandler. Proehl stuck his 190 pounds into Mann's breastbone, and the right tackle and guard wedgeblocked him back. A back and left tackle, meanwhile, stuck it to Marshall. Neither got within five yards of Chandler. Chandler threw a seventeen-yard strike to Hill. Three plays later, Bugel had the biggest win of his life.

"See what that proves?" he said, after a half-hour of clicking the play back and forth so that I'd memorized it. "The great ones are great. But you're not helpless against 'em."

I noticed, over time, that Bruce Smith complained a lot for a man who made $1.5 million a year.

Actually, his moods varied with his physical condition, which happens with most players. Late in 1990, he strode into an Italian restaurant in Buffalo on Friday night, on top of the world, not caring who saw him or bugged him, and telling a couple of dinner guests, referring to the game at hand, "We're two nights and a wake-up call from kicking their ass." In 1991, his left knee started hurting, and a black cloud came over him, and he got some racist mail in his home mailbox that scared his wife. Fans questioned his pain threshold when he became a totally ineffective player in 1991 after what his surgeon said was a relatively minor arthroscopic procedure. In mid-1991, driving to a TV appearance, the cloud rested on his forehead. "I'm so sick of feeling like this," he said forlornly. "My knee feels like there's a burning sensation that's going to explode. I keep trying to play and it's not ready." He wanted to resign from life after the Bills' second Super Bowl debacle; he was drained and limping and mad and stupefied all at the same time. "I wonder if that was me in my uniform," he said glumly that night after the Redskins' victory, walking up the tunnel to the off-season. "Sure didn't feel like it." He was enraged if anyone blocked him below the waist. Preparing for his early-season game with San Francisco in 1992, watching films upstairs in Rich Stadium, in a dark defensive meeting room, I thought he would have been happy. The previous day, he'd made a triumphant return in his first real game back after all his knee problems, and the quarterback he'd camped out with all afternoon, Jim Everett, said after the game, "He was in on me so much I could smell what was on his breath. I told him, 'Bruce, you've got to stop eating onions the night before games.' "

"Nah," Smith said, watching film for the second time this day. "The previous game is history every Monday. I can't do anything about it. It can't help me."

He complained about all the rules the offenses had to their advantage. "They can hold me and grab me and cut on my knees, and the league took away the head-slap from the defense. We can't do anything. I firmly believe they make rules in this league to protect everyone except the defensive linemen." He complained about leg-whipping, the practice of some teams to kick opponents as though it were a perfectly innocent residue of a block when in fact it's intended to cause mayhem and pain.

"One time, I had a player from another team come to me before a game and say, 'Bruce, be careful. Watch yourself. Protect yourself, they're trying to put you out.' This was 1990. I won't tell you what team, but I will tell you the coach has been fired," he said.

Then I realized the reason for all the complaints and moans. Bruce Smith, like many players in football, can't quite get the end of his career out of his mind, even when surrounded by the most beautiful of families in a cushy living room with gigantic TVs and more friends than he knows what to do with. He was a gunfighter, and everywhere he plied his trade there were men not just out to stop him, but to stop him by any means possible.

"In the business we're in, you shouldn't expect to play a long time, and you shouldn't expect to live a long time," he said. "Basically, I'm giving up my body to support a better lifestyle for me and for everyone close to me. Any time I go out there, it could be my last time. And is my contract guaranteed? No. Is this lifestyle guaranteed? No. The position I play, the way I get beat up every single game, you think about things like that, no matter how much glory comes your way."

There was a Western on the gigantic TV in the background, and just then some other brave gunfighter lost a duel. Shot in the chest. Bruce Smith never saw it happen.

But on that November night in Miami, such dark thoughts were very far away. Richmond Webb and Keith Sims saw to that. Rewind the tape now, and go back to that game. In the closing minutes of the game, Smith, who played every snap of the fifty-five defensive plays it took to beat the Dolphins, had the biggest smile I've ever seen on him. With two minutes to go and the Bills' offense running out the clock, Smith nodded at me and came over.

His right arm was bleeding from a cut near the elbow. There were seven major spots of grass stain on his pants, mostly all over his rear end, and his shirt was a puzzle of south Florida soil and grass and soaked splotches from the sweat. The jersey was torn and worn and out of shape from Sims and Webb and Weidner grabbing it all night. The right shoulder pad hung awkwardly out of the jersey, like it had been yanked out. There must have been a faucet on the top of his head, because the sweat, even with the temperatures falling into the low sixties around midnight in south Florida, was dripping off his face in virtual rivers.

He was walking fine. The adrenaline hadn't worn off yet. The pain would wait until tomorrow.

"Unbelievable," he said. Exhausted, he couldn't stop smiling. "What a feeling. What a war out there."

This is what a great pass rush and a great pass-rusher can mean to a game. He can mean the game, that's what he can mean. And this night, he just did.

Later, he said, "My role with the team is simple. I may not get a sack. But I'm a presence. I'm there. They know I'm there. That's important. I harass the quarterback enough, and some quarterbacks are going to get jittery. They get what we call happy feet, dancing around there. It's important just to put the thought in their head: There's somebody there. Somebody's after you. Then they can't think as clearly. Then they feel hurried. That's my impact. I can be overwhelming, but it's important that at least I'm there."

Wideouts and Corners

WARFARE AT MATCH PLAY

In the beginning, there was just good hard football—tough football, running football, the world dominated by big bruising backs. And it was good. But then came artistic passers and fast, deep receivers—fast men, perhaps the world's fastest—and it was still good, and the TV ratings were even better. But coaches, who most love what they can control, did not think it was good, and they devised zone defenses and bump-and-run coverages, and they slowed the thunder-and-lightning passes to a dull roar.

And the lords of football saw their game and feared that it was growing too dull and slow, and they changed the rules to let the receivers flow free, and passes rained down again, and the lords were happy. But the coaches fretted. All right, they said, if you won't let us stop the receivers from running down the field, we won't give the passers time to find them. And the Taylors and Smiths and Dents were unleashed to wreak terrible havoc upon the passing game.

But all things are cyclical, and each strategy leads to counter-strategies. As Joe Bugel has shown us, the great pass-rushers *can* be stopped, if you apply enough resources to the task. If you spread the field, present enough options, and focus on the most dangerous threat to your offense, you can give your passer time and create the individual matchup you want between a wide receiver and a cornerback.

This is the NFL today. At no time since the original development of the zone defense has this pairing been so critical. Never has there been such a premium placed on the athletic gifts of the players at these two positions. The wide receiver no longer just runs his routes; he must run, read, react, and do so with lightning quickness and in total synch with his quarterback back in the pocket. And the cornerback must do more, bearing the burden of the defense's increasing inability to force the action, while matching wits and skills with a phalanx of receivers who are getting bigger and faster every year.

Twice a year, the quintessential matchups of the nineties are played out on the fields of the AFC Central, embodied by three prodigiously talented athletes:

Pittsburgh Steelers' cornerback Rod Woodson, who grew up in Fort Wayne, Indiana, a track and football star; Houston Oilers' wide receiver Haywood Jeffires, from Greensboro, North Carolina, a basketball and football star; and another Houston wide receiver, Ernest Givins, from Tampa, Florida, a baseball and football star.

These three fellas can play—anything. Woodson barely lost a 100-meter hurdles race against Roger Kingdom, the reigning Olympic gold medalist, in 1987. Jeffires outscored Danny Manning in a state high school championship game. Givins was scouted for his baseball prowess in high school. Their skills help make the modern NFL as popular as it is and as compelling as it is.

When Houston plays Pittsburgh twice a season, one of the best athletes ever to take an NFL field—Woodson—is matched against a lithe high-jumper with huge hands—Jeffires—and a tough little Ping-Pong ball with gluey hands—Givins. When Woodson and the quick, young Steeler secondary come up big, Pittsburgh should win. When Jeffires and Givins dominate, Houston, an aerial show waiting to happen every Sunday, does win.

"I love these games as much as any I play," Woodson said a few days before the Steelers' 1992 season began, at Houston. "They're so great because any play when our defense is out there can be the play that decides the game. Houston's so dangerous, and they rely on their great receivers so much. You've got to play every play like it's the biggest one of the game."

Where are the teams with the antiquated, predictable passing game? New Orleans and Kansas City have the defenses and the pounding running games to get to the Super Bowl, yet they've combined for just one playoff win since 1980 because they haven't built sophisticated pass offenses. Every team in the 1992 AFC and NFC Championship games—Miami, Buffalo, Dallas, and San Francisco—was at least close to state-of-the-passing-art. Just as Woodson versus Givins/Jeffires is crucial in the Pittsburgh–Houston series, wide receivers and cornerbacks all around the league were being recognized as franchise players as the nineties dawned.

"Watch this," Michael Irvin says.

He's in an offensive meeting room at the Dallas Cowboys' practice facility. Irvin, who leads all NFL wide receivers in guile, has the video control in his hands, and there's a game up there on the big screen. Dallas at Washington, 1991. Washington came in 11-0. Irvin caught nine balls for 130 yards against all-world cornerback Darrell Green, including the clinching touchdown pass. Dallas won, 24-21.

Irvin lets the tape go forth. The images on the big screen tell it all. Starting from the left wide receiver slot, he runs about twelve yards straight downfield, shakes his shoulders a little bit, stops almost dead in his tracks, and turns to face the quarterback, Steve Beuerlein. The timing on this pattern is such that, by the time Irvin has fully turned to Beuerlein, the pass is already in the air, winging its way to Irvin's gloved hands. So as Irvin turns . . .

Well, let him explain. He freezes the tape.

"As I turn," he says, "a lot is going on. I've got to locate the ball and focus on it, because it's going to get to me in a split second. I've got to get ready for Darrell behind me, because I know he's coming up. I've got to figure out where I'm going to catch it—if it's going to be high or low or outside or inside—and how I'm going to keep my body between the ball and Darrell. And I've got to start thinking about running with the ball when I catch it."

He unfreezes the tape. In slow motion, the play continues.

As the ball approaches Irvin, Green, who even looks quick in slo-mo, is recovering. His body has flown four yards past when Irvin stopped to turn, and now he's pumping his legs, taking three sprinting steps at Irvin; as the ball is inches from Irvin's hands, Green flies at him.

Here—it's almost an imperceptible thing—Irvin seems to turn his body into a shell. The body becomes concave. His shoulders come forward. His rear end pushes out. His arms reach for the ball. The combined effect is to build a little house for the ball; Irvin's arms are the front door, and his gut is the living room. And now the ball spirals into his hands with a slap we can only imagine; quickly he nestles it away tight to his stomach. Maybe four-tenths of a second after ball hits skin, all 170 pounds of Darrell Green catapult into the spinal column between Irvin's shoulder blades, just below the shoulder pads. Irvin sinks like a stone, the breath momentarily going out of him. But he pops right up like he never felt a thing—which, with the adrenaline that pumps when you've caught a ball for a first down on the man some people say is the best cornerback in football, is true. "I usually never feel a thing, I'm so excited," Irvin says.

This is not ballet. It is grace in the face of violence. It's the most compelling one-on-one match we watch every autumn Sunday in living rooms from Maine to Mission Valley.

"Look at how much went into that," Irvin says, "and look at how many things could have gone wrong. I could have slipped. The pass could have been a split-second late. The pass could have been off to one side. The pass could have been high. If the pass is off, I still get the shit beat out of me, and all for nothing. It's amazing when you think about it, that so much goes into the catching of one ball. All the timing you build up with the quarterback, all the work you do to build that timing and trust in the offseason, all the work you do knowing that the cornerback is doing the same kind of work in the offseason, trying to get better. It's so challenging, so violent, so hard. And it looks so easy. That's the strange thing."

Just then, fellow receiver Alvin Harper, who starts on the

other side of the field from Irvin, sticks his head into the room.

"You working out, Alvin?" Irvin says to him.

"Oh yeah," Harper says, and he pops out.

Irvin continues. "You know, when Alvin came here last year from college, he was shocked. He'd say things like, 'Man, you're never open in this league. I was always open in college.' I'd say, 'Open? I'll tell you what open is. Open's when the damn corner is just breathing down your neck and not smacking you. Open's when you've got an inch.'

"The game's so physical and so close that the thing between the receiver and the corner is almost like two power forwards going at it. When you catch the ball, it's like you're boxing out for a rebound, and the corner's coming over the top trying to get the rebound from you. It's the best confrontation in the game. I love it."

"Let's watch some of this," Albert Lewis says.

It's late in the 1991 season, and Lewis, the Chiefs' all-pro cornerback, has just decided this day to have arthroscopic knee surgery. This will end his season, but he feels he has no choice. He can't sprint, and a corner who can't sprint is like a tiger without teeth. Lewis could go out there and scare people because of his reputation, which he'd been doing when he could stand the pain this season, but he couldn't make any plays. He hasn't felt right all season because of a bothersome and sometimes painful cyst behind the knee.

Now, with a trace of longing in his voice, he sits down and starts to talk about what we're about to see. It hurts him so much to watch. What he puts on the big video screen is a taped reel of Jerry Rice tearing the New Orleans Saints to shreds. Nine catches, 154 yards. And angst from Lewis.

See, the Chiefs and 49ers, being in opposite conferences, play at most once every three years. So Lewis, at most, faces the best receiver in football, Rice, once every three years—unless they happen to meet in the Super Bowl. Fat chance. Lewis was nine the last time the Chiefs made the Super Bowl. Now he was thirty-one. The next time the Chiefs and 49ers would meet, in 1994, Lewis would be thirty-four, and probably out of football.

So here he is, he thought, with one last chance to play the best, and his bum knee won't let him do it.

Lewis is a thin, handsome, very serious man. Unemotional, too, except on the field. So it was strange, after a couple of days with him, to see him show emotion at the sight of the silent video running in front of him on a big screen.

"Damn," he spits, watching Rice make plays. Lewis is downright morose. "I can't believe I'm going to miss this. This kills me. I was looking forward to this. It was going to be like Ali and Tyson, a real heavyweight fight."

(Two days later, Rice was informed how down Lewis was about not facing him. "He is?" said Rice, genuinely pleased Lewis would want to face him so much. But Rice was also genuinely pleased not to have to face Lewis. Someday, Albert Lewis will be discussed by the Pro Football Hall of Fame committee in Canton, Ohio; his replacement, Jayice Pearson, won't. Rice could see a potential big stat day staring him in the face.)

Lewis is distraught. The cornerback mentality is—well, it's just different from the mentality of other positions in football. Lewis is eloquent about it. He can hide his emotions and be introspective and smile slightly and give you meaningless answers to the usual questions, but this subject he loves. Just loves it. His response is the essence of the position.

He gets up, flexing his wounded knee. He wants to be out there, eating up some poor wide receiver.

"In one sense," he says, "you have no fear. In another sense, you have fear every waking moment of your life. Every play you have to know you can be totally exposed out there. It's a one-play-at-a-time career. If I don't have fear, I might relax, and if I relax, I'm vulnerable. They can beat me then.

"I live for the feeling—to walk into the tunnel before a game and let out a deep breath and know that I'm about to go against the best athletes in the game, every week. Nothing else matters. You're living on the edge, every second of the game, and it's so exhilarating. And different. Every Sunday, no matter who I'm playing, I know they've been working on ways to stop me and to challenge me. It's a chess game. I know if I don't disguise what I do and if I stop the same play the same way every time, they're going to figure out a way to defeat me. And I know if I'm not confident, they'll be able to defeat me too.

"Every time I don't make a play, I'm shocked. It's like [in the 1990 playoffs] when we're playing Miami, and I go for the interception against the Dolphins late in the fourth quarter, with the game on the line. I missed. Mark Clayton catches the ball, and he scores the winning touchdown. After the game, people keep asking me about the play, and I tell them I'd do the exact same thing again. I would. Sitting here right now, thinking back on the play, I'd do the exact same thing, the exact same coverage. You can't doubt yourself. You can't change how you play if one thing goes wrong. That has to do with something I feel strongly about.

"You're fighting a war out there. It's the war of confidence, and you've got to win it to be successful in this league. I'm not going to lay back and react to how the receiver plays. I'm going to attack. I'm going to put my ass on the line. Like on the Clayton play. All I'm thinking out there is, 'Make the play!' I'm not thinking that I should be cautious because the game's on the line. It's instinctive. It's like when I watch tennis, and I watch John McEnroe play, I know how good he is. But I just figure if I devoted my time to the sport, I could beat him.

"That's how a cornerback has to think."

What are the most important positions in the game today? Most fans and experts would agree that quarterback is number one. After that, you hear about left tackles, big-hitting safeties, the great pass-rushing linebackers and defensive ends, and the game-breaking backs.

I'd argue that today, right after quarterback, the most important guys are cornerbacks and wide receivers, numbers 2 and 2A, in either order. You couldn't have made this argument a generation ago, when a great receiving season was fifty catches for 800 yards, but today it's a whole new world. Look at the Super Bowls since 1985. Every winner has had a solid running game—San Francisco, Chicago, the Giants, Washington. But the 49ers had the greatest quarterback of his day, Joe Montana, and the Giants had a blazing-hot quarterback in one of their wins, Phil Simms, and the Bears and Redskins both had passing games that could carry them in any game. The AFC champs— Miami, Denver, Buffalo, Cincinnati—all had Pro Bowl quarterbacks and deep-threat receivers. The passing game has become crucial to the success of a good team, and blunting it crucial to a great defense. Since the league last expanded, in 1976, the percentage of passes caught by wide receivers in the NFL has risen from 40.7 percent to, in 1991, 58.1 percent.

"We're the game today," says Houston's Jeffires. In 1990–91, Jeffires had the most prolific back-to-back seasons (190 receptions) in NFL history. "The running backs and quarterbacks used to be the mainstays. Now, we're about equal to the quarterbacks. We're taking the spotlight away from everybody in the game."

It's tougher to quantify the importance of corners, because the best ones often don't have the best statistics. But coaches know, front-office guys know, and the players know. "Great corners ought to get more consideration for things like MVP awards," says Ernest Givins, "because they can control what an offense does, just by their presence. They can force an offense to avoid a huge chunk of the field." In 1991, one of the most fiscally conservative teams in the league, Pittsburgh, with one of the smartest men in the league running the club, Dan Rooney, smashed its salary structure to bits to tie up Rod Woodson for three years. The Steelers had never paid a player a million dollars a year; they paid Woodson $1,450,000 annually. The Packers faced a similar situation in 1992, drafting cornerback Terrell Buckley with the fourth pick in the draft and laboring all spring and summer to sign him. Late in the summer, Buckley called Deion Sanders, on the road with the Atlanta Braves, to ask his confidant and former cornerback teammate at Florida State for advice. Deion spoke volumes: "Don't get down," he told Buckley. "Hey, you've got the power here. You're playing the spot they need. Don't give in. They've got to have you. You know it, they know it. They'll come up with the money." And they did—just as the Falcons had with Sanders.

Deion went through a heated series of negotiations before signing a new football contract in September 1992. But he knew he had a hammer in the talks, because the Falcons relied so much on man-to-man defensive coverage, and because he was a great man-to-man cover player, and because the Falcons were moving into a new domed stadium and needed Sanders's drawing power. The flashpoint of the talks, and their real importance, came just after Sanders told the Falcons' brass in a face-to-face meeting that he wanted $2,000,000 for the season, in some combination of salary and bonuses. That would be $400,000 more than Chris Miller, the Atlanta quarterback.

The Falcons' long-time owner, Rankin Smith, Sr., said in an annoyed voice, "What team pays the defensive back more than the quarterback? That's crazy."

Sanders shot back, "Why don't you let me go free, and we'll see!"

The Falcons understood. The Falcons, gun to their heads, paid.

Add the threat of punt- and kick-returning, which all of the corners above do, and their salaries seem quite fair, in the context of the prevailing financial insanity of all sports. Each had a punt or kick return for a touchdown in 1992. By midseason 1992, these three corners—Woodson, Sanders and Buckley—were being paid more than half of the NFL's starting quarterbacks, more than the 1991 leading receivers in the NFC (Irvin) and AFC (Jeffires), more than any of the Pro Bowl safeties, more than any offensive lineman, and on a near-par with Lawrence Taylor ($1,833,000), Reggie White ($1,513,000), and Bruce Smith ($1,500,000), the premier pass-rushers of the day. "Don't go comparing me to Lawrence Taylor, because I do more things for my team than he does," Sanders says. "Compare me to Dan Marino."

The following statistics show two reasons why the Woodsons and Sanderses are so badly needed today.

Here is a breakdown of total National Football League receptions at recent five-year intervals, with the figures signifying the percentage of balls caught per position each season:

Position	1976	1981	1986	1991
Wide receiver	40.7	42.2	45.6	58.1
Running back	42.4	40.0	35.7	28.3
Tight end	16.7	17.5	18.5	13.5
Other	0.2	0.3	0.2	0.1

At the same time, collegiate passing is markedly up, which means, ostensibly, that more and better receivers are being developed for the NFL. "For the last ten years, year in and year out, wide receiver has been the deepest position in the draft," general manager Dick Steinberg of the Jets said in 1992.

Here are the average per-game rushing and passing statistics in major-college football games in 1980 and 1990:

	Rush Att.	Rush Yds.	Pass Att.	Pass Yds.
1980	95.3	356.6	46.6	303.7
1990	86.1	335.3	56.6	394.8
Change	-9.2	-21.3	+10.0	+91.1

There's one more reason for the passing game's rise: The league wants to see it. Offense sells. Defense doesn't. Almost every rules change of the past fifteen years has helped the offense put points on the board, not aided the defense in taking them away. And now, with the NFL facing a crucial point in its television history—the TV contract is up for negotiation after the 1993 season, and the networks are threatening to lower the $32,500,000 average annual payments to each team because of stagnant ratings—exciting games are more important than ever. "The NFL needs us," Jeffires says, correctly. "We're the circus. Not just in Houston, because of the wide-open offense we play. Everywhere. The passing game has never been as important."

Even the hard-bitten guys see that. Career coach Walt Corey, Buffalo's defensive coordinator, knows the real deal in football. "TV has made such an impression on our game, whether we want to admit it or not," he says. "And TV wants excitement. TV people appreciate good defense; I really believe that. But TV people are just like the fans. They want to see the home run. They want the big play. And we have to keep the TV people happy, because they've got to keep the advertisers for our games happy, and they're all happy when there's lots of scoring." Ergo: Pass the ball to very fast people, and get very fast people to cover them.

Now you know something about the importance of wide receivers and cornerbacks in today's football.

. . .

To understand the matchup, understand that nowhere in football is there such raw emotion or such definite finality as in a duel between a great corner and a great wideout. It doesn't happen all the time, the way it used to; today, teams play lots of zone defenses in which safeties, the last line of football defense, or extra cornerbacks help cover the best receivers. It's rare for the best corners, like Green, to take on the best receivers, like Irvin, in single-coverage for much of a game.

But in some important games through recent NFL history, this one matchup has determined who wins and who loses. Often during a season, a game turns solely because a cornerback bests a wide receiver or because a wideout burns a corner. And sometimes, a season ends with Bobby Thomson suddenness.

The Giants and Rams were in overtime in the NFC playoffs in January 1990, with Los Angeles on the New York 30. The Giants lined up eight players near the line of scrimmage to stop the Rams from running the ball any closer to a game-winning field goal. Split wide right were Flipper Anderson, very fast, and one Giant, corner Mark Collins—out on an island together, soon to decide the fate of the game. Jim Everett, the Rams' quarterback, took the snap and dropped back, eschewing a handoff to running back Greg Bell as the Giants flooded the line to stop the run. Collins tried to bump Anderson off his pass route but barely tipped him, and Anderson got a one-step edge flying down the right sideline. Everett floated a rainbow toward the right corner of the end zone. Collins leaped to deflect it near the goal line, and his middle fingertip missed the falling spiral by six inches. Anderson caught it. He kept running, too, through the tunnel to the Rams' locker room, stopping only to open the door. When his Ram mates charged into the room, there was Anderson, jumping up and down like a kid who'd just gotten a Beagle puppy in his Christmas stocking. They charged into him with such intensity that Anderson was knocked to the hard floor, bruising his jaw in the joyous melee. The Rams went on to the NFC Championship game the next week.

Here's where the cornerback mentality comes in handy. A corner has to have something in his mind that keeps telling him, over and over: Forget! Forget! Forget! If you've made a great play or a play that cost your team the season, forget it by the time you get back to the huddle! Because if you're getting drilled and you keep thinking about getting drilled, your mind starts to wander. You start to think: *Oh no! Don't throw it at me!* Atlanta threw a heavy blitz at Joe Montana in 1990, leaving pedestrian cornerback Charles Dimry in man coverage most of the game against Jerry Rice. Rice caught thirteen passes for 225 yards and five touchdowns. Dimry got run out of Atlanta, signing with Denver as a Plan B free agent the next winter and playing in anonymity.

The Falcons lost faith in Dimry after that game, and others like it, that season. But Mark Collins didn't lose faith in himself. Collins is from the Albert Lewis school of corner confidence. After the Rams knocked the Giants into next season with the Flipper Anderson catch, Collins stood in the locker room and told reporter after reporter—there must have been ten waves of them—the same thing. He was stoic, professional, totally unbowed by sending the Giants home for the winter instead of to San Francisco for the NFC title game. "That's the life of a cornerback," he kept saying, over and over, never losing patience. "You make ten good plays, and one bad one, and all anyone wants to talk about is the bad. If you're going to play cornerback in this league, you've got to accept that this is your life."

"It's a mental position much more than a physical position," Minnesota defensive coordinator Tony Dungy says. He was a safety with Pittsburgh and San Francisco in the seventies. "You can have a bad game if you don't make two plays. You can be ninety-five, ninety-seven percent efficient on a given day, but you've got to shoot for 100 percent. And that gets to some players. They can't adjust to one play ruining their day, and they don't make it."

"In college, I played safety and running back and wide receiver, and I returned kicks," Woodson of the Steelers says. "I think now, playing cornerback, that the corner is the hardest position, along with quarterback, to play in this league. In some ways it's tougher. The day-to-day, play-after-play responsibility is so big at both corner and quarterback. But if you think about it, a quarterback can go fifteen of twenty and have a great day. You go eighteen of twenty as a cornerback—eighteen times you cover well, twice you're beaten for big plays—and you've had a terrible day. At corner, you're basically on an island. Say I'm an offensive tackle, and Reggie White's on me. I'd be more at ease there because I know I'm going to have help blocking him. If I'm on the corner, and I'm covering Haywood Jeffires man-to-man, and he's one of the best receivers in football, I know if I screw up and he gets a step on me, I've just cost my team seven points. With all the great receivers in football now, you face that kind of pressure every week."

Receivers actually have it easier, mentally. A wideout can drop a couple of passes during a game, even a long one, but if he catches seven passes for 111 yards, he's had a good day. If a cornerback plays good coverage—not necessarily preventing completion, but keeping the damage to a minimum—on all but two of the throws in his direction, and one goes for a touchdown, he's wearing the goathorns after the game.

There's never been a time in NFL history when the game's been so pass-happy, and when cornerbacks have been so important. There just aren't many great ones. Look at the lengths to which the Falcons went for Sanders in 1992, making him the highest-paid defensive veteran in history—even though he was going to miss four games to play baseball with the Braves. "Deion," said Atlanta VP Ken Herock, "can without question be a Hall of Fame football player. Plus, we really need him."

Why is it so hard to find great corners? The answer lies in the requirements of the job. First: speed. Wide receivers know where they're going, and wide receivers are getting faster and faster; all four starting Falcon receivers in 1992, for instance, ran the forty-yard dash in 4.5 seconds or less. Cornerbacks, optimally, should be at least as fast as the fastest wideout they play, with the quickness and maneuverability to make up for the tricky patterns wideouts are running. Second: size. The Jets' top four receivers in 1992 were all between six-foot-two and six-foot-four. Rob Moore would have six inches on Darrell Green if they played. "We definitely use our height to our advantage when we play," says Moore. But it's not just height. These guys are big.

Rice is a lithe but surprisingly tough six-foot-two and 205. Art Monk, the all-time receptions record-holder, is six-three, 210. Ed McCaffrey of the Giants is six-five, 215. The Dallas starters, Irvin and Harper, average six-foot-three, 202. Corners have to be able to handle them physically. Third: expanded job responsibility. As if coverage isn't tough enough, corners today are being asked more and more to help out in run defense. They have to be bigger, to ward off linemen and blocking backs coming at them. So cornerbacks have to be all things to all coaches. And today, the really good ones are extremely valuable.

These increased demands are, naturally, triggered by the growth in the role of the wide receiver. Teams have done more and more to make receivers their prime offensive weapons. Three teams—Atlanta, Houston, and Detroit—were among the NFL's final eight in the 1991 playoffs, and all three of them ran four-wide-receiver offenses that were offshoots of Mouse Davis's run-and-shoot. Davis is a sort of nutty professor of pro football. He took the crazy-quilt run-and-shoot (four wideouts, one back, no tight ends, a mobile quarterback) from college football to the United States Football League to the Lions of the NFL and most recently to the ill-fated World League. In exile now without a job, in part because his ideas are too radical for the mainstream NFL, Davis still sees his offense being run in Detroit, and his disciples, Kevin Gilbride and June Jones, are offensive coordinators in Houston and Atlanta, respectively. Running four wide receivers, Davis says now, is no longer the hodgepodge or radical offense football conservatives once thought. "It's a rational approach to a winning offense. Coaches everywhere can see that the game is becoming much more wide receiver-oriented rather than a slug-mouth game. Wide receivers give you more production than big backs."

It's been fascinating to watch the recent evolution of the game. "When I came into the league," says quarterback Ken O'Brien, drafted in 1983, "it seemed like every team had one quality receiver. Now the depth is unbelievable." High schools and colleges slowly but surely are going more and more to wide-open offenses. When Davis held a run-and-shoot clinic in New

Jersey in 1992, almost 300 coaches overstuffed a group-meeting room; some had to be turned away.

They're all using receivers more, almost regardless of how good the receivers are. The schemes today just seem so well-suited for the pass to succeed when the run is blunted, especially with so many defenses gearing up to clog the middle (especially Philadelphia, Kansas City, and Washington) and stop the big backs. When San Diego got off to an 0-5 start in 1991, coach Dan Henning quite literally changed his coaching philosophy from run-oriented to passing—and he had led the league in rushing two years straight. "We'd been running the ball out of necessity, because of a lack of [good] receivers," he says. "So we're playing our fifth game, against Kansas City, and we play close to perfect. No turnovers. We outgain them 311 yards to 182. Our backs rush for 156. And we lose, 14-13. I'm walking off the field, saying to myself, It doesn't work. In today's football, it just doesn't work. The next week, we go to play the Raiders in a game we have no business winning, we run four wide receivers, twice as much as I ever have, and we win 21-13. We didn't win all the time with it, obviously, but we beat New Orleans with it."

The changes are attracting great young athletes to the game. One of the best receivers in the game today, Minnesota's Cris Carter, came to a fork in his road in 1984, in high school in Ohio. He was a basketball-football star with a brother, Butch, playing in the NBA. Truth be told, Cris would rather have been the next Mark Aguirre than the next Steve Largent. "But I decided to make football my primary sport," Cris said, "because there were so many more jobs in football, and I thought to be a great football player would be easier than being a great basketball player."

Lots of players today had to make similar choices. Woodson, a four-time Big Ten high-hurdles champion, broke Renaldo Nehemiah's collegiate indoor record in the fifty-five-meter hurdles. "If he concentrated on track," Purdue track coach Mike Poehlein said some years ago, "he could have been another Jesse Owens or Carl Lewis." In 1987, during his rookie-year contract holdout with the Steelers, Woodson trained for the first time since high school in outdoor track. After two months of training, he lost that 100-meter hurdles race to Kingdom by eight-hundredths of a second, 13.21 to 13.29.

Jeffires and Givins, the star Houston receivers, had choices too. "I wanted to be a basketball player," Jeffires says, and he certainly could have been one. He led his Greensboro Page High basketball team to a state championship as a senior, outscoring teammate and current National Basketball Association star Danny Manning in the title game. Jeffires was a terrific rebounder and shooter.

"My first love was baseball," says Givins. His dad played minor-league ball in the Indians' organization, and Givins was one of the best hitters in greater Tampa as a high-schooler. Scouts told him he'd have a chance to play professionally. His strengths were his eye, his mental toughness, and his intelligence. He says his career path changed when he faced Gooden in a high school game and struck out on three pitches. Not that guys like Gooden were invincible; he just figured, correctly, that being the tough son of a gun that he was, he'd have a better chance being a great player in football than he would in baseball.

So Woodson went to Purdue and Jeffires to North Carolina State and Givins to Louisville, where they honed their football talents. Givins got to Houston in 1986; Jeffires landed in Houston and Woodson in Pittsburgh in 1987. Now the fates of their teams rest in their hands on many Sundays. Can Givins turn a routine twelve-yard catch over the middle into a long touchdown play? Can Jeffires outleap the Pittsburgh defenders five or six times a game for big chunks of yardage? Or can Woodson disrupt both of them, smashing into them or into quarterback Warren Moon on a surprise blitz, or lurking behind one of them until a Moon pass goes into the air, attacking quickly to intercept?

Twice a year they face each other in key games. Seldom have they been as important to the outcome of one of these games—and to their teams' entire seasons—as they were on September 6, 1992, at the Astrodome.

Early September, 1992, Pittsburgh:

"I was up late last night," Woodson was saying, in the finished basement—no, the shrine to his athletic achievements—of his home. He lives in a woody suburb, Wexford, north of Pittsburgh, with his wife, Nicki, and daughter, Marikah. Nicki was upstairs fixing chili for dinner, and Marikah was outside, playing in the turtle sandbox. All was right with Woodson's world, especially now, with the season three days away and his strained calf muscle responding so well to treatment. He'd heard it pop in a preseason game eleven days earlier, but today it just felt like a nagging pain in his left leg. Nagging pains he could deal with, but you can't cover Ernest Givins or Haywood Jeffires with a popped calf muscle. The twenty-two hours he'd spent rehabbing the calf muscle—swimming, Stairmastering, massaging—in the past eleven days had obviously paid off. Now, mentally and physically, he knew he'd be ready to face the Oilers, annually his toughest test as a cornerback.

He'd been up late the previous night studying with Nicki. The new Steeler defensive coaching staff had given each of Pittsburgh's twenty-one defensive players an identical videotape that week so they could take it home and pop it into their VCRs. The tape showed the Oilers' plays from the last two preseason games and from late games from the 1991 season, separated by down and distance. For instance, one series of plays was labeled, "First and second down passes with TD." This means, to the Steelers, all passes on first and second downs with two receivers on each side of the field. There are quite a few of these, because the Oilers play lots of four-wide receiver formations with the receivers split equally on either side. Another is labeled, "First and second down passes with TD Switch." This means all passes on first and second downs with the two receivers on the right or left crossing with each other near the line of scrimmage and running the other receiver's pattern. "They just try to confuse you doing that," Woodson said. "But the thing is, if you've studied them doing this thirty times on film, then it happens in the game and, boom, you know it right away, and you're not confused."

Why, Woodson is asked, was Nicki up late with him the previous night?

"She was helping me," he said. "I gave her our defenses, all written down and circled, and I'd be watching first and second

97

down passes with TD, and she'd call out our different defenses to quiz me. And I'd just figure out with every different defense where I'd be on every particular play, and we'd do it over and over again for two, three hours."

Nice wife, he's told.

"Well, she's not a football fan," he said. "She's kind of got that attitude, 'Well, I'll do it because I love you.' She loves me, and she loves the fact that I'm playing this game. I get involved, and get her football-minded, and she's really a great help to me."

It took Woodson a while, but he's grown to like homework and video study. A couple of days earlier, at the Steeler offices in the bowels of Three Rivers Stadium, he'd spent two hours with me, teaching me how to watch film. The minutiae is incredible.

"It is an amazing thing, and I never really thought of it playing in college or my rookie year," Woodson said. "I always thought, just go out there and play. Let your athletic ability take over. Uh-Uhhh. My first year here, I was like, films? Forget about it. I want to get out of here and have a life, cultivate a life outside of football. I just winged it. And I just didn't play well, because I wasn't in tune with what the rest of the defense was doing or what the offense was trying to do to me. I played on instinct, football instinct. And then, Rod Rust, our defensive coordinator at the time, he got to me and told me, 'You have to understand the concept of football if you're going to play it the best.' And I'm thinking, 'Yeah, right. What's this guy talking about?'

"What he meant was you had to understand the philosophy of an offense in order to play well against it. I just always thought you watch film to pick up little tendencies guys have, like how they move their shoulders or how they try to fake you. I just figured, it's me against them, and let the best athlete win. I never knew there was an exact pattern to what each team does based on things like down and distance. So Rod Rust taught me football. I started studying the Bengals, the Browns, and the Oilers, the teams in our division that we play twice a year, and I tried to learn everything they do. I started studying film. I learned this: No matter how complex an offense is, it only has so many formations and so many things they do out of each formation. You can learn it. It takes work, but you can learn it. And I did.

"Like with the run and shoot in Houston, they can only do so much. They've got only four receivers out there and one back and five linemen. They can't run the ball a lot; they've only got like five running plays. They've got to throw. So once you learn their adjustments and their splits—how far each receiver lines up away from the tackle or the tight end—you can play well.

"When you learn everything, it's like you have a computer with you right out there. If you line up at cornerback and see the receiver line up in a certain way and the back line up in a certain spot and the motion guy get in motion to a certain area, the computer in your head starts working and, boom, you know what they're going to do. You know where the ball's going. Basically, this eliminates the thought process for you. So while as a rookie I'm just standing out there and reacting to the moves the receiver makes when he makes it, now I can anticipate what the receiver's going to do before he does it. I know where he's going, so I know where I'm going to go. It's second nature. Like with a calculator and you just add up two huge numbers and it's right there, the offense does something and, bang, it happens and I'm not shocked. I'm not even surprised.

"Everything has names. Once you learn the names, you don't have a problem understanding what's going on. If the offense has two receivers on two different sides, that's twin. If they have three on one side and one on the other, that's yellow. Two receivers and a tight end and a back all on one side, that's black. It's so easy once you learn the words and what they mean.

"You've got to know the words and the different defenses out there if you're going to succeed. In the huddle, you might have just gotten belted or smacked your head on the turf or something, and you have to be able to focus on the next play-call. The strong safety makes the calls in the defensive huddle. Against Houston, he might say, 'Flush, flush,' which means four wide receivers in the game—you know, flush, four of a kind in cards [like calling a 61 play "Mantle," it's more important that the players remember these names than that they be accurate]—and then the play, like Okie three backer, which is one of our zone defenses. But Houston's hard to prepare for, because even when you know all the things they're going to do, you can't do the same thing all the time because if you do, they've got things called rule-busters. Which means if you start anticipating what they're going to do and show them you know exactly what they're going to do and play the same type of defense every time, they have in their package the ability to read what you're doing and then do something else. I mean, last year, we're playing Houston, and we still had [wide receiver] Drew Hill [since departed for Atlanta] covered perfect, just like the films said we should. But he read what we were doing, and he had such a great rapport with Warren Moon that he was supposed to just do kind of a double-bend-in pattern with Givins, and Drew saw the seam between our two DBs. Instead of him just going across the middle, like he was supposed to, he ran right up the seam of our defense, and Warren hit him for a long one."

Woodson felt like a kid cramming for a college final this week, for a couple of reasons. One, the defensive coaching staff was all new. Head coach Bill Cowher came over from Kansas City, defensive coordinator Dom Capers from New Orleans, and secondary coach Dick LeBeau from Cincinnati. This meant new ideas for combating what the Oilers did. Not revolutionary things, just different things. LeBeau, for instance, encouraged the defensive backs to play their most physical game, because he was convinced the Oiler receivers could be intimidated. Capers urged them to disguise their coverages so things like the long Drew Hill play wouldn't happen again. Cowher brought some ideas from secondary-rich Kansas City, and he changed Woodson's position. That's the second reason for Woodson's cramming: Cowher moved him from right corner to left corner, his more natural position, which meant that for the majority of this game Woodson would be playing Givins, who was one of the most physical receivers in the game, instead of Jeffires, one of the great and slippery finesse receivers in football.

Cowher also taught him about disguising his intentions. Cowher saw from film study that when the Steelers were in a zone defense, Woodson would be looking straight at the quarterback, which was a tipoff to the quarterback, similar to the look the Browns' cornerbacks gave Boomer Esiason. Cowher taught Woodson to change up his looks. "Dan Marino and Bernie Kosar do that," Woodson says. "They'll look right at the corners to see if they're in zone or man, and if they can make eye contact with you, they know you're in zone."

It was a new world for Woodson, with the new coaching ideas and the new position and the new responsibilities and the new disguising. Adjusting to the new position would be the toughest thing, especially this week. Against Jeffires, Woodson could focus on one man. Against Givins, Woodson would be drawn into following Givins in motion on probably forty percent of the plays, and when he wasn't, he might be confronted with a sweep running at him, the Oiler line leading running back Lorenzo White. He would also be blitzing more from this spot because he'd be closer to Moon. The slot receivers, Givins and Leonard Harris, are inside the wide receivers, Jeffires and Curtis Duncan, so Woodson was much closer to the action and the traffic now.

"The main reason we did it," he said, "is because most offenses are right-handed, and they're naturally going to look to the right first to make plays. That's the left side of our defense. So if you move me over there, I'm going to get most of the action, plus I can help stopping the run. Last year, let's say against Houston, I was on the right side of the defense playing Haywood, and I was just out there on an island, not involved in much of anything except stopping Haywood. Now, moving over, I'll be covering Givins in the right slot, and I'll go everywhere with him, and I'll be much more involved in the game. Givins is one of the toughest receivers in the game, probably the toughest. I've never seen him knocked out of a game. But you have to put that thought in his mind, especially on a crossing route, that when he comes across the middle or when he catches anything, he's going to get tattooed. Then you hope their arms start to get a little bit shorter. On a lot of guys it does. But not, I don't think, on Givins."

That day at practice, Woodson pulled backup cornerback Richard Shelton aside. Shelton was going to have to play Jeffires on some downs in the game, and Woodson wanted to get him ready. "Sometimes," Woodson told Shelton, "Haywood'll come to the line of scrimmage and he'll touch any part of his body, like he's adjusting his uniform or something. It's a sign. He's telling Warren he's going to run a quick look pass. He's seen something in our defense that tells him to run a quick look pass. So as soon as the ball's snapped, Haywood's going to come out a few yards and just stop."

Woodson also told Shelton that sometimes Moon would throw Jeffires, in essence, a jump ball. Moon would see Jeffires covered, but he knew he had such great leaping ability that he'd trust him to go up for the ball and get it, even against a great corner like Woodson.

LeBeau spent much of the day telling his defensive backs, "Remember to knock the crap out of them." As Woodson said, "We've seen how rough Philadelphia played them last year, and Philly beat them down in the Dome, and we think that's the way to play them. Philly hit those guys so much they didn't want to play football anymore. Their receivers were like, 'Warren, you catch the ball. Let me throw it to you and *you* get hit with a forearm in the face.' They broke Givins's nose. [Those receivers] can start getting alligator arms, and they start dropping the long pass."

At dinner, Woodson seemed at ease. He didn't know what Sunday held for him, but he did know he was ready for it. In between bites of chili and cooing with two-year-old Marikah, he talked about his upbringing in Fort Wayne, in a racially mixed family. His dad was black, his mom white. Some Fort Wayne parents told their kids not to play with Woodson because of his parentage. White kids called him nigger and zebra; black kids called him yellow boy and white boy. "My parents taught me never to back down, never apologize for who I was," he said. "Stuff that happened to me growing up makes something like switching from right cornerback to left cornerback seem so insignificant."

He couldn't stop thinking about the game.

"Switching," he said, "I think is going to be a plus for me. I'll be more involved in the game, and when I'm more involved in the game I play better. The last couple of years I'm sitting out there at corner and sometimes I'd get lackadaisical. I'm excited now. I can't wait for Sunday."

Nine hundred miles away, Jeffires and Givins and the Oilers didn't believe the news.

"Why would they switch Woodson?" Givins said. "Why would they put him on me? Watching the preseason games, I can't tell what Woodson's gonna do, because everybody bull-shits in preseason."

"I read in the papers they might do it, but I won't believe it until Sunday," Jeffires said.

"We've heard it," receivers coach Chris Palmer said, "but I can't figure it out. Jeffires is coming off a 100-catch season, and you just figure they'll put their best horse on him."

We're in southwest Houston, near the Astrodome, at the Oilers' training facility, a smallish place by NFL camp standards, located in an industrial park. The Oilers had just come off the practice field after their Friday workout, and Givins sat down.

He is a happy man. First of all, he's one of the most interesting players in the league—engaging, full of bravado, tough enough to be a linebacker—and, at five-nine and 172 pounds, he's probably the guttiest player around, pound for pound. In 1991, against Philadelphia, he was hit away from the play with a forearm to the face by Eagles safety Wes Hopkins. He saw stars and wobbled back to the huddle.

"Haywood," he said to Jeffires in the huddle, "is my nose messed up?"

"No," Jeffires said, pointing to the left side of his face, "but it is way over here. You're finished."

"Damn," Givins said. "Must be broken."

He went to the Oilers' sideline, had the nose cracked back into place by a trainer, and then had the trainer stuff it with gauze so it wouldn't flop around out on the field and he wouldn't miss any time. He was back for the next series.

He never said a word to Hopkins.

"You don't say a word to assholes," Givins said. "If you're going to cheap-shot me, I never say anything to you. Never. All I want to do is get back on that field and show you that I'll beat you. His time will come. I live for things like that."

Givins plays the right slot, the spot between the right tackle and the right wide receiver. He calls it the hell position. On running plays, he has to help block defensive ends and outside linebackers. If the running play goes far, he has to get up and block the corners and safeties downfield. On passing plays he has to elude a bump at the line of scrimmage, then beat coverage from a cornerback and quite often a safety, deciding which way to go based on the coverage he sees.

The Houston system makes it doubly hard for a receiver, because the slot receiver has to know more than any player in football besides a quarterback. To demonstrate, he grabbed my notebook and drew a football line of scrimmage, with Xs for the offensive players and Os for the defenders.

"People wonder why it takes so long for a receiver to come into our system and contribute right away," he said. "They wonder why Haywood was so screwed up as a rookie. Well, it takes two solid years to learn the system, and three to get out on the field and do something. It's not till your fourth year that most guys are ready to play instinctively. You can play before that, but you'll be messing up a lot."

He drew himself running out a few steps from the line, and then drew the free safety coming over to what would be Givins's deep zone. "Here, I just find the open slot because I can't go deep. It's covered," he said.

He drew himself running out a few steps from the line, and then drew the free safety staying deep on the left side of the field, away from Givins. "Here, I can find the open seam and take it, and Warren can look for me deep," he said.

He drew six other configurations, with corners and nickels and dimes chasing him all over the field, talking about what reads he has to make. His job always is to draw coverage with him, so that the wide receivers can be in single coverage and Moon can hit the wide guys—Jeffires or Duncan—for big gains. Givins takes the most physical abuse because he's running in the middle of the field so much, and because if you're running in the middle of the field against five-, six- and seven-defensive back coverages, you're going to get hit by a lot of defensive backs.

Givins has trained himself not to care about the big hits.

"I can't," he said. "If I do, my career's over. Done. I'm finished. I pretend when I'm going over the middle that I'm in a big stadium, just me and the quarterback, and all I'm doing is focusing on the nose of the football, nothing else. I hear nothing else. I feel nothing else. I see nothing else. I'm watching the football, all the way in, and then I'm tucking it in, so that nothing humanly possible can break the ball away from me. If I get the crap knocked out of me then, fine. I've got the ball. If I don't concentrate like that, the ball's going to come out, because you're thinking about all those other things.

"I've been knocked unconscious a lot. You don't feel pain then. You don't feel it until you wake up maybe on Tuesday, because of all the adrenaline you're playing with. You notice that when I get knocked unconscious I usually still have the ball tucked in, don't you? When I get knocked out, I love waking up and hearing people say to me, 'Hell of a catch.' Then I just want to get off the field so I can come back in on the next play. When I just get the crap knocked out of me but I'm not knocked out, first of all I'm surprised that somebody could make me lose my bearings. You're like, Here, wait a second, let me gather myself together. You're down a couple of seconds shaking off the cobwebs and then you're back in the huddle. You never let them know they've stung you. Never."

At practice earlier in the week, Palmer sidled up to Givins and told him Woodson might be switching over to him from Jeffires's side. "Fine," Givins said. "If that's the case, bring him on. I want him."

What troubled the Oilers in this particular week was the unexpected. They didn't know for sure if Woodson was moving to the left side. They didn't know whose defense they'd be seeing—LeBeau's from Cincinnati, Cowher's from Kansas City, or Capers's from New Orleans. "We have to school ourselves for so many things," Palmer said, sitting in the offensive meeting room. "I'll be upstairs [in the press box] for the game Sunday, and I might say down to [offensive coordinator] Kevin Gilbride after the fifth or sixth play: 'Kevin, it's the Cincinnati package,' or 'Kevin, they're doing Kansas City stuff,' and then we'd go about adjusting to them. But then again, our offense is an offense of adjustments anyway."

He flicked on the video projector, showing me why if Moon is on and Jeffires is on and Givins is on it won't matter what kind of scheme the Steelers throw at them.

"This," Palmer said, "is what we call a One Wrap. This Steeler defensive back is going to try and help out on any of our crossing routes, and you see on all these other receivers they're getting good coverage. Woodson's locked up on Jeffires, and he turns, and Warren sees Woodson is slightly inside Jeffires . . ."

And Moon threw about seventeen yards upfield for a streaking-then-stopped-dead Jeffires. If he threw the ball eighteen inches further to the left, it'd zoom out of bounds. If he threw the ball eighteen inches to the right, Woodson would tip it away; twenty-four inches to the right and Woodson picks it off. But it was zero inches to the right or left. Woodson lunged and didn't come close. Jeffires reached up with two hands and snagged it.

"I don't know if people appreciate Warren's greatness," Palmer said. "I mean, he throws most of his passes just like this. If he plays like this, we're in pretty good shape."

The Oilers' plan doesn't change from week to week. Their receivers have set patterns on every play, though these can change as the receivers run downfield and see the defense's reaction. The whole thing works because Moon is laser-accurate and because his receivers know what they're doing, and because the offense is never the same on any two plays.

And because of the man eating potato soup and sipping grapefruit juice at Houston's that night.

The first thing you think of when you meet Haywood Jeffires is that this guy wouldn't hurt a fly. He has an ear-to-ear, Magic Johnson smile, and he backs it up with a laid-back, easygoing personality. At a supple six-foot-two and 201 pounds, he looks like a ballplayer—a basketball player, smooth and big-handed and athletic. After your second and third meetings, he's so warm and open you'd think this was your brother, not your interview subject. You sit down with the guy, and he's so friendly, and ninety minutes are gone, and you say, Where'd the time go, Haywood?

He doesn't have a lot of reverence for football. It drives the coaches nuts—"Haywood's not the most serious guy about his football," Gilbride says—and probably detracts from Haywood's long-term goal to be one of the greatest players ever. He's almost the football antihero, the guy who succeeds while flouting the system. But he does it so good-naturedly that it doesn't sound bad or disrespectful. It sounds like common sense.

"I don't bang my head against the wall about football," he said. "I think coaches overdo everything. I don't think watching a hundred hours of film every week accomplishes much. I don't believe in the film theory, that watching a lot of film every week makes you such a better player. Film's a waste of a lot of time. Let's just go out there and play. Hey, beat your man straight up. That's the challenge of football. Can I beat my man, and can Warren get me the ball? All these schemes and different plays, they're crazy mind games. I don't pay any attention to them."

He does, however, pay attention to Woodson.

"He's an absolute machine," Jeffires said. "He looks like he's cut from a rock, doesn't he? I get jitterbugs lining up across from him. I'd rather have the lesser guy across from me, to be honest with you. It's not less challenging; I'll still see Rod during the game. I just find if Warren's looking for me early in the game it's easier for me to keep my focus. Sometimes, if I'm not getting the ball, my concentration goes off."

So Moon feeds him. Moon's philosophy, he told me, is to get the ball to all four of his receivers by the end of the first quarter. That means each one of them gets the feeling that Moon's looking for him early, and so they stay on their toes every time they run downfield, even if they're not the primary receiver.

Just because Jeffires seems devil-may-care about football, that doesn't mean he doesn't want to be great. "If I caught eighty balls next year, the season would be a total loss. If I don't get a hundred again, I'll kill myself. The thing I want people to say about me when I'm finished is: Who is the next Haywood Jeffires? I want to be that good."

Different goals, different minds. The receiver wants the ball, the yards, the catches, the glory. If a subpar opponent makes it easier for him, so much the better. Not the cornerback: He wants the biggest challenge, the most responsibility. He wants to shut down the best. It's the most vivid matchup in the sport.

In the hours leading up to a game, Woodson likes to watch a movie in his hotel room, then go to sleep. Jeffires likes to chatter. Givins is a bit more intense, especially on the day of the game. Fellow receiver Leonard Harris has said to him, "Ernest, be calm! Why don't you relax?" But Ernest can't.

On the morning of the Pittsburgh–Houston game, a noon kickoff, Givins was the most focused of the three, walking the field, plugged into his CD player. The repeat button was pushed over and over again as he listened to a Michael Jackson song, "Remember the Time."

"I listen, over and over, because I want to keep reminding myself of the last time I played these guys, whoever we're playing," Givins said. "I want to remember what happened the last time: who played me, how I did, how we did. Remember the time, remember the time. I spend the pregame recalling past times."

The Astrodome is an obnoxious building in which to watch football. First of all, it's a dome; there's one strike against it. Second, the PA system blares a constant stream of soft and mild rock, even between plays, stopping only when the quarterback gets under center. It's distracting, and it's dumb. And it's not just this place where it happens; unfortunately, football's packagers think people in the stands want to hear snippets of Phil Collins and Michael Bolton and Madonna and Hammer nonstop. They don't.

When Woodson, Jeffires, and Givins finally met in the season-opener on the floor of the Astrodome, the story of the game was told right away, in the season's first four plays, while the Temptations screamed: "Ain't Too Proud to Beg."

One: Jeffires, with lesser-light Richard Shelton covering him, streaked up the left side of the field, stopped, and felt the thud of a Warren Moon pass in his midsection. Eleven yards. First down.

Two: Jeffires shaked-and-baked three sprinting steps upfield and turned to his left. Bang. Moon's ball was right there again. Five yards. "When we noticed Rod really *had* switched," Jeffires said later, "well, we took advantage of it right off. We entered the game still thinking there was a good chance Rod was going to play me. I looked up there and saw this new guy Shelton, and the coaches said, Let's feel this guy out. Let's attack him. Let's not let him get comfortable out here. Let's get him thinking."

Advantage, Jeffires.

Three: The Oilers began to establish the run, sending Lorenzo White up the middle for eight. Woodson was in on the tackle late, coming off coverage of Givins to pound into the pile.

Four: "Fifty-two buster, fifty-two buster," the Steelers called in their huddle. That was one of their standard defenses for the Oilers: four defensive linemen, one linebacker, and although it was first down, six defensive backs, because the Oilers throw so much on first down.

Woodson noticed right away the Oilers were in TD with no motion. (Remember? Two receivers on either side of the field, stationary.) He wouldn't have to move with Givins to the other side of the field; he could stay here and think. From film study, Woodson knew a lot about Givins's tendencies on this play. "They pass about seventy percent of the time out of this formation," he said to himself out on the field, remembering the lessons from the Wednesday night video session with his wife. And Givins, he knew from studying, would streak straight upfield about eight or nine yards, then read the two deep safeties to see how they were playing before committing to a route. Woodson knew Givins could either stop and do a classic sandlot buttonhook—just turn around and wait for the ball in the gut—or he could exploit a deep seam caused by a moving safety and go deep. Woodson figured he'd stay short; that was his best guess. "The one thing you know playing these guys," Woodson says, "is that they only do a certain number of things out of each formation. If you study, you can learn what they're likely to do."

Givins, from his right slot position at the Houston 36, streaked upfield about ten yards, into a seam between Woodson and dime back Sammy Walker. Because the safety was behind him trying to foil a long pass to Givins, Woodson thought that Givins would probably cut off the route at eight or nine yards and curl back toward Moon. It was Woodson's job to watch Givins's hips—"Always watch hips, because a guy can't go anywhere without his hips turning that way"—and to catch up when Givins stopped. And Givins did stop, at about eight yards, and Woodson saw Moon's arm in motion toward him, and now the race was on. The pass was a bullet, and Woodson strained, strained, strained to get there, his legs churning toward Givins from three steps away. All of this happened in about a second. The pass was five yards from Givins, traveling at seventy miles an hour, when Woodson lunged ahead of him, bumping him noticeably with his right shoulder on the way by.

"You don't even notice any of that," Woodson said later. "You notice the ball, and you go for it, and if you hit anybody on the way to the ball, you hit him. You have to concentrate only on the ball. I didn't even know I hit Givins until I saw the replay."

Woodson intercepted the ball in full gallop, weaving through traffic for sixteen yards on the return.

Boos cascaded down from the stands—not at Moon, not at Givins, but at the officials. Woodson jostled Givins, and pass interference could easily have been called. Givins hollered to the official nearest him, "He pushed me over! Interference! Didn't you see that?"

"I probably had pass interference on him," Woodson said in the locker room later, smiling. "But they didn't call it, so I guess it wasn't interference."

Advantage, Woodson.

The first four plays were a perfect microcosm of this game—and, incredibly, this season—for both teams. Houston would get some yards, make some plays, score some points, wreak some offensive havoc, just like the Oilers always did. Pittsburgh would bend and bend and scratch and claw and make a big defensive play—and draw life from that. From the first game of the season, here in the Astrodome, to the last game of their playoff seasons, the Oilers would seem a better football team by every measure but wins. The Steelers won the top seed in the AFC playoffs, while the Oilers had to scramble in as a wild card. No one could quite figure out why, but the Oilers made the mistakes, while the Steelers converted mistakes into points, and the record will show the Steelers were better in 1992. Four plays into the season, it was as if the die had already been cast.

Givins got Woodson back later in the quarter, just one play after getting forearm-popped by a Steeler linebacker. A play broke down at the Pittsburgh 11, and when a play breaks down, defensive players are told to just get to the nearest receiver and cover him man-to-man. Woodson blanketed Givins, who was just behind Jeffires at the back of the end zone, and it looked like Moon threw to Jeffires and just overthrew him. "I'm a pretty good leaper, but not that good," Jeffires said later. "That ball was in the stands."

But somehow, Givins leaped high in the air, a good thirty inches off the ground, caught the ball on the tips of his fingers, and then on his way down, instead of falling awkwardly as any normal person would do, he pointed his ten toes straight down at the green AstroTurf that lies just before the wide white end line. "Like Baryshnikov, or Biletnikoff," laughed Jeffires. "Poetry in action. Beautiful." The ten toes hit the green, and the ref's hands went up. Touchdown!

"I tried to go up for the ball," Givins said, "which was way beyond me, at a forty-five degree angle, and then come down with my toes in. I didn't think I was going to be able to."

Woodson's shoulders sagged. He was speechless. Later, he said, "Just an unbelievable catch by Givins. I'm still not sure who Warren was throwing to. Fate was on their side." Moon said the ball was intended for Givins. But it looked like it was intended for the guy in the fourth row of the end-zone seats.

Givins had taken a brutal hit over the middle on one play and came back to make a truly remarkable catch, with fingers that must have little vacuum cleaners on each tip, at the back of the end zone on the next.

Advantage, Givins.

Houston led 14-0, and it looked bad for the Steelers. Pittsburgh rallied some because of their defense—confusing Moon with their chameleon coverages, a mix of Cowher, LeBeau, and Capers stuff—and picked Moon off three times in the first half, keeping the game tight. The key here was something Capers did on the Monday before the game. "He brought us Houston's tendency sheets, and we found out how true they were," Woodson said. "We couldn't believe what we were seeing once we watched film. Once one receiver did one thing, we knew what the other receivers were going to do. That really started to help us as the game went on."

Still, Houston just looked better. Moon kept taking what the Steelers gave him, the six-yarders to Jeffires on the left sidelines and the eight-yarders to Curtis Duncan on the right. "We felt great," Givins said, "and we were making big yards, just like our offense is supposed to."

And Givins taught a lesson to a young Steeler.

With fifteen seconds left in the half, Houston, up 17-16, had a third-and-goal from the Pittsburgh eight. The Steelers called 52 buster again, the dime defense with two deep safeties: Carnell Lake and rookie Darren Perry, an eighth-round pick playing his first game as a pro. Houston receiver Leonard Harris came in motion from the left slot to the right, which suited Givins just fine. He figured, standing there at the line: Now Woodson has to figure out who he's going to take—me or Leonard. And if he doesn't take me, I've got a nice seam against a deep zone to exploit.

"I knew this play perfectly," Woodson said later. "The motion receiver makes it trips right. [Three receivers on the right side, with Jeffires, alone, at the left hashmark.] The back, White, always steps to Jeffires's side to try to take some of the coverage to the left, but Moon almost always looks right to throw. Givins and Harris are going to run inside routes. If I take Harris, a safety has to come over and take Givins. If I don't take Givins, he becomes the seam-reader. He goes up the seam of our defense and waits for someone to cover him. When somebody gets on top of him, he just stops and turns to Moon and then he hopes he gets the pass. But if nobody gets on him, he streaks into the end zone, and he can score."

One of the deep safeties, Perry, bit on White's movement left at the snap of the ball, heading to that side. Woodson took the motion man, Harris, but Perry, instead of inching over and then sprinting over to cover Givins as he loped into the end zone, never made a move toward Givins until it was very late. Givins was thinking: Nobody picked me up! Throw it! Throw it! This was probably the easiest touchdown catch of Givins's life, a floater from Moon right in his breadbasket, Perry coming over in flailing coverage a second or so too late.

Elapsed time of the play: three seconds.

"Darren!" Woodson said to Perry, shouting to be heard over the din of the Dome. "Scoot over! You gotta scoot over on that play!"

Perry just hung his head.

Woodson said later, "It's not a secret, what Houston's going to do. The problem is, for a rookie, it's hitting you all at once, and to memorize every tendency is pretty hard."

Advantage, Givins. Houston led at the half, 24-16.

But Woodson flat-out won the game in the second half.

It was a brilliant move to bring him closer to the action; he played like a combination of outside linebacker, safety, and cornerback in the final thirty minutes.

Houston led 24-19 midway through the third quarter. On first down at the Pittsburgh 43, Moon went back to pass and suddenly faced Woodson blitzing from his right. Now, understand that the new Steeler regime decided to blitz Woodson more than it had in previous years, because it knew he was fast enough and burly enough to make a quarterback quake the split-second he saw Woodson coming. Here he came now. Lorenzo White was there to block him, and he dove for Woodson's knees, trying to knock him off his pins. *Woodson leaped four feet in the air, right over White!* He steamed toward a stunned Moon, sticking his right hand high in the air. Moon's pass stuck him right in the palm, and it fluttered past Woodson, far short of Duncan.

Woodson was steamed that White would try to clip him at the knees. He, like most defensive players, was especially enraged by guys who go for the knees, because he can't function without his knees, and he thought offensive players should block defensive players at the shoulders and sternum, not lower, where careers could be lost on one block.

White and Woodson pushed and shoved each other a couple of times after the play, like players do about fifty times every game. And then Woodson said, "Lorenzo, I know what you're doing, buddy. You better stay up high, because I'll just fly right over you every time."

Two plays later, Woodson was still energized by White's attempted low hit. After a pass to Duncan for eight yards, on third-and-two at the Steeler 35, Moon gave the ball to White, and he tried to sweep left, away from Woodson's side. Woodson leaped over a prone Oiler lineman and a lunging Steeler teammate like they were high hurdles on the Purdue track and chased White down, tackling him from behind for no gain. It was a very memorable play; White looked like a sure thing for a first down, and a first down would have meant at least three more plays that would have put the Oilers into position for a field goal. The Oilers seemed headed for a 27-19 lead or even a 31-19 lead with a touchdown here, until Woodson hurdled two guys and chased White from behind like a coyote after a sheep.

On the sidelines, Cowher, coaching his first game, had veins popping in his neck, exhorting his defense and exulting in Woodson's great plays.

On fourth down, Houston coach Jack Pardee eschewed the fifty-two-yard field-goal try for another play. Moon threw incomplete.

So on those two plays, Woodson kept his team within a touchdown of the Oilers. When he got to the sideline, Cowher was waiting for him. "That was a hell of a play!" Cowher screamed at him, eyes bulging. And everyone on the defense slapped everyone else, and the offense went out on the field fired up, and Cowher took off his headset and went to a clump of defensive players on the bench and screamed, "THAT'S A GREAT JOB DEFENSE! GREAT JOB! GREAT JOB DEFENSEWAYTOGETAFTEREM!" It all flowed out of him so fast, like a volcano.

The Steelers' offense drove for a field goal to make it 24-22, but then Moon the magician was back. Early in the fourth quarter, he drove and drove the Oilers, looking for the clinching touchdown. With eleven minutes left, he had them first-and-goal at the Pittsburgh three, and the crowd could smell 31-22.

Moon sent White on a sweep right. Givins and Woodson were in hand-to-hand combat, Givins blocking Woodson with his forearms, Woodson trying to shuck off Givins in time to stop White. In the nick of time, he finally tossed aside Givins, and White slammed into him like a car hitting a wall. They both went down, with a Steeler linebacker ramming Woodson's back from behind. The breath came out of Woodson as he fell turf-ward, and he lay there for a moment, stunned and catching his wind. But he had stopped White again for no gain.

Second-and-goal now, from the three. Woodson was gasping. The Oilers had a short huddle, and then Moon took the snap from center. He faded right, looking, looking, looking—and Pittsburgh linebacker Jerrol Williams dove at him, grabbing his waist, and then he threw one of the stupidest passes of his life, an absolute wounded duck toward Jeffires and Givins, who were sprinting around, doing anything to get open in the left-central section of the end zone.

"I couldn't tell you who I was throwing to," Moon said.

"We couldn't have been the primary receivers," Jeffires said, referring to himself and Givins. "Everything he saw was black and gold and white there in the end zone, I'd think. He must have been throwing it away, I figured."

"I was shocked," said Steeler backup quarterback Bubby Brister, watching from the sideline.

"I was shocked," said Woodson, watching the ball float right toward him. "What was he doing?"

The ball wafted into the middle of the end zone, into a fire drill of players who'd been chasing or chased for the seven seconds since Moon got the ball and started running around. "I'm looking around," Woodson said, "trying to figure out where Givins is and hoping he's not going to knock it away. I'm saying, Get there ball, get there!"

It got there. Woodson picked it off, leaping at the goal line, and sprinted fifty-seven yards until exhaustion, and Jeffires, caught up with him.

Less than two minutes later, the Steelers scored the go-ahead touchdown, and they kept the Oilers from scoring on their last two possessions. Pittsburgh won 29-24.

For the day, Woodson had seven tackles, two interceptions, three passes batted away. Givins had four catches for forty-two yards and two touchdowns. Jeffires had seven catches for 117 yards. The four Houston wide receivers caught passes for 306 yards, but Woodson made the biggest plays of the day.

"He just has a feel for what we do," Jeffires said. "I don't know how to explain it."

The answers could be found on a videotape back in the Woodson home, and in the physical ability of the best athlete on the field, the well-honed skills that let his body do what his mind tells him he must.

Now came the emotional release.

The Astrodome clock ticked down through the final minute, and the Steeler defensive backs were defiantly giddy down on their bench. They bear-hugged, pads crashing into each other. And Woodson went from player to player, screaming: "WE DID IT! WE DID IT!"

And then he went to each of them again, slapping right hands with them hard, eyebrows scowling. With each handslap of D.J. Johnson and Larry Griffin and Richard Shelton, he screamed in a sing-song voice, "Fuck them! Fuck them! Fuck them!" And then they woofed at each other for a few seconds, howling some unintelligible sounds of exultation. The howls and the fuck-thems were for the whole wide range of emotions spilling out. There was a look in Woodson's eyes, a wide-eyed kind of maniacal yet happy look, as if he'd just won the lottery and the heavyweight championship in the same day. He and the other defensive backs had spent weeks looking forward to this day, hoping they'd be able to stay in the game with Moon and parry with him and win more battles than they lost and beat up the wide receivers and conquer the Oilers' Astrodome advantage. They'd done all that. They'd defeated Moon and his top-flight receivers, outhustled them, outfought them, outthought them, and the energy release was absolutely amazing. They were screaming like kids on the playground now, and the fans behind their bench were taunting them for being so giddy. The fans screamed really intelligent things, like: "You guys SUCK!" and "Get the fuck outta town!"

And now Woodson led his defensive-back peers in waving patronizingly to the crowd. "See you in Pittsburgh! We're gonna whip your ass again!" Woodson hollered at them. And the defensive backs whacked each other around a little bit more, releasing some more emotion. They should have been exhausted enough to need about sixty-four hours of sleep, but here they were, waving to the fans and jumping around still, on a high people outside sports cannot reach or understand.

Out of the corner of my eye I spied Bryan Hinkle, a Steeler linebacker I know well from being around the team over the years. Hinkle was drafted by the Steelers in 1981, fifteen months after they won their fourth Super Bowl, and he is much closer emotionally and in spirit to the stoic old Steelers—Jack Lambert, John Stallworth, Rocky Bleier, Donnie Shell—than to these new pups. He's a big believer in winning with a dignified reserve.

Hinkle surveyed the scene of the defensive backs woofing back and forth with the fans, and he saw me, and he shook his head sadly.

A couple of weeks later, Hinkle and I had a chance meeting in the Steelers' hotel lobby in San Diego, where they'd play the next day. I reminded him about his disapproving look toward Woodson's bunch that day.

"I didn't think you'd notice," Hinkle said, breaking into a surprised grin. "That's just the way things are today. It's not really my game anymore."

In so many ways, he's right. The game belongs to these exciteable—and exciting—young Givinses and Woodsons.

Running Backs
SEE, FEEL, DO

Once upon a time in the yards and sandlots of northeast Wichita there played a kid named Barry Sanders. And he trained and trained and trained to be a National Football League running back, even though he didn't know that was what he was doing.

The game Barry played in northeast Wichita was called Tackle the Man with the Football. It's called other things in other towns—Every Man for Himself, Kill Him Until He's Dead, Pigpile, Dodge Football—but the rules are, basically, that there are no rules. One kid takes the football at one goal line, and he tries to run through a group of other kids to the other goal line, and all the kids try to tackle him. No two runs are ever alike. And Sanders, always one of the smaller kids in the neighborhood, took his life in his hands every time he took the ball at one goal line and headed for the other.

BAM! He'd get sandwiched by two kids trying to tackle him, and . . .

SQUIRM! He'd weasel his way out of that one, and juke on the patchy grass (half-dirt, half-grass usually) to the right, where . . .

STRIP! Two bigger kids would grab his right arm, where the football was cradled, and try to knock it out, and they'd succeed, and the ball would go spinning into the air, and then he'd have to be a receiver, and he'd leap to grab the free ball, and . . .

OOOOF! He'd be gang-tackled, and try as he might, the ball would pop out when he hit the ground, and one of the other nine kids on the field would grab it out of the dust and start running toward the goal line, and—of course, in this game there are no timeouts, because what do you think this is? The NFL?—so he'd get up and Barry would start chasing the guy with the ball, and . . .

BLOCK! He'd level the guy closest to the guy with the ball with his two crossed forearms exploding into his chest, just like an offensive lineman might do, and the guy would fall like so many dominoes, and he'd steal the ball from the guy with it, and he'd sprint across the goal line, and he'd exult, and . . .

"It was great fun," Barry Sanders says. "It wouldn't matter how many guys we had, two or three or twenty, we could always play it. It was every man for himself on the football field or in somebody's front yard or on some lot. I was pretty good at it. That's one of the things that influenced me in becoming a football player. And it was probably pretty good training for my job now."

Precisely. This kids' game is the essence of what it takes to be a great running back in football today. Running backs can't just be runners anymore. They have to be runners and blockers and receivers.

Today's back has to be the most complete back of any NFL era, because so many teams employ so many receivers and play so many three- and four-wide receiver combinations. Barry Sanders is usually the only back in Detroit's backfield. Ditto Thurman Thomas in Buffalo, Lorenzo White in Houston. If they can't block, they're going to get their quarterback killed. If they can't catch, they can't give their quarterback a good outlet if the wideouts are covered. And when they run, without the aid of a blocking back to lead, it's much more like the game on the Wichita playgrounds than it used to be. Every team used to have a gritty blocking back to clear paths for the great runner; now fewer than half the teams have them. Ricky Watters in San Francisco has Tom Rathman. Rodney Hampton with the Giants has Jarrod Bunch. Emmitt Smith has Daryl Johnston in Dallas. The Vikings use Randall McDaniel, a 275-pound guard, to block for

Terry Allen in short-yardage situations. Sanders has himself.

In the nineties, more and more backs are being asked to be multipurpose. The best backs are like Dennis Rodmans with a shot, John Dalys with a short game. The best backs are the Michael Jordans and the Barry Bondses, the guys who can do it all. Thomas can run and catch, and he's a good enough blocker to keep Jim Kelly from getting killed. Same with Barry Foster of the Steelers. Emmitt Smith can run and catch, though he isn't asked to block much.

Sanders, on the average, catches only two or three passes a game for his team, the Detroit Lions, though he's caught as many as nine in a game; the Lions keep saying they want Sanders to catch more passes out of the backfield, but they never follow up on their intentions. This is in part because he's the best runner in the game, and when he's effective running the ball, why swing passes out to him and risk the incompletions? He's also a selfless, willing blocker, even at five-eight and 203 pounds, one of the best running-back blockers in football. Sit down and watch a game tape with Dan Henning, the Lions' offensive coordinator, and you get a lesson in football physics and leverage and violence, because three or four times a game, Sanders throws himself into a blitzing linebacker or cornerback or safety, and he knocks him down like a bowling ball hitting a moving headpin. No, you don't get very confident as a defensive player rushing the quarterback with Barry Sanders in the way.

The development of the multidimensional back is just the latest step in the evolution of what used to be the most important position in the game. The formations were so varied in the early years of pro football that sometimes the quarterback was the running back, or vice versa. In 1933 and 1934, an American Indian named Lone Star Dietz coached the Boston Redskins and installed the double-wing formation—two tight ends, two wingbacks outside the tight ends, a step back from the line, and one quarterback. The quarterback ran and passed and handed off on reverses from his single-setback position. "Many years ago," offensive football curator Sid Gillman says, "the tailback was the quarterback—the passer, the runner, the guy who was the nerve center of the offense. Lots of offenses were being created on the fly, and many of them had one thing in common: They didn't want the back to be more of a thrower than a runner. There was one formation called the Dead-T, with a quarterback under center and three running backs behind the quarterback, parallel to the line. Curly Lambeau ran that in Green Bay. Runners just dominated the sport."

In 1934, rookie running back Beattie Feathers of Chicago ran for more yards than the league's leading quarterback, Arnie Herber of Green Bay, made through the air, 1004 vs. 799. The NFL's leading passer in 1944, Frank Filchock of Washington, threw only 14.7 passes a game on the average.

The league lived by the old Woody Hayes saw for much of its first fifty years: Three things can happen when you throw, and two of them are bad. The great running teams became the great teams, period. "I'm convinced people just didn't know the passing game and they were afraid of it," Gillman said. "Whatever the reason, running backs really dominated the early days of football."

Paul Brown, the pioneering Cleveland coach, was the mentor of many great young football minds in the fifties and early sixties, and he built a team that lived by the run. Marion Motley and then Jim Brown dominated the league, Brown leading the NFL in rushing for five years in a row, from his rookie season in 1957 to 1961. In 1963, he averaged 133 rushing yards a game in again leading the league. Vince Lombardi won with the run in Green Bay. Then, in Miami, as the tide began to turn toward the pass, Don Shula followed old coach Brown's lessons and stuffed the ball down the NFL's throat with a perfect 17-0 season in 1972. The Dolphins' leading receiver that year, Paul Warfield, caught twenty-nine passes. Miami's run-pass ratio that year: 613 runs, 259 passes. Think of that Dolphin team; you don't think much of Bob Griese, the (questionable) Hall of Fame quarterback, because he missed most of the season with injury. It's likely you think first of the three running backs, Larry Csonka, Mercury Morris, and Jim Kiick.

Although Gillman, then the San Diego coach, and the rest of the new whiz kids from the American Football League made pro football more wide open in the sixties, the running back remained the primary hero until the seventies, when a series of profound rules changes made the modern passing game possible. The running game would never be the same.

"Three things happened," Gillman said. "Not many people talk about the first. Early in the seventies, they moved the hashmarks in, and that helped the passing game tremendously. When you move in the hashmarks, you allow more room for the outside receivers to run their routes. That began to take some of the game away from the backs." The hashmarks, formerly seventeen feet from the sidelines, were moved to—and remain today—70 feet nine inches from each sideline.

The other changes are the ones most often discussed. Before the 1977 season, a new rule allowed defensive players only one contact of offensive receivers. Formerly, defenders could beat up the receivers all over the field, as long as the ball wasn't in the air to them. Then, before the 1978 season, the league said defenders could bump receivers only within five yards of the line of scrimmage. And it ruled that offensive linemen could, within the plane of the body, use their open hands to block defenders.

The run-pass ratio throughout the league had steadily progressed toward parity through the years. But the backs stayed at the fore until the rules changes benefiting the passing game in the seventies, as these numbers showing the percentage of running plays compared to passing plays prove. (The numbers beginning in 1963 include American Football League statistics.)

NFL Plays

Year	Pct. run–Pct. pass	Comment
1933	71.6%–28.4%	Nagurski, Grange rule the landscape
1938	67.1%–32.9%	Halas popularizes the T-formation
1943	63.0%–37.0%	Only Washington, Chicago start passing
1948	59.3%–40.7%	1947: 'Skins throw for 3,300 yards
1953	53.0%–47.0%	Graham, Waterfield, Van Brocklin shine
1958	54.9%–45.1%	Paul Brown leads running surge
1963	50.6%–49.4%	Wide-open AFL influence showing
1968	53.4%–46.6%	Conservative coaching still dominates
1973	59.4%–40.6%	Everybody's doing it the Dolphin-Redskin way

1978	57.6%–42.4%	But here come the rules changes . . .
1983	50.3%–49.7%	Bill Walsh, Dan Fouts lead passing trend
1988	49.0%–51.0%	'88: Thurman. '89: Barry. '90: Emmitt.
1992	46.8%–53.2%	Only one team has more yards rushing than passing

Indianapolis, Buffalo, and Minnesota learned valuable running-back lessons late in the time line of this chart. Two of them were quite painful.

In 1987, the Colts, foundering in their four-year-old Indianapolis home, engineered a monster trade for disgruntled Rams runner Eric Dickerson, thinking a dominant back was going to lead them to the promised land. Well, it would have been nice if they'd *gotten* a dominant back. Defenses ganged up on Dickerson, because the Colts didn't have an adequate passing game to take the heat off him, and Dickerson never was the type of back to be a swing pass-catcher. And the Colts didn't have the front line to block for Dickerson either. The trade was a disaster, netting the Colts one playoff game in his five Indianapolis years. "We learned the quarterback has to be your primary building block," Indianapolis general manager Jim Irsay said, looking back.

In 1988, the Bills made the smartest draft choice in recent NFL history. While other clubs were scared away from Oklahoma State running back Thurman Thomas because of senior-year knee surgery, the Bills had team physician Richard Weiss probe and twist and spy into Thomas's knee in an extensive pre-draft evaluation. "What I saw," Weiss said, "was a knee fully equipped to keep doing the things he'd been doing in college. I had no reservations recommending that we draft him." One club's damaged goods was another club's treasure trove. For four straight seasons beginning in 1989, Thomas, the Bills' second-round choice in 1988, led the NFL in combined rushing-receiving yards, and became the running-back blueprint every team studied. He could catch and elude as well as he could run and elude. He saved a team a roster spot by playing runner and receiver at a Pro Bowl level.

In 1989, the Vikings thought they were a running back away from winning a Super Bowl. And so they traded what turned out to be six players and six high draft choices to the Dallas Cowboys for running back Herschel Walker and two draft picks. Disaster, as you know, ensued. This was a classic case of a selfish back, Walker, who could only hit a hole when it was huge and only catch and run in the wide-open field, pulling the football wool over a naive GM's eyes. Minnesota general manager Mike Lynn was so smitten with Walker that he decided to pay anything, no matter how ridiculous the price for him. The Vikings didn't begin to recover until new coach Dennis Green took over in 1992. For years, they'll be suffering for Lynn's trade because for three years they didn't have a prime draft choice.

The moral of the story: A running back with varied skills is an important piece of the puzzle. But without those varied skills, or without the rest of the puzzle, there's no picture to see.

What makes a great multi-purpose back? The answer is elusive; most of them are doers, not thinkers, and their quotes always come out seeming antiseptic. It's like when you're a kid and get off a roller coaster for the first time, and your mom says, "What was it like?" You say, "It was great! Oh, it was unbelievable!" Your mom has no idea what you've actually just felt. Only you know. Everyone else can only watch and imagine.

The essence of the position is walking the walk, making the play—without, most likely, having any idea how you've done it.

"I pretty much think the same thing on every play," Barry Sanders said, sitting in the offensive team meeting room at the Silverdome in the spring of 1992. He was watching some film of himself, not flinching or smiling or emoting. "Try to make as many yards as you can and keep going until you can't go anymore."

The play that ran again and again, by demand of some visitors in the meeting room, happened in 1991, at Minnesota. It might be the only play anyone's ever seen where ten players actually had a chance to tackle a player and failed.

The game was scoreless in the first quarter, Detroit ball on the Vikings' seventeen, first-and-ten. The Lions lined up in their typical Silver Stretch alignment of that season: two wide receivers split far outside, two slot receivers between the tackles and the wideouts, five offensive linemen, quarterback Erik Kramer and Sanders in the backfield. The Vikings had five men on the defensive line, a middle linebacker, and five defensive backs, four of them playing head-up with the four Lion receivers. The fifth stood about twelve yards behind the line of scrimmage, at about the Viking five-yard line.

As Kramer took the snap, the Viking middle linebacker rushed Kramer, trying to get by the Lion left guard, who made the block. Sanders sprinted left and up toward the left slot receiver, while Kramer sprinted to that side too. Suddenly he shoved the ball into Sanders's gut. Just as suddenly, there was a scrum at the left side of the Detroit line. No opening. Not a sliver. Sanders bounced into the back of the left tackle. Right here is where half the backs in the NFL would burrow for two yards, be happy, and live to fight another fight.

As the scrum enveloped Sanders, one Viking stayed free of the fray—the left outside linebacker. A well-coached fellow, this Viking. He just wanted to see, somehow, if Sanders, who was being surrounded by five Lions and five Vikings, would bounce outside like his coaches had said he might. In an instant, Sanders nimbly bounced out of the pile and back a couple of yards behind the line, pivoted on his right foot, and headed for the waiting Viking linebacker. He was out of the scrum, and the guys in the scrum fell over each other trying to refind Sanders.

Sanders threw his left shoulder two inches to the left.

The Viking linebacker threw his right foot a foot to his right, matching Sanders's move.

Sanders's fake.

Sanders turned to the right again, away from the gap he was faking toward, but the linebacker was too far gone now to matter, and as Sanders flew by him, all the poor guy could do was grasp at air and flail his arms ridiculously.

Sanders sprinted sideways a couple of yards more, then moved upfield. Uh-oh. Another trap. From his left came a defensive back with a good angle on him. In front of him was another defensive back, waiting for him on the balls of his feet.

Pffft! Sanders put on the brakes again, and the guy from his left flailed past, hitting and missing, and Sanders threw a quick shoulder to the left to fake the other defensive back, and now he was at the eight, and he could see the goal line, and two defensive backs—one from the end zone, one from his left charging hard—were coming at him, ready to sandwich him at the two.

Sanders dove between them, and they both missed. Sanders landed about a yard deep in the end zone.

What comes to mind after seeing something like this? And then seeing it over and over again on tape with The Great One Himself sitting in the next chair, clearing his throat occasionally because of a slight cold but otherwise not saying anything or feeling anything? The Gale Sayers quote comes to mind: "Thurman Thomas is a great back. Emmitt Smith is a great back. But I would pay to watch Barry Sanders play. He turns me on." That's what Gale Sayers thinks of the guy, and after watching this play, you can see why. What an incredible display of making people miss.

"Thank you," he said.

"I think, being smaller like I am, that I started to realize as a kid on the sandlots that I'd have to make people miss instead of plowing through them. Obviously, I can't do that. So all my life I've tried to be a squirming, twisting, jumping runner. I think in some ways my size has helped me because I've been able to practice this style of running for so long. It's the only way I've ever run the ball.

"There are a lot of different styles for running backs, and I'm not saying my style's the best," Barry Sanders said. "I think any back who has confidence in himself, who has heart, who physically can be a threat on every play and who has durability can be a great back. Sometimes you're tired, and there's a blitz coming, and you know you could give minimal effort and get by, but my parents always taught me that whatever you do, you should do the best. That's what I live by."

The Prototype's toothpaste was getting hard now. Toothpaste does that when it stays on the brush for forty minutes, and the toothbrush-holder is waving it around like a wand. But when Roger Craig is talking about his passion, white teeth can wait. As can most things.

And on this cool 1992 Indian Summer day in Minnesota, where Craig still didn't feel quite at home after a career in California, he wore a warm and excited look discussing the state of the NFL running back. Craig naturally has a twinkle in his eye anyway, and he loves to talk. For a few weeks now, since he wasn't playing much with the Vikings, no one talked to him much anymore. So in his little corner of the Vikings' locker room, in the comfy Minneapolis suburb of Eden Prairie, he was a willing talker, almost professorial. And the topic suited him. The position of running back, even in the time he'd been in the league, had changed greatly—and had done so to follow his example.

"Everything has changed," Craig said. "Bill Walsh changed it forever. Now, if you want to be a great back in this league, you've got to be an all-purpose back. You've got to run, you've got to catch, and—this still is so underrated—you've got to block. I was helped by the fact that I played fullback my first four years in the league. I blocked for Walter Payton in the Pro Bowl after my third year. It wasn't until my fifth year that I played running back. But by that time, my blocking skills and receiving skills were pretty sharp, and they've never left me."

Life as a running back was elementary for Roger Craig in college, at Nebraska: All he had to do was run. He didn't have to block much as a running back his senior year, and he caught about as many passes as the right guard. But then, in 1983, he went to the 49ers as a second-round draft pick, and on the first day of a weekend orientation camp in California, Bill Walsh told offensive coordinator Paul Hackett, "Let's throw Roger a few passes coming out of the backfield and see what happens."

Hackett threw Craig forty passes that day, and forty more the next day. Craig caught seventy-seven of the eighty. The rest is NFL history. Craig played his first four years under Walsh as a fullback, the most prolific per-season pass-catching fullback in history, with 292 catches in four seasons. In 1985, from the fullback position, Craig had one of the best seasons a back has ever had: Each time he touched the ball that season, he gained an average of nearly seven yards—4.9 per rush, 11.0 per pass. And he became the first back ever to rush for 1,000 yards and receive for 1,000 yards in one season.

When the beefy Tom Rathman became the regular fullback for the 49ers in 1987, Craig was moved to running back. In 1988, he rushed for 1,502 yards. He caught seventy-six passes.

He's the only player ever to start in the Pro Bowl at both running back and fullback—playing fullback with Wendell Tyler in the mideighties, and running back with Rathman later. That's a pretty nice portfolio right there.

It will be a sad misconception if, somehow, Bill Walsh goes down in history as a finesse coach of the passing game who lived on Joe Montana's arm. Walsh lived on the legs and the forearms and the hands of Craig, too. Think of Craig in your football replay memory bank. It's likely there's no overriding memory. Maybe you think of him galloping through the line, his knees coming up so high, his legs chugging like pistons. Maybe you remember him catching a blitzer, saving Montana from a violent sack. Maybe you remember him catching a quick little screen from Montana, turning on a dime upfield around the corner and sprinting for twenty yards. Maybe you remember him lowering his shoulder into somebody's gut on a determined run, because he never just tiptoed out of bounds when there was another two yards to be had.

Whatever your memory of the guy, it almost certainly won't be as vivid as your Montana memory or Rice memory, which is unfortunate and misleading. The NFL ranks its teams every year by yardage gained; under Walsh, with Montana and Craig ensconced in the backfield, here's where the 49ers ranked among the league's twenty-eight teams:

	Overall	Rushing	Passing
1983	4	8	5
1984	2	3	4
1985	2	10	5
1986	3	10	2
1987	1	1	2
1988	2	2	10

In the years the 49ers won the Super Bowl, with Walsh, Montana, and Craig all there—1984 and 1988—they were actually better running than passing, compared to the rest of the league.

"They tried to label us a finesse team, but we always could rush, and you've got to be a powerful team to rush the ball well," Craig said.

"The running back is so misunderstood—our running backs in San Francisco and really running backs everywhere." His brows started to furrow seriously. "People think we take the ball, find a hole, rush for as much as we can, and that's it. That's so wrong. Our job's almost as complicated as the quarterback's, and we actually have more to do. There are so many elements to the job that people don't see."

Craig listed the key points of what it takes to be a great back in the nineties.

"One, unselfishness. That's number one. If you're in the NFL, you must have some talent. As a running back, you carry some of the weight of the team on your shoulders. You're in for a lot of big plays, and you're responsible for whether or not your team succeeds. And you're out in the forefront in practice and with the press and in meetings. You've got to be team-oriented. If you have to run a lot that week to win, you run. If you've got to block a lot that week to win, you block. Same with catching the ball. You've got to be able to do it all successfully, and it can't matter to you what you're called on to do. Like if your biggest role a couple of weeks in a row is blocking, you've got to do it and be happy about it, because it's going to help the team win. You know, I can see what kind of a back a guy is by watching him fake on play-action. If he's really selling on play-action, giving his all, diving into the line, making everyone on defense think he's the one with the ball and not the quarterback, then he's a back I want on my team. If he just goes into it half-heartedly—like, don't hit me, I'm faking—I don't want that guy on my team.

"Two, a back's got to be physically and mentally tough. Don't give up when you're hit. Don't give up when you're hurt. Don't be gun-shy. Bang in there, even if you know you're not going to get many yards. That's the one thing you can never let the defense know. You can never let the defense be able to say, 'We got him! He's gun-shy!' When I get my brain scrambled, I might not know where I am, but I guarantee you I'll get back up in a hurry and run back to the huddle, just to show them, 'You'll never beat me.' We were playing Washington a couple of weeks ago, and two of their young running backs came up to me after the game and said, 'Man, you run hard. After ten years, you still run like you're fresh.' I'm rubbing off on younger guys. I like that. The other thing about being tough is learning to play with pain. You've got to do it, all the time. In '86, I played with a posterior ligament tear in my right knee. I've played with a separated shoulder, cracked ribs, concussions. Against Denver once, I got a gash over my eye, and the blood wouldn't stop. But I played, wiping the blood out of my eye. We're warriors. We can't stop. Running backs are modern-day gladiators, getting beaten up every Sunday.

"Three, attitude. I can't emphasize enough that you can't let down, no matter what the situation is. Things can steamroll on a team, and you've got to be the guy to get things going back in the right direction. My last play as a 49er, I fumbled in the 1990 NFC Championship Game, and we lost the game, and—I couldn't believe this—guys were saying I lost the game, getting on me in the press about it. That was tough. And then I went to the Raiders as a free agent, and my numbers weren't great, but I still led them in rushing. Why? Because I was still a good player. I knew I was. I'd had too many great days and too many great games with the 49ers to let that one play screw up my career. You have the attitude that you're going to succeed on every play."

Now for the physical act of running with the ball.

"Size and speed," he said. "My ideal back for my system would be six-one, 215 pounds. Big enough to take the pounding, quick enough to be a great receiver, fast enough to get around the corner, strong enough to be a good blocker. That's the big three, as I call 'em—running, passing, and blocking. It'd be Marcus Allen, but a little faster. Marcus Allen has been a tremendous back. Marcus Allen with 4.4 or 4.3 speed would terrorize the league like nobody ever has.

"Last thing: vision. It's some knack you develop as a kid. Instead of waiting for the play to unfold, you react. You just know it's there. Sometimes, you get a young guy, and he gets overwhelmed with everything involved in the play and the game and he gets to thinking too much instead of just relaxing and seeing the field. What separates good players from great players is that vision, that knack, that ability to think when times are tough. A coach can draw up a play on the board, but it's not going to hit that way. You run to daylight. It's easy for a coach to say after the fact, 'Why'd you cut back on this play? You should have stayed wide.' Then we look at the tapes the next day and we all see why. Then they understand, because then they can see what I saw."

Craig talked some more, mostly about blocking. He is obsessed with blocking, because he is obsessed with teamness, and he thinks blocking is the best way for a back to show he's a team player.

Asked about memorable games, Craig picked a queer one. San Francisco versus New England, 1989. He rushed twenty-two times for sixty-six yards. He caught three passes for fifty-five yards. But he threw some memorable blocks.

"After we played the Patriots," Craig said, "I got a long letter from Raymond Berry, their coach at the time. Coaches never write letters to players, but he wrote me this long letter. He told me it was a pleasure watching me do so many things in our game. He told me how well I did them. I thought, wow. I like that. I'm proud of that. I mean, I'm proud of the fact that I've caught more passes than any back of all time. But I'm prouder of things like that letter, things that show respect from other people in the league. I can remember John Robinson, when he coached the Rams, would show his backs tapes of me running, and he'd say, 'This is what it takes to be a running back in the league.' That's the stuff I'm proud of, because that's what I think means you're a good back today."

There's one other thing Craig wanted to stress. "The times I think I've run my best is when I'm confident, and I felt I could control the field. It's like how Magic Johnson could do things on the court. You relax in the open field, because you can think more clearly and run faster when you're relaxed. Relax, relax, relax, I tell myself. The key to running is relaxing. You dream, and you visualize, and you just feel it. Sometimes, on game day, I wake up in the morning, and I feel . . . light, almost . . . I wake

131

up and feel like I want the ball. It's almost like I go into the stadium that day and I'd do anything to get the ball that day. You'd beg for it. And there are certain times where I *have* begged for the ball, I want it so bad."

The act of running is so hard to define, hard to explain. It's almost zen. It's so deep, and there are so many things we as outsiders can't know, because it happens so fast, and so much of it is simple reaction, culled from years and years of just doing it.

Most backs can't explain what they do. "I just do it the way I've been doing it since I was a kid," Sanders said. "It's hard for me to explain it. Some of the things I don't even think about. They just happen. And we'll be watching film of them the next day, and I'll be surprised I did them."

One of the only backs capable of verbalizing the process is Craig's San Francisco heir, Ricky Watters. This, then, is the zen of a football running play, through the eyes and ears and emotions of Watters, talking in front of his locker at the 49ers' training facility in Santa Clara, California.

You break from the huddle and . . .

"First of all, I'm looking across the line to see what defense they're in. I look at them to see what the linebackers are looking like, maybe look into their eyes and see what they might be thinking. Try to see, anyway. Sometimes you can tell by the way they're cheating up on the line. They're cheating up into a hole, and their foot's back like this. [Watters put his right foot behind and to one side.] They might be in that hole, but they might not be rushing from that hole. They're going to be rushing from a different hole. So you kind of watch what the linebackers are doing to see what you might run, if you even get the ball."

What can you see in their eyes?

"You can see if they're keying on you. If one of the linebackers is keying on you, he'll look right at you and study you, and then you know if they've got you. If you come out of the backfield, you know he's going to stick you. And if you run, he's going to be the guy right on you. Other guys will look at you and then they'll look away, at the quarterback, or at the fullback. But when a guy locks onto you, you see it in his eyes and you feel he's going to have you whether it's a run or pass. It gives me an idea of what I'm going to do when I come out of the backfield. If he's inside of me, I know if I've got an outside pass route all I've got to do is come out and I have him beat just by the position of our bodies. So I want to get up into him [bump him] and nod to the inside, and then I have an advantage to the outside. Whereas if he's outside, I have to go into him straight up and fake him to the inside, then move outside."

What do you hear? The crowd?

"No, I focus the crowd out because I'm intent on what we're doing and what the defense is doing to us. I can hear [quarterback] Steve Young, because he might call an audible. I hear the defense yelling things and calling out formations, but we don't know what they mean."

So you're lined up, the ball's snapped, and . . .

"First of all I've got to take my deep breath. Every time. Especially if I'm getting the ball. I will take the breath . . . [he breathes in deeply, not letting it go, and struggles to talk for a moment] . . . and then the snap count comes. As soon as Steve says, 'One,' or 'Go,' or whatever the key word on the snap is, I let it go . . . [he exhales audibly] . . . and that's when I blast. That allows me to relax my whole body and then explode."

The breath's important?

"Yeah. I suck it up and then WHOOOM! It's kind of like the effect of pushing off, like a rocket or something."

After the breath?

"Then I'm reading my keys, and everything's in fast-motion. Say it's a running play, and I have a pulling guard or tackle. Whoever it is that I'm supposed to read as I go across the line of scrimmage—either I'm reading [guards] Guy McIntyre or Roy Foster, or I might be reading [fullback] Tom Rathman, to see how they light into their men. If they're on the outside, then I know I'm going to cut outside. If they're blocking inside, I'm going inside. You read your block, then follow it."

After that?

"Then it's just me. I'm just looking at which man is coming that I can beat or that I can mess up an angle on. They're all taking angles to the ball, right at me. So sometimes I'll get in there,

133

instead of just running straight up the field, and I'll give 'em a little juke this way or that, to try to get them to freeze for a second or put some doubt in their minds about where I'm going. Then I'll explode."

Do you see colors? Holes? What? What are you seeing?

"I look for a hole. Say they have black jerseys on, like the Falcons or the Saints. I see the black, and I'm looking for a break in the black. I don't want to see a wall of black. If I see a little break in the black, then I have to hit it—NOW—I can't wait, I can't kind of just go in there, I have to hit it."

And if you get through there?

"And once I get through there, it just feels like . . . well, it's almost like I've been underwater and I can't breathe, and as soon as I come out of the water, it's like AAAAAHHHHHHHHHHHT!!! That's how you feel once you get past those jerseys, into the open field. Because, like, BLAM! then I'm in the open, like I'm out of the water. Then my eyes get wide and I feel real good about myself, and my energy is really pumping, my adrenaline is going . . ."

And . . .

"I just start looking again for the jerseys, because you just don't know. They could be coming from anywhere, from this way or that way or in front of you. You just have to have your eyes open and react."

Do you make your moves without thinking?

"All the time. All the time. Somebody will just dart at you, and, you know, you can tell by where they're coming from. If they're coming from the left, you've got to dart this way [to the left, in front of them, juking the imaginary guy right here on the locker room floor]. Because if you try to dart [to the right], their momentum's coming in such a way that you know they're going to get you. So if you see them coming, then all of a sudden, at the last second, you just shift back in the opposite direction and they miss you—if you've made a good move."

Do you hear anything now?

"Oh yeah. You hear people grunting coming after you. They're like, AAAHHHHH!, coming after you and if they're missing, they're all like, AHSHITTT!, cussing. It's a lot of fun. Tom

Rathman makes fun of me because I talk when I'm running the ball. Not many guys do, I guess. I'll go, 'OH YEAH!!! THAT'S IT RIGHT THERE! THAT'S IT!' And he says I get him excited because I'm like, 'OH YEAH, TOM, THAT'S IT!' I'll say something like that while I'm running."

You mean, while you're breaking into the open?

"Yeah! Or sometimes before, when I'm breaking through the line. I'm kind of quiet, then, as soon as I, like, bust out of the water, I might just burst out and say, 'YEAH THAT'S IT! OK!' And one time I was running with Roy, and Roy went outside, and I went outside, and they kind of stopped us. The next time, Roy went inside, I bust inside, I say, 'YEAH, ROY!' I'm running right by him and I'm like, 'YEAH, ROY! THAT'S WHAT WE GOTTA DO RIGHT THERE!' You're feeling the game, you're into the game, you're excited, you're in your zone."

How about getting hit? Does it hurt?

"You know when it hurts? Like if you get hit, even with a good shot, you don't feel it at first. It's like, POW, but your adrenaline's going, you're so high, you don't even feel it. And you get up, and you're walking back to the huddle and that's when it starts to sink in. You realize where you've been hit and how hard. You might say to yourself, 'Man, that was a good hit.' And you realize that was a good shot. When they hit you, at first, you never think it's a good shot. At first, you just feel like you've been stopped. Then maybe it starts to hurt, and you get up, and it's like, it hurts. But then it just fades away, because you're getting ready for the next play. Unless it's a real severe injury."

How about the breathing after you whoosh out of the backfield?

"I just try to relax, stay calm."

Even though you're talking so excitedly sometimes?

"Yeah, even though I'm talking. It's exciting, but the one thing I've got to do is stay relaxed. That's what they always tell you as a running back. Stay relaxed. And if you watch my body, it's kind of moving in such a way that you can tell I'm relaxed, totally relaxed, when I'm running, because I can move so naturally."

And so the moves come naturally?

"Yeah. I'm just reacting to whatever I see out there. If I see someone dart this way, I'm darting that way. It's all happening, but I try to stay calm."

Playing the Run

You have to react to play running back. But you have to think to play against running backs.

In a week, there are four main characters who scheme to help a defense gain advantages over a great all-around back. In 1992, the four characters were a scout-team back, a defensive coordinator, a defensive line coach, and a defensive player keying on the back. They talked about their jobs and their lives preparing to face one of the great ones, Barry Sanders.

The Scout-Team Sanders

"See you tomorrow, Barry," Vinson Smith said.

Michael Beasley, a practice-squad player with the Dallas Cowboys, did not reply, because he was used to being called Herschel.

"Hey, Sanders!" hollered Ken Norton, Jr.

That's right, Michael Beasley said to himself, finally getting it. I'm not Herschel Walker anymore. I'm Barry Sanders.

Later, Beasley explained that, on Sunday night, he ceases being the running back the Cowboys are playing that week and he becomes next week's back. So, with the Cowboys having disposed of Herschel Walker and the Eagles that afternoon, now he had to turn his attention to imitating Barry Sanders that week in practice.

"I do film study every week on Barry Sanders," he said. "I do it Sunday night when I'm watching the highlight reel on ESPN. That's all I need to see. He's been doing the same things ever since he's been in the NFL. He's elusive, quick, powerful, and strong, and he's got a low center of gravity that's tough for tacklers. I'm not new to what Barry Sanders does. The thing he also does well that people don't give him credit for is blocking. But I'm not really focusing on blocking this week. I need to focus on being elusive, which is fine with me because that's the type of running style I have. I need to be good at it too, because if I go

136

out there this week and just go through the motions, the defense may get the wrong idea of how well they're progressing during the week. Maybe they'll get a false sense of security.

"I do know I'd love to be him. I'd love to have his opportunity. That sprint draw is just an incredible play. It's every back's dream. We ran it a few times yesterday, and I'd love to run it in games someday. You have so much freedom to pick your hole and to run where you want. A week like this is so great because, imitating Barry Sanders, the coaches basically just give you the ball and say: Be a player. Run to daylight. Don't get hit. Find the hole."

The Defensive Coordinator

"There's always something nagging at me in weeks we play the Lions," Dave Wannstedt said during one such week. This was about ten weeks before he took the head coaching job with the Chicago Bears, where he'll face the Lions twice a year. He wasn't thinking about opportunity advancement now, though. "I always come back to one thought: Barry Sanders can beat us on any single play."

Most of the Lion running attack in 1991 was centered on draw plays. They'd just spread out, give the ball to Barry, and let him do his damage. "This year," Wannstedt said, "we can see they're doing much more conventional stuff, like running the Washington counter-gap. When we met with the players, we told them: They're getting the ball to Barry a lot more ways this year. We might see them in two tight ends, two receivers, and one back. Or we might see them in four wides and one back. Or we might see them in three wides, a tight end, and a back. But however they do it, the guts of the game plan hasn't changed very much. It starts with Barry Sanders. It ends with Barry Sanders. In their game against Green Bay last week, on one play, six guys missed a tackle on Sanders. Six guys! The speed, the power, the strength—that's what I have to get across to the players this week. I want them going into that game thinking: I can't miss a tackle this week."

The play that troubled Wannstedt preparing for Sanders was the sprint draw. On the sprint draw, the quarterback, Rodney

Peete, takes off toward one side or the other on a semirollout, and he hands the ball back to Sanders, maybe six or seven yards deep in the backfield. And instead of Sanders hitting the hole closest to the line, which might be the easiest thing for him, he hits whatever hole he sees. And when that closes up, he bounces off and hits the next hole he sees, and he keeps doing that until he's tackled. "We watched probably thirty of those," Wannstedt said. "There's not five of the thirty that hit in the same hole. So, unlike most backs who give you a pretty good idea where they're going from watching the tapes, the Lions don't give you any idea."

And the screen pass. That troubled him, too. Wannstedt sidled up to rookie safety Darren Woodson on Thursday before the game and said, "You know when you defend against a screen normally, you're just supposed to contain it? Here, against Sanders, you have to contain and make the tackle, or try to make the tackle." Wannstedt saw right away that Woodson knew. Why? "Because," Wannstedt said, "against the average back, he'd just have to contain him from making a big play to the outside and turn him in to the inside. With Sanders, because he's so quick, you can't count on the inside support helping out."

And one more thing. The speed. The game was being played on Detroit's AstroTurf. "There's a potential to have a tremendously fast game," he told his players on Saturday. "All the tackling drills and practice stuff we did this week, it's all going to be so much faster tomorrow. It'll be like when we used to play Oklahoma in college. They have an unbelievable percentage of scoring on their first offensive series, because it takes defenses a while to adjust to the speed of the offense. You just can't simulate it totally in practice."

When the game came, the Lions showed the Cowboys a completely different look early. They were playing two tight ends, one of them in the backfield like an H-back, and they were using him to wham-block the defensive tackle. It was the old Redskin Wham, which the new offensive coordinator, Dan Henning, brought with him from his former coaching job in Washington. On the Redskin Wham, the tight end is like a lead blocker taking on the defensive tackle. They'd been using the two tight ends, usually out where tight ends normally play.

The first time, Sanders bounced around left end for fifteen yards. The second time, Sanders ran around right end for fourteen yards.

Then Sanders ran in the hole over left guard for thirteen, and he made four yards on a sprint-draw to the left. Luckily for the Cowboys, Peete threw an interception just then, so Wannstedt and the Cowboys could regroup. He figured that as long as the Lions kept those two tight ends in they wouldn't score a lot of points, because they'd have to go on long, grind-it-out drives, and he had confidence his defense wouldn't allow many of those.

As it turned out, they didn't have to do a lot of wholesale changing the rest of the day, because when Dallas went up 7-0, the Lions went to their usual four-wide look that the Cowboys had spent so much time preparing for. "At halftime, although Sanders had eighty-eight yards, there was a confidence in the locker room, because we felt good about playing against the four wides, and they'd already shown us they were only going to run what we'd prepared for." While in most weeks, the defensive coordinator's vocabulary is peppered with words like "contain," "plug the gaps," and "support the run," when you face Barry Sanders, it's back to Wichita: Tackle the man with the football. Dallas won 37-3. Sanders got his 113 yards, and he was magnificent at many points of the first half. But in 1992, with the Lions, he was an island.

The Defensive Line Coach

John Teerlinck, the defensive line coach of the Minnesota Vikings, leaned forward in his chair. "Let me tell you about my first experience with Barry Sanders," the fleshy Teerlinck said, warming to the task. He was in a sterile conference room at the Vikings' practice complex in Eden Prairie, in between morning and afternoon sessions with his linemen. An intensely interested, loud, and good-natured guy, Teerlinck is a favorite of the writers everywhere he coaches. That, recently, had been at Cleveland in 1989 and 1990, at the Los Angeles Rams in 1991, and with these Vikings in 1992. Assistant coaches are the gypsies of the NFL. Most of them never met a franchise they didn't like.

"Barry's a rookie," Teerlinck said, hands gesturing. "It's 1989. We're contending for the playoffs that year in Cleveland with a pretty good team—that's the year we went to the AFC Championship game and lost with Bud Carson as head coach. Anyway, we go into this game thinking—the Lions have, I think, one win at the time—that they've got just one back in the backfield, and we'll just play the pass. Well, at the end of the first quarter, Barry's really hurting us, and we're there on the sidelines saying, Well, time for a new strategy. Whoa. We get into halftime, and we totally redo our game plan to stop Barry Sanders. He was beating us by himself. What I'm saying is, any other team that had one back in the backfield, we'd have been fine. This guy was the exception. We shut him down better in the second half, but the damage was done."

Teerlinck and coach Bud Carson directed a stunting second-half defensive plan. At the snap of the ball, the Browns stunted their defensive tackles and inside linebackers, switching positions with each other and moving into the gaps the Lions saw at the same time. This forced Sanders to read the defense on the run. The whole thing became a fire drill for Sanders, who improvised his way to a seventy-one-yard second half. But it was enough, that plus what he did in the first half, for a 13-10 Detroit win. Sanders got 145 yards.

As a position coach, Teerlinck can be more focused than Wannstedt. Wannstedt has to see the big picture. Teerlinck sees the world as it affects his three players, or four, depending on the scheme of defense, whether it's a 4-3 defense or 3-4. He's coached both. Teerlinck, in a week his team plays the Lions, has two jobs. He contributes to the game plan on Monday and Tuesday, suggesting fronts and philosophies with the three other defensive assistants; he funnels ideas to the defensive coordinator—in this case, Tony Dungy with the Vikings—and they arrive collectively at the decision on how to play that week's opponent. Then, the rest of the week, Teerlinck gets down in the trenches, energizing and educating his players for the task ahead.

On Monday of a Detroit week, especially when the Lions were battered on the offensive line as they were in 1992, Teerlinck starts to think about whether the Vikings have someone who can shed Lomas Brown, the Lions' Pro Bowl left tackle. Then he starts to figure out which Viking defensive fronts will work best against the Lions' offensive line. "It's such a fine balance," he said. "You try to figure out what it is you want to stop, and in stopping that, you might open up a whole 'nother can of worms. Like when you play Houston. They spread you out, obviously, with the run-and-shoot offense, and if you choose to take away their wide guys, Jeffires and Duncan, then you're going to have trouble stopping whatever inside game they have. That means trouble with Lorenzo White, their great running back." Teerlinck puts the Viking linemen in the eight or ten defensive fronts they'll be using that week. Then, using the scout team, Teerlinck simulates exactly how the offense will block the defensive linemen. "Wednesday's chaotic," he said. "I've got to get our plan from the blackboard to the playing field to the players' heads."

More of the same Thursday and Friday, with technical fine-tuning. Teerlinck says line versus line is just like a chess match with real people. What fake does the man across from you take? What's his best move? How do we counter what he does well? Which hand does he use best? Does he have telltale clues on whether the play's going to be a run or pass? On third and long, should you hit the guy across from you with a power move or a speed rush to the outside?

"I like to have what I call thinking soldiers playing on my side," Teerlinck said. "Especially against a Barry Sanders. When my players come off the field, I ask them, 'What's working?' I use their input. They're out there, doing the job. They're out there, trying somehow to bring guys like Sanders down. They know what's happening better than I do. My job is to put them in the best possible position to succeed. Imagine the biggest detail and the most minute detail, and a position coach has to be concerned with them all. In Los Angeles once, we were playing San Diego at home, and one of the defensive linemen shows up five minutes before the game. He says, 'I went to San Diego. I thought the game was there.' That taught me a lesson. You've got to tell everybody everything, no matter how obvious it seems. And the little things . . . one time this year, we're going to Tampa, and I ask one of the guys, 'What kind of shoes you bringing for the trip?' He says he's bringing grass shoes. And I've got to ask him, 'What kind of grass? Turf Bermuda? Bluegrass? Or the sandy surface like they have in Cleveland?' Different lengths of cleat are good for different grasses."

Often, different teams have radically different approaches for facing a player. Teerlinck laughed when asked about the differences in preparing for Sanders with the Rams in 1991 and Vikings in 1992.

"Well, I'm with the Rams last season, and my first meeting with him a couple of years before left quite an impression," he said. "We're setting up our game plan normally on a Tuesday, going around the room, with the coordinator, Jeff Fisher, asking for ideas how to defend the Lions. And the whole plot centered on Sanders, obviously. We're sitting around thinking what we can do to overcome our problems, and I keep thinking of Sanders squirting out of every hole and being so quick no one can catch him. And I think of the Rocky movie, the one where Burgess Meredith puts Rocky in the box with the chicken and tells him to catch the chicken. That'll teach quickness.

"Jeff says, 'How can we simulate practicing this week against Barry Sanders? We don't have a back that quick, who moves like that. How can we get our people accustomed to that kind of movement, that kind of speed?'

"I said, 'We gotta be like that Rocky movie and go out and get a chicken and make 'em catch it.' Everybody laughs. But we said, what the heck, let's do it.

"Now here's a problem—finding a chicken in Los Angeles. It's not like we're in Kansas City and can go to some farm and get a chicken. We called around, and we found a Vietnamese market in downtown Los Angeles that sold live chickens. They asked what kind of chicken we wanted. We told them we wanted a mean chicken, one that could peck your eyes out. We decided to buy two of them."

Why?

"Because we had Al Wright, a nose tackle, on the roster then. And he weighed about 320. We were afraid Al might fall on the chicken and ruin our drill. To make it even better, our equipment guy took a couple of those rubber sleeves the linemen wear on AstroTurf, and he put the number twenty on both of the sleeves, and he slipped 'em on the chickens.

"We made two mistakes, though. We put 'em in a cardboard box and covered it so they wouldn't get away, and I think they got kind of groggy. We got all the defense in a big circle, and we said, okay, case of beer for whoever catches a chicken. This is what it's going to be like trying to catch Barry Sanders. We can't simulate him. This is the closest thing. We dump the chickens out, and everybody catches 'em. They're just not moving. And the guys are saying we had California chickens because they're so laid-back. If we won that week, we were going to give out rubber chickens as game balls."

What the Rams ultimately did was something Teerlinck and the Ram staff had seen the Bears do to Sanders: rush the two defensive ends about three yards upfield, then face the ends in toward the backfield and try to collapse the pocket by blocking the offensive tackles into it. On Sanders's rushes, this would take away much of the inside gap between tackle and guard, because there wouldn't be the gap there that Sanders was used to. Sanders would be stuck in traffic inside and have to run outside, where, the plan went, there'd be a linebacker and a safety waiting to come off their assignments to focus on Sanders.

This, some defensive coaches in the league say, has been the most effective way to corral Sanders. "You make the field smaller," Teerlinck said. "He wants to spread the field out so he can open the rushing lanes and create more chaos. But the way we played it, in this defense, you take one step up the field and close it down, squeeze the box, squeeze the pocket." The Rams held Sanders to fifty-seven yards on twenty-six carries.

The new Viking staff thought this was a good strategy too, and so this is how they defensed Sanders in 1992. With one added stress. "Chris Doleman and Henry Thomas get cut and get chop-blocked a lot. We told them, 'You've got to stay alive. Go down, and get right back up, ready, because he could be coming right back at you. We need 100 percent effort to stay alive. Get up in one piece, because the ball's coming back to you.' We had our line running the ropes, high-stepping through the ropes, that week." Agility. Balance. Alertness.

"Every week we have to coach different," Teerlinck said. "In a Detroit week, we coach the guys to stay alive, stay up. Barry'll show up on any play, anytime."

The Keying Linebacker

A half-hour before the Packers played the Lions at the Silverdome in 1992, Green Bay's assistant equipment manager, Bryan Nehring, padded up to linebacker Johnny Holland in the end zone, where Holland, in full uniform, was warming up for the game.

"Helmet fits?" Nehring said.

"Yeah, fine," Holland said.

"Got enough air? You need some?" Nehring said.

"I'm okay. It's fine," Holland said.

A word about the helmet. There are air pockets in the helmet, and the air pockets can be inflated, to allow the wearer a snug fit. Equipment guys can pump up the helmet just like you pump up a basketball or football, with a pin and air pump. And today, inside that size 7 1/4 helmet resided one of the Packers' most important players. Johnny Holland would need a particularly snug helmet, because he planned to be banging it on Barry Sanders a lot.

As Holland warmed to the occasion, he thought about his workday ahead. Over the PA system, Bonnie Raitt's "Let's Give Them Something to Talk About" wafted over the speakers into the half-filled stadium, and that's exactly what Holland intended to do. If he and his mates could stop Sanders that day, they'd give Detroit something to talk about, all right. Holland's job was to patrol the area behind the defensive line, often keying on Sanders. He'd have to shed blockers and not be fooled by Sanders's moves. He knew that from his six previous games against him. And he knew it from a week's worth of video and practice he'd just experienced.

The Packers played a 4-2-5 defense against the Lions much of the time—four defensive linemen, two linebackers, five defensive backs. "Six in the box," Lions offensive coordinator Dan Henning calls it. "Six guys up front—maybe four defensive linemen and two linebackers, or three and three—and five defensive backs. That's how a lot of teams play us. They get these six guys up against our line, then rush upfield and try to box Barry in." The linebackers were Holland and George Koonce, an inexperienced greenhorn Green Bay coach Mike Holmgren was trying to make into a player. Holland was his personal tutor. Holland played left linebacker, Koonce right, and they had to work in tandem or else the Lions would perforate the defense right in its heart.

Holland is the perfect man to play against Barry Sanders. He's obsessed with his sport, striding purposefully from group to group in the pregame warmups, a six-year veteran encouraging the kids or firing up the old guys. Not yelling, just talking, in an encouraging way, the way a good mother prods her three-year-old just learning the alphabet. At six-two and 232 pounds, he has a body-builder's torso and a track man's legs. He's brute-strong enough to play inside linebacker and fast and quick enough to play outside linebacker. He can blitz and he can drop into coverage. He loves the big hit. He loves the game. And he loves playing against Sanders. "Are you kidding?" he said a couple of days before this game. "You've got to love playing against the best, and Barry's the best I've ever seen. You get so excited to play a game like this because you're playing one of the best guys ever at his position."

Once, during the week, when the defense was watching tape, a voice ordered the tape halted in midrush by Sanders, a particularly stunning one, one where Sanders left three Tampa Bay Buccaneers in his wake.

One player said: "No!"
Another player said: "God!"
Another player said: "Oooooh!"
Another player said: "Incredible!"
All those comments just kind of bunched together and formed Holland's outstanding memory of this week. And so as he was getting ready down on the plastic-grass-covered cement floor of

the Silverdome, he thought of Sanders. Holland, who is not a holler guy, now did his only hollering of the pregame warmup. "Hey D!" he yelled to the defense. "We gotta get to that ball today. Gotta corral that Barry Sanders."

Holland said to George Koonce, "Let's go, Koonce. Gotta fly today. Gotta fly to the ball. Gotta take shots at him. Gotta take shots at him."

Sanders, of course.

To substitute linebacker Burnell Dent, he crouched low and readied for a hit. "C'mon. I'm just like Barry. Hit me!"

"CRACKLEOOOOMMMMPHHHHH!" was the next sound you heard, the sound that happens when pads hit pads and breath leaves men.

"I think I'm a good match for Barry," Holland said during the week. "In practice, I try to sprint back from plays, because I think that's a way I can improve my conditioning. That's how I've made a lot of plays in my career—by conditioning. I run to the ball no matter where it is on the field. You can't take a break on Barry Sanders. If there's one play when you're tired and can't go full-speed, that's the play Barry'll break it. That's the philosophy all eleven guys on defense have to take, because if they don't, one of those guys is going to hurt you during the course of a day. Some of the things he does, there's nothing you can do about 'em. I've seen him make five guys miss on a play. Some teams, they sit back and let him make his decision where he's going, and then they go after him. You have to take the initiative and go after him and hope your teammates go after him. He's never done. He goes into piles of five or six guys and pops out for a touchdown."

The Packers' favorite defensive call today will be "Packer South." In this 4-2-5 alignment, Holland and Koonce are the spies on Sanders on most pass plays. If he darts toward Holland's side, Holland covers him; same thing with Koonce's side. Naturally, with Detroit quarterback Rodney Peete being right-handed, it's more likely he'll throw to the right, and it's more likely Sanders will run to the right. That's the left side of the Packer defense, toward Holland. The Packers like that.

On the second play of the game, Sanders ran around left end

for two, into Koonce's arms. That left the Lions with a third down. Peete threw a screen to Sanders that Holland snuffed out short of the first down.

Next series. On second-and-eight from the Green Bay twenty, the Lions driving, Holland was chatty in the huddle. "We need a play now, need a play," he said, and then Sanders showed what makes him so dangerous. Peete tossed him a screen pass to the right. "I got contain! I got contain!" Holland yelled, trying to seal off the outside running lane and turn Sanders inside. But Sanders threw Holland a fake upfield, like he was going to turn the play up into the hole. Holland bit. ("I say you can't bite on the guy's fakes," he'd later say, "but I'm human. It's not easy.") And Sanders ducked outside and up the sidelines for a six-yard gain, averting a possible no-gainer.

(Later, on the sidelines, defensive end Bryce Paup called Holland over. "When they're wide," Paup said, ". . . when they're running wide, try to stay outside. Try to stay wide, okay?"

"Yeah," Holland said, launching into playspeak. "I'll try to stay outside. I know that one time Barry . . . came around outside, I got forced in by him and let him go outside. I'm gonna try to get upfield more and force him inside. I was playing too off.")

Here's one play in the Sanders–Holland duel, in the stream of consciousness way NFL plays seem to happen:

Late first quarter, Green Bay up 7-3, Lion first down at the Detroit twenty-six . . . The Packer defense and Lion offense run on the field . . . Holland, the defensive signal-caller—he has played every defensive snap for the past two months—looks to the sidelines to the play being signaled in. "Packer! Packer!" he says above the rock-music din in the Silverdome . . . Then he looks over again, to complete the call. "Packer South! Packer South! Ready?" He claps his hands. He moves into position behind his defensive front, between the end and tackle on the left side of the Packer defense.

"All right, Koonce! C'mon, Koonce!" he yells to the neophyte, six yards away, for no apparent reason, just chatter . . . He rocks on the balls of his feet, crouched a bit low, like a shortstop waiting for a grounder. And he starts to study the Detroit offense.

Holland stares at Sanders's eyes, which don't dart nervously. They move. They look at Holland, then over to Koonce, on the right side of the Packer defense, then at Peete, then at Holland again, all in three or four seconds . . . Sanders is alone in the Lions' backfield, three yards directly behind Peete.

"Blue 90! Blue 90!" Peete yells, once to the left, once to the right.

"Hut!" and the ball is snapped.

Sanders fakes inside, then jogs out to the right, about three yards behind the line of scrimmage. Holland, right leg over left, left leg behind right, follows each Sanders step. And the ball is wafting in the air toward Sanders.

"Ball!" Holland yells.

Sanders catches the ball, then moves forward with it, looking for any hole he can find. He has a lineman in front of him, but Sanders is only using him for interference, because he never really follows his blockers the way the old Vince Lombardi textbook said to. He glides and fakes and dekes and shifts until he can find an opening or until he gets buried. And now it's beginning to look very much like he's going to get buried. Holland follows each Sanders move. ("But you look at his hips," he would say later, echoing Rod Woodson's words about Ernest Givins. "His body can't go where his hips don't go.") Sanders, for a split second, can't seem to find a hole, which isn't unusual in this season . . . A Lion lineman lunges at Holland as Holland continues to follow Sanders and fill the hole Sanders wishes for, but the blocker only deflects Holland's left side. The blocker has done nothing to stop the inevitable . . . Sanders jukes to the outside, stepping a yard past the line of scrimmage, and then he lunges straight ahead, knowing in a millisecond he's going into the arms of Holland and somebody else but hoping he can somehow power through them.

That last paragraph lasts 2.8 seconds of real time.

He churns his legs, which are suddenly being grabbed at by a Packer safety, LeRoy Butler. Holland stops on a dime. He attacks Sanders, crunching shoulder pads with him, and he simultaneously puts his arms around Sanders's chest.

There is a loud collision sound—BAM!!!—as pads hit pads.

Sanders tries to surge forward, even for an inch more.

"AAAAAAAAAHHHHHHHHHH!" Holland says as he steer-wrestles Sanders backward and Sanders fights with everything he's got to go forward.

It's not a fair fight. Holland has thirty pounds on Sanders, and the entwined Hollandsanders starts to fall floorward.

"OOOOOOOOOOOOOFFFF!" is the next sound. It is the sound of Sanders hitting the ground and Sanders gasping and Holland gasping, all at the same time.

"OVER GENTLEMEN!" is the next sound. It is the sound of the umpire, Chad Brown, rushing in to break up the fallen bodies, telling them the play's finished.

"MFLTPKEETPEKOONCEWAYTOGORRRRRRRRRR!" is the next sound. It is the sound of Holland, with his jaw forced shut in the pile for a millisecond and his mouthpiece preventing intelligent sound anyway, telling Koonce he done good.

Sanders is speechless, expressionless, emotionless as the pile disengages. The players unfold themselves, test to see that everything's still intact after the collision with bodies and plastic grass covering cement, and get ready for the next play. Sanders starts to walk back to his huddle. Holland jogs back.

"Way to fly to the ball, baby!" safety Chuck Cecil hollers in Holland's face once he rises.

Here's how this play would look on the official play-by-play sheet later: 1-10-DL26. R.Peete pass to Ba.Sanders to DL32 for 6 yards (J.Holland; G.Koonce).

And this is what makes Sanders so good. He got six yards out of the play, six yards out of a three-yard play, six yards when his primary blocker missed Holland, six yards with three Packers zeroing in on him. He caught and he bulled, two essential elements for good backs today.

And this is what makes Holland so good, too. The biggest offensive threat in football didn't get away, and Holland wasn't even breathing hard. He was ready for three more quarters of collisions.

The Packers won the conflict with Sanders, who rushed twelve times for thirty-eight yards and caught five passes for thirty yards. Holding Barry Sanders to sixty-eight yards is a terrific day. They also won the game, 27-13.

Holland, though, led the league in humility after the game. "I never saw a pattern the whole game, and that's one of the things that makes playing Barry so tough," he said. "Everybody gives you some kind of pattern, something to show you what they're going to do on a certain play. But Barry, he just invents things."

The great running back, especially having so many jobs today, is football's Van Gogh. You know his brush strokes, and you're going to know it's his canvas at the end of the run because of how he cuts and twists. But you don't know exactly what he's going to paint, because every painting is different.

A quarterback has assigned reads to make. A receiver has precise routes to run. A lineman has an exact area to clear. A pass-rusher has a certain hole to hit, and a defensive back has a definite area or man to cover.

A running back starts out being assigned a hole to hit. Then, more than any player in the game, he creates, and he feels, and he bursts, and he stops, and he goes, and he evokes.

The great ones do, anyway.

Special Teams

THE HIDDEN GAME

"The offense doesn't set the tempo! The defense doesn't set the tempo! Special teams set the tempo! Special teams will win or lose this game today!"

Washington coach George Allen, to his team, 1971

When Steve Tasker of the Buffalo Bills is out socially with his wife, and they're not in the company of Bills followers, and Sarah Tasker is introducing her husband to friends, this is how the conversation always goes:

"This is my husband, Steve. He plays for the Bills," Sarah says.

"Oh, isn't that nice. That must be exciting."

"Yes, it's really fun," Steve says.

"What exactly do you do? What position do you play?"

"Well," Steve says, "you know when they kick the ball? When they kick it, I chase it."

"Isn't that . . . interesting."

Or something like that.

Tasker, at his locker at Rich Stadium in Buffalo, told the story. He is small for a football player, about five-foot-ten and 185 pounds, with a surprisingly cherubic, unmarked face and curly blond hair. "That's how it usually goes," he said. "But let me tell you, there's a lot of guys out there, like coaches or very serious fans, who think they know football, and maybe they even know a little about football. They can talk about strategy or ask an intelligent question about why we might do something in the course of a game. But if you ever run into a guy who claims he knows about special teams, I mean, there's no way. No way at all. Punting, point returning, kicking off, kickoff returning, punt-blocking, field-goal kicking. They don't spend any time doing what we do. It's one of the most completely specialized areas of sports, with some incredibly technical stuff. Everybody always says it's chaotic, but they don't have any idea how much precise scouting and film work we do. I've never met anybody outside of the NFL who could hold an intelligent conversation about special-teams play in professional football."

Special teams have been with us for as long as football has. But they've only been coached in a concentrated way for the last quarter-century and have only been crucial to most teams for the past few years. They still are football's great unknown, both to the friends of Steve Tasker and to the most rabid of football followers.

Special-teams play is also football's best example of the art of violence, of bodies colliding full speed, of players wondering if this punt return or kickoff will be their last.

But this is all you need to know about their importance: Special teams are the only major variable left in pro football today, which means that the clubs with the great ones have a huge advantage over the clubs with the lousy ones.

The differences can be incredibly subtle, and sometimes only true insiders can see them. When Buffalo kicker Scott Norwood missed the 47-yard field goal that handed the New York Giants Super Bowl XXV, New Orleans kicker Morten Andersen was providing color commentary for a European telecast of the game, and on the replay he noticed that holder Frank Reich hadn't rotated the laces properly toward the goalpost before the kick; the laces were off to the side, and Andersen pointed out what a difference that could mean aerodynamically, and how it certainly would have pushed the kick inside the right upright if the laces were pointed properly. The kick sailed wide right by thirty inches.

Special-team failures stick out for all the world to see. In the fourth week of the 1991 season, six games came down to made or missed field goals, and one of the misses had a huge effect on the rest of the year. At Washington's RFK Stadium, Houston's Ian Howfield blew a thirty-one-yarder that would have won the game and thus knocked Washington from the ranks of the unbeaten. That one-game margin cost Houston the home-field advantage for the playoffs, and they had to travel to Denver, where the Broncos won on a last-second miracle John Elway drive. Howfield was long gone, cut just a day after the miss. Such punishment is increasingly common for kickers, although one of the most flagrant goofs in recent history led to no such fate. In the 1985 NFC playoffs, one of the best punters in the league, Sean Landeta of the Giants, barely grazed a punt deep in his own territory in a scoreless game; the Bears recovered for a touchdown and won 21-0.

Special-teams play can help make history. Houston led Buffalo 35-10 in the third quarter of their AFC Wild Card playoff game in January 1993. The Bills, having just scored, were kicking off. They had twenty-four minutes to score at least twenty-five points, and everybody in the place knew the Bills would have to try an onside kick very, very soon—everybody except Houston special-teams coach Richard Smith. He had his regular kickoff-return team in the game, including five men on the front line who were mostly lead-handed linebackers and linemen. As Buffalo's Steve Christie advanced for the kick, the Oilers on the front kickoff line started *retreating,* assuming this would be a regular deep kick. Insane! Christie squibbed. The ball bonked off an Oiler right back into Christie's hands, and fifty-six seconds later, the Bills had scored again. Buffalo rebounded from a thirty-two-point deficit and won, 41-38.

These teams are so important, and it's such a fire drill every year to put them together. When teams scour college campuses, they're not scouring them for punt-blockers or punt-chasers. Special teams are what teams think about once their rosters are near to closing in late August each year. And the annual

153

turnover and remake of special teams became tougher each year in recent seasons because of Plan B free-agency, where the marginal players on every roster were set free each year to seek small fortunes with other teams. One of the last guys on every roster is the long-snapper, the center who snaps the ball on punt, field-goal, and extra-point attempts. One long-snapper, Frank Winters, went from Cleveland to the Giants on Plan B in 1989 (for a $125,000 signing bonus), from the Giants to Kansas City on Plan B in 1990 (for a $75,000 signing bonus), and from the Chiefs to Green Bay in 1992 (for a $100,000 signing bonus); in turn, Cleveland, New York, and Kansas City all needed to look for and train long-snappers when Winters left. In 1992, San Diego lost its three best special-teams players on Plan B, and the Chargers spent training camp totally rebuilding all their special-teams units.

Lots of special-teams freaks—head coach Marv Levy of the Bills and defensive coordinator Rusty Tillman of Seattle, for instance—will tell you that special teams have as much to do with winning in the NFL as offense and defense. That's probably a slight exaggeration, although the specialty zealots have a case. In today's average NFL game, there are about 145 plays—sixty on offense, sixty on defense, twenty-five on kicking and punting. That's seventeen percent of a game's plays, approximately, spent with the special teams on the field. But about thirty-four percent of the points in recent NFL seasons have been scored with special teams on the field (field goals, extra points, punt and kickoff returns for touchdowns), and huge chunks of the field are exchanged on special-teams plays.

The point is, it's a vital aspect of the game that even the best fans gloss over. "The thing that's glaring about the game today," says Dick Vermeil, the former Eagle coach and current TV analyst, "is that there's so much parity and competition and intense scouting, more than ever. With that evenness, teams have to lean on something else to make the difference. I think special teams are the biggest dimension in winning and losing football games today."

Vermeil helped give birth to this dimension. The science of special teams was invented by the late George Allen on the floor of the Los Angeles Coliseum on December 8, 1968. That's the day Allen knew he had to make special teams a separate discipline. The previous day, the Colts had won at Green Bay, raising their first-place National Football League Coastal Division record to 12-1; Allen's Rams, 10-1-1, needed a win to keep pace with Baltimore. The Rams, unbeaten at home at this point of the season, were prohibitive favorites over the 6-6 Bears, who had been crushed by the two other premier teams in the league, Baltimore and Dallas, earlier that season. A win by the Rams would make the Baltimore–Los Angeles game the following week at the Coliseum a match for the division championship and the only playoff spot in the division. There were, of course, no wild cards in those days.

With the Bears up 7-3 in the second quarter, Chicago's Clarence Childs dodged a couple of feeble tackle attempts and returned a Ram kickoff eighty-eight yards. This set up a Bear touchdown run and infuriated Allen. How can we be tackling so poorly? What can we do about this? The Bears stunned the Rams 17-16, knocking them from the playoff race. Allen's mind raced, from that day into the offseason.

"I was on the road that winter recruiting southern California for Stanford," Dick Vermeil says. "And I got a message to call George Allen. You want to know the whole story? I had a bunch of friends who liked to play games with me. I mean, they'd leave messages for me saying Ara Parseghian called. Once they told me Bear Bryant called. I'd call these guys back, and it turns out they'd never called me. I debated about calling George back, but I did. When he said, 'This is George Allen,' I said, 'Yeah, right, and I'm Knute Rockne.' He finally did convince me after about five minutes, and boy, was I embarrassed. Anyway, he wanted to interview me for a coaching job. I went. We talked about this new position he was creating to coach the kicking teams. He wanted a young guy with enthusiasm who he could train, and he gave me the job."

Although Allen needed a special-teams coach, he didn't need anyone to tell him about the importance of every single play in a game. "Invariably," Vermeil says, "he'd walk up to you twenty or thirty minutes before a game and ask you some simply unbe-

155

lievable question. We'd be on the road somewhere, and he'd come up to me at 12:30 or twenty minutes to one, and he'd say, 'Do you know where the sun is going to be at 1:30?' He'd want to make sure you covered everything with the return people, because he wanted you to be able to tell the return man if the sun might be in his eyes at a certain point of the game. Really, it wasn't that unbelievable, because you had to know the answers to questions like that on special teams. You had to know the most minute things."

When Allen went to Washington in 1971, his special-teams coach was Marv Levy. They turned the teams into game-winning units, and marginal players like Rusty Tillman became stalwart special-teamers. "George Allen was so far ahead of his time, probably about twenty years," said Tillman, now the Seattle defensive coordinator. "It's only today that we're stressing special teams the way George did back then. Back then, you could gain such an advantage on other teams, because not many teams spent much time on them. George's greatest talent was making every player on the field feel like he was the single most important player on the team. Every game, he'd come up to every special-teams player on our team and say, 'The special teams are going to win the game today.'"

In 1971, the Redskins could win games on special teams, and their kamikaze guys did. Today, they couldn't get such a large advantage. The Cowboys, for instance, have a full-time special-teams coach, Joe Avezzano, and a kicker coach, Steve Hoffman. "I know how many games a year are decided by the kicking game," Dallas head coach Jimmy Johnson said.

A lot. And special-teams play is as complex as the other 120 plays each game. Which is why Dante Scarnecchia has such an important job.

Dawn is breaking in the foresty northwestern Rhode Island town of Smithfield, which means it's time for Scarnecchia, the special-teams coach of the New England Patriots, to get to his training-camp worksite at Bryant College. At 5:50 A.M., Scarnecchia pads across the campus to the rotunda, where the Patriots have their meeting rooms and offices, to get ready for his day. He's the first one at work. He has a lot to do. Today, he will teach about forty-five New England Patriots how to return a kickoff from the right side of the field.

Scarnecchia is a lifetime football coach. "It's what I always wanted to do, even when I was a kid. My dream job," he says. He is forty-four, and he works sixteen hours a day in training camp and about thirteen during the regular season. He doesn't see his wife and two kids nearly as much as he'd like, but this is what he does. He is a muscular and fit five-foot-ten, with wavy black hair graying at the temples. It's apparent when he puts on his kicking-team videos that he's intensely interested in his work, a teacher with fifty holdover students each summer and thirty new kids. He has to mold all his special teams fresh each summer, with only a few guys in the same spots, so he has to stick to the same basic tenets every year and teach, teach, teach.

There is a page he hands to every special-teams candidate every summer. It's a very uninspirational page of type, kind of a Joe Friday just-the-facts-ma'am list of special-teams reminders. Here is what it says:

New England Patriots
Kicking Game
1. Effect a smooth transition in ball possession.
2. Provide positive field position for our offense and defense.
   a. Offense—Return game.
   b. Defense—Coverage.
3. Protect our kickers/Block kicks.
4. Score points—PAT, FG, KOR, PR, blocked kicks returned for TD, stripped balls returned for TD.
5. Make good things happen.
   a. Cause/Recover fumbles.
   b. Great coverage.
   c. Down a punt inside our opponents' 10-yard line.
   d. Block kicks.
   e. Execute good fake punts and field goals.
   f. Onside kicks: Load/Surprise.

"Most of us don't start out as special-teams coaches," Scarnecchia says. "I was an offensive line coach for eleven years before I changed to special teams, and I consider myself lucky. The more you see of special teams, the more you realize how important they are to the game, even though I realize they're a mystery to a lot of people. So I know my job's important. Now, I'm not a brilliant person who has all these ideas to revolutionize the game. I just want to make sure that we have a smooth transition every time the ball changes hands in a game. That's number one. Don't make any mistakes. Make all positive plays when the ball's changing hands. And then, if we can, try to make positive yardage. We think there's about twenty yards to be exchanged on punts, yards we can push them back if we're punting or yards we can gain if we're receiving.

"With players, we just try to tell them the impact special teams can have. In compiling a roster, you've got to be good enough to play on offense or defense to make the team. That's number one. Then I have to take the guys who can play special teams the best and mold them into a unit. I think most of them understand the significance. They play between twenty and thirty snaps a game, and their role is to have an impact on the game. You never can predict how that impact is going to come."

This day, Scarnecchia gathers most of the running backs, defensive backs, and linebackers in a team meeting room at Bryant College. This is the usual talent pool for special teams: Quarterbacks are too important, wideouts too fragile, linemen too slow. The room looks like any big classroom in any college in the United States, with seven rows of long tables and swivel chairs bolted into the floor behind them, the tables each having room for ten students. Scarnecchia stands in the front of the room, lecturing like an Econ 101 prof, using graphics from the overhead projector and a pointer just like a real teacher. He'd said earlier, "A special-teams coach has to be just like a teacher. Exactly like one. Because you're teaching something they don't know and they have to know to be good at their jobs. You have to be a motivator and a psychologist and a listener and someone who can get them out of their funks, back to learning."

Here he was teaching 32 Right Return 2 Deep. "We had sixteen returns of 32 Right Return 2 Deep last year, and we averaged 20.9 yards a return," he told the team. "That was a terribly productive return for us. Our intent this year is to call it more, to use it more."

Each of the eleven players had a specific job, and Scarnecchia was explaining each guy's role in intricate detail as they looked at the sheets in front of them, which was the same as the sheet on the overhead projector. Each kickoff formation starts with a formation that looks like this:

L1 L2 L3 L4 L5 K R5 R4 R3 R2 R1

With the Patriots, as with most teams, every player on the opposing kicking team is assigned a number. Each guy on the kicking team has an assigment, obviously; they don't just go get the ballcarrier. On the return team, Scarnecchia names his players after the positions on the field: safeties for the return men, backs and ends for the middle backers, and offensive line positions for the front liners.

Similarly, the kickoff-return game, which Scarnecchia is now teaching, has specific assignments for each guy. On 32 Right Return 2 Deep, for instance, the Patriots' R2 player would line up around the New England 20, forward and to the right of the double-safety return men. Here's how Scarnecchia dictates the R2 assignment, in the special-teams playbook and now to each player in the room: "Drop ten yards in front and to the return side of the safety that catches the ball. Just before the ball is caught, yell 'GO!' Block the opposing R2 with inside-out leverage." There are eight different special-teams units: kickoffs and kickoff returns, punts and punt returns, place-kicking and blocking, onside kickoffs and onside returns. Imagine, if the R2 has to play on seven of them—not an unusual number—all the assignments he must memorize. Then think what happens if he gets knocked woozy or if he has to play real offense or defense because of an injury or if he has to substitute for an L3 who gets hurt, and think what happens if . . . it can get pretty involved.

Back to 32 Right Return 2 Deep. Scarnecchia tells the team: "Try to blow the guy up. Hit him in the earhole. Really get after him."

Isn't that the essence of special teams?

"It really is," Scarnecchia said later. "Guys like Steve Tasker, Reyna Thompson, what's great about them is that their effectiveness and productivity haven't diminished as the years go on. See, what happens is that guys who are great on special teams usually get a chance to play regular roles on offense or defense at some point, and then they're not used as much on special teams. So if you get three or four years of great special-teams play out of a guy, that's really good. It takes an extraordinary kind of player to give you a career of great special-teams play, to know they're not going to be starters. They have to know they're going to be as valuable to the team as a lot of the starters. You've got to be football-smart to know that."

(A quick detour into motivation in the nineties: In 1990, a head coach came into his office on a Monday morning and took out a white bank envelope, the kind the drive-through teller hands you when you cash a check from your car. The white envelope contained ten $50 bills. This coach had on his roster a thirty-one-year-old player on the downside of his career, who'd gone from being an every-down defensive player to a backup, and so now the player needed to play special teams to be valuable enough to keep around. The previous day, the player had made two huge hits on the kickoff return team, and the coach wanted to reward the hitting. The player would get $100 for the special teams hit of the week, the coach decided, and he'd get $50 for the lesser hit, as a runnerup. The head coach wanted this guy to win the money. [The other $350 goes for other special-teams plays.] "I've got to keep him interested, and $150 will keep him interested," the coach said. "It's amazing what cash means to players. They don't have to pay tax on it, don't have to tell their wives, don't have to do anything but put it in their pocket." The coach is asked, Why do you feel you have to keep him interested? "Well, I need him to play a role in some of our defensive schemes, but I can't keep him around unless he shows he's no different from the other guys. If you're not a regular, you have to play on special teams. That's it. So now, this guy'll be motivated, because he knows I'm watching how he plays on every play, and he knows he'll be rewarded for good plays. He's not just out there filling a hole. Hey, everybody does this. It's not just me.")

Scarnecchia will be our tour guide through the key jobs of the special teamers. We'll look at Tasker, an all-around special-teams performer who last season made the Pro Bowl squad for the fourth time; long-snapper Sam Anno of the San Diego Chargers; holder Rohn Stark, who doubles as the Indianapolis Colts' punter; punt- and kick-returner Mel Gray of the Detroit Lions; kicker Gary Anderson of the Pittsburgh Steelers; punter Sean Landeta of the New York Giants; and his former partner in the league's most dangerous punting game, Reyna [pronounced Re-NAY] Thompson. Thompson, a cornerback when he's playing defense, is known as one of the best gunners ever to play pro football. A gunner is the man split very wide on the punt team, and his job is to outfox usually two blockers who are in his face at the line of scrimmage and go downfield and tackle the punt-returner or down a punt.

Special-Teams Ace
Steve Tasker, Buffalo Bills

Scarnecchia: "To play on several special-team units, you have to have the physical requirements—the speed and the quickness and the toughness. But I think as much as that, as much as anything, you have to have pride in doing the job. Because a lot of times no one notices. But twenty-five times a game, these guys will have the chance to influence the outcome of a game. And no one in football approaches this kind of job in a more workmanlike, professional way than Steve Tasker."

Tasker was sitting in a film room at Rich Stadium, staring at the screen, trying to find the right words to describe the chess match he plays every Sunday. "Sometimes, you try to think what the other guy's thinking across the line from you so you know what to do to beat him," he said. "But then you think, Well, he's going to be thinking I'm thinking that, so now I have to think what he'll be thinking so I can . . ."

He is asked, "Have you ever seen a move called *The Princess Bride?*"

Tasker laughed. "I just saw it! Iocane powder!" And he couldn't stop laughing.

See *The Princess Bride* and you've seen Steve Tasker's football pesona. *The Princess Bride* is a storybook romantic comedy. A heroic character named Westley is chasing a character named Buttercup, who has been kidnapped by a brilliant but evil character named Vizzini. Westley outduels Vizzini's henchmen and finally meets and matches wits with Vizzini. Vizzini fills two goblets with wine, and Westley takes the goblets, hides them, and puts Iocane, a lethal powder, in both goblets. Vizzini thinks Westley has put the Iocane powder in only one of the goblets, and he sets about trying to figure out which goblet to drink.

Tasker is Westley. The other team, collectively, is Vizzini.

Vizzini says, "Are you the sort of man who would put the poison into his own goblet, or his enemy's? Now, a clever man would put the poison into his own goblet because he would know only a great fool would reach for what he was given. I'm not a great fool, so I can clearly not choose the wine in front of you. But you must have known I was not a great fool. You would have counted on it, so I can clearly not choose the wine in front of me."

And on they go, until Vizzini distracts Westley, then switches the goblets, and then they drink. Vizzini laughs uproariously at Westley, because he got Westley to drink from the just-switched goblet in front of him. Then Vizzini keels over, dead.

Westley tells Buttercup, "They were both poison. I spent the last few years building up an immunity to Iocane powder."

Why is this perfect Tasker? Because if he can't outquick 'em, he has to overpower 'em. If he can't outquick 'em or overpower 'em, he has to outsmart 'em. This is his job, every Sunday.

You knew a Tasker growing up. He was the indefatigable kid, the one who loved sports, the one who was one of the best athletes in town and might have been the best if he'd only been four inches taller and twenty pounds heavier. Approximately 99.99 percent of these guys become Marines or carpenters or teachers or stockbrokers or coaches. The other one-hundredth of a percent become Kevin Johnson of the Phoenix Suns and Bip Roberts of the Cincinnati Reds and Tom Waddle of the Chicago Bears. And Steve Tasker of the Buffalo Bills.

He has risen very high in his profession, which is chasing punts and blocking kicks and whamming return men. Bill Parcells, the former Giants coach who won Super Bowls in 1986 and 1990, says, "You know what the last thing we did at practice on the Friday before the second Super Bowl was? We imitated Steve Tasker. I thought he was one of the most dangerous players in the game, and I wanted to make sure our players, as they left the practice field for the week and started thinking about the game, had Tasker on their minds. So I had our fastest guys, guys like [cornerback] Perry Williams, line up in number 89 [Tasker's number] and imitate him for our punt-return team."

Only Kansas City's Albert Lewis, with eleven blocked kicks in his career, has more among active players than Tasker, with six. "I learned about blocking punts from studying Steve," Reyna Thompson says. "You look for a telltale sign from the center. They all have little habits. One center had this habit of, every time he was about to snap, he'd bump his arm against his knee, like a reflex action. I see Steve on film getting such a great jump off the ball, and I'm thinking, he must have seen this, because on every snap, he's gone when the guy bumps his knee. It's just a split second. But you've got to have some advantage. There's always something, and Steve finds it."

Back to the film room with Tasker. He's wide-eyed enough to be enthusiastic, but he's been around the block enough times to know the business. When he played for Houston as a rookie in 1985, he suffered a knee injury, causing him to miss nine games. The team gave him a check for $10,000, which he thought was to cover a workman's comp settlement. His next check from the Oilers was for $20, and the checks for $20 kept coming until he'd repaid the $10,000 out of his own paycheck. When the Oilers tried to do the same thing in 1986 after another knee injury to Tasker, he got a lawyer.

But he knows how good, all in all, he has it. And his attitude is a big reason why he's good. "I love playing special teams because I love playing football," he said. "I love being a professional athlete. I mean, if I was sitting on the streets or working at a Kmart just because I didn't want to cover a kick, that'd be ludicrous. My attitude is, every year, I've got to make myself valuable to this club."

Tasker is a gunner on the punt team, a rusher on the punt-rush team, an R4 on the kickoff team. Whatever his role, he cites one important factor for almost all special-teams play: momentum. Keep going. "Keep moving upfield. Never get knocked off your feet. As long as I do that, I've got a chance to make headway into making a play."

Tasker, like Thompson, has made his mark on punt coverage. In fact, in 1991, the Bills had the best punt-coverage season since big rules changes went into effect in 1973. Before then, all ten coverage players could leave the line of scrimmage before the ball is punted. Now only two can. In 1991, the Bills allowed only fifty-three yards on punt returns. Think of this, if you're not amazed: There were ten individual returns of at least fifty-three yards in the league in 1991. The Bills punted fifty-four times, and gave up fifty-three yards. Buffalo special-teams coach Bruce DeHaven said it was Tasker's finest year.

There are 100 ways to make plays on the punt team, 100 jukes and stunts and fakes to be used. In 1991, against New England, Tasker found number 101. In the first quarter, Buffalo punter Chris Mohr hit a forty-three-yard punt to the New England 30. Tasker, working against a double-team, appeared to get frustrated—waving his arms, almost curling into a ball, appearing stuck halfway downfield between the two Patriot defenders. For a split-second, Tasker paused, like he was quitting. The defenders paused, thinking they'd finished off the great Tasker. Suddenly, Tasker sprinted outside both of them and made a beeline for the punt returner, who hadn't called for a fair catch. BOOM! Tasker leveled him for no gain.

All the cleverness and planning and counterfakes can't mask the fact that the end result is a collision, often a remarkably violent one. In the first game of the 1992 season, Tasker lined up as the left gunner against the Rams. First quarter. No score. Tasker wedged between his two blockers at the line, sprinted downfield toward return man Vernon Turner, juked the Ram

guardian in front of Turner, saw the ball out of his upper pe-
ripheral vision floating toward Turner, watched Turner crouch
a little and spread his legs, timed his run at Turner with the arrival of the ball into his chest, had one final thought of "Pull the
trigger!" sprint through his mind, and

WHAM!!!!CRACKLE!!!!

He let Turner have it with the crown of the helmet right in
Turner's breastbone. Turner went airborne, the wheeze of
breath leaving him as he flew through the air backward, landing
flat on his back. Tasker would feel a shooting pain in his upper
back in a few minutes, but now all he could feel was the sweet-
ness of a great hit, the crack of a grand slam in the bottom of the
ninth, a twenty-foot jumper to win the game at the buzzer.

He opened his mouth to scream but could barely hear himself.
The crowd, he noticed, was going berserk, the same sound
they'd make after a long touchdown bomb. And his teammates,
swarming him, were all screaming as loud as they could, gut-
teral screams, screams of exultation. "GREAT HIT!!!" teammate
Mark Pike screamed, whacking him hard with an open hand
across the helmet.

The crowd, nutso, urged on the fired-up defense. The Bills
stopped the Rams on three downs and scored on three of the
next four series. Buffalo 40, Los Angeles 7.

"If you're going to get a pain in the back from that," he's
asked, "why not just tackle the guy? Why try to kill him?"

"Because I can," Tasker said.

It's the night before the Bills' January 1993 playoff game with
Houston, and Tasker is at Billy Ogden's, an eclectic little restaurant just south of downtown. Tasker, telling this story, doesn't
smile. "Hey, the ball might get jarred loose, and we might get it.
The guy might think twice about returning it the next time, call
for a fair catch and give us better field position. Plus, the boys
love it. They get off on it. It picks up the team.

"You know, if the NFL announced tomorrow that in football
games from now on bats are optional, everybody would carry
Louisville Sluggers. It's a violent game. You don't go through
high school and college football then make it to the pros
through such a filtering system if you can't hit somebody very

hard and take it when somebody hits you very hard. If you can't take that risk, don't play. You want to hit somebody as hard as humanly possible. You want to go down there and you"— Tasker grits his teeth here, keeping them gritted for emphasis— "want to destroy them. It's a high. Sadistic? Yeah. But it goes with the territory. You don't like it, stay home and watch TV."

But still, is this gratuitous violence? Why does the good clean fun have to include this macho, destruction-for-destruction's-sake mentality?

Tasker thought for a minute. He's a thoughtful, well-spoken man, not even remotely demented, as these passages might make him sound. He wanted to be sure I understood why the big hit is his football holy grail.

"When you grow up, especially in a Christian home, you're taught, don't fight. Never raise your hand against another. And yet you get mad sometimes and you want to. That goes on through school and college, and then you get out on the football field, and there's . . . there's a kind of justified violence. Everyone in the world, watching on TV and in the stands, says to you: You have the right to hit that guy as hard as you possibly can within the rules. It might be barbaric. But there's not a guy in the stands or sitting at home who wouldn't love to go out and dish out the same shots I give out.

"I mean, I make one of those hits, like on Vernon Turner, and everybody on the team is patting me on the back. The crowd is roaring. Even Marv Levy, who never says anything, gives me half a smile, like, That was a great play. You feel like you've done something big to help your team win, and you've gotten everybody so energized. You get a dose of that, and you don't care if your back hurts a little bit. Immediately, you want to get right back out there and do it again. It's like taking a pill. A drug. Then it wears off, and you want another one. Last week, I missed our game with a knee sprain. Well, I felt like I was in detox. I couldn't take it. There was this game going on, we were losing, I know I could have helped, and I'm just standing there, pacing, not able to do anything, totally helpless. I ate a twelve-ounce bag of sunflower seeds in the first half. Do you know how many sunflower seeds that is? I felt like I had the shakes, missing that game."

Then he paused. He paused because a forty-five-ish lady was shyly approaching our table, interrupting his intense gaze on me. He looked up at the woman and nodded, and she moved a couple of steps closer.

"Hi, Steve," she said.

"Hi," he said.

"I just wanted to tell you good luck, and go out there and kill them tomorrow," she said.

"Thank you," he said, and she padded away.

" 'Kill 'em,' " he said. "See? See what I mean?"

It was only when the question of his wife's feelings came up that Steve Tasker got serious.

"We were watching the playoff games on TV today, before I came over here. Somehow, on TV, the players seem bigger than life, and I watch and I think, That's a different game than the one I play. When I play, they're all guys like me. Anyway, I've been hurt some this year. I've had a broken hand, some sciatic nerve damage in my back, a sprained knee. And I think it gets to my wife sometimes. I was getting ready to leave today, to come here and then to go to the hotel where we stay the night before games. Sarah usually wishes me luck and I leave. Today she said, 'I don't want you to go.' I looked at her, and she said, 'I don't want you to go out in that dangerous world.' "

Steve Tasker's world is usually more dangerous for the other guys.

Return Specialist
Mel Gray, Detroit Lions

Scarnecchia: "The job your return man does is almost totally dependent on the quality of the special teams. I want something positive to happen with my returner. If he gets me five yards in a tough situation, that's good; fifteen, that's great. Just get positive yards."

In 1991, Gray became the first player in NFL history to lead the league in kickoff returns and punt returns in the same season. And he really can't remember much about it. Mentally, Gray gets so locked tight in a zone on a return that he doesn't know what he's done until he watches films the next day.

So when Mel Gray tried to unlock his mind to explain his job, he couldn't.

"As soon as I get out there, everything shuts off," he said. "I step on the field, and the world goes away. I don't feel the weather. I don't hear the crowd. A minute ago, on the sidelines, I was nervous and tense and pacing around, but now, when the ball's in the air, I have no feeling about anything except catching it and doing my job. I get the ball, and I know exactly where I'm supposed to go, whether it's a middle return set up or a left return or a right return.

"But as far as knowing what I do, I don't. Somebody might say, 'Nice return,' or something like that, and as far as the moves I put on, I won't know what I did. I watch the film the next day and I say, Wow, I didn't know I did that. I'm always surprised when I see the films."

Gray was asked about the return that clinched the punt-return title for him in 1991, at Lambeau Field in December. The Lions had played five straight warm-weather games, and here they came into Green Bay on a day when the temperature reached eighteen below zero with the wind chill.

"Before I go out, our kicker, Eddie Murray, is standing on the sidelines, all bundled up, just freezing, and he asks me how I'm feeling. I say, 'I'm taking it all the way.' The special-teams coach, Frank Gansz, tells me just before I go out to let it go if it's over my head because it's so windy. So I set up at the right hash, about at our thirty, and I remember thinking how I've got to be careful with my footing, because it's so slippery and damp. That's about the last thing I remember. The rest of my memory comes from the film."

Here's what the film showed: Green Bay punter Paul McJulien spiraled one over Gray's head, and instead of letting the thing bounce in the awful conditions, Gray, disobeying Gansz, turned around and caught the ball like a receiver would, on about the eighteen. He turned to run the right return, which Gansz had ordered if there was to be a runback, and he noticed that the wedge captain and two other guys had missed their blocks. After bursting through the initial traffic, Gray had two Packers to beat. He juked left, then right, making the two Packers stutter-step, and then Gray burst right through the middle of them.

Watching the films back in Michigan the next day, the Lions let out a whoop when Gray burst through. "How'd you do that?!" somebody yelled. "How'd you get outta there?!"

Gray didn't know. "You watch the film, and returning a punt's like driving fast down Broadway in the rush hour. Returning a kickoff, you have a little more time to let something develop. A punt, it's just bam-bam-bam-boom, all-out, in a second. You've got to be crazy, or have total confidence in yourself. With me, I think it's a little bit of both. I'd still rather be doing something else, because this is so dangerous. But this is what I do. And I'm determined that if this is what I do, I'm going to be the best in the world at doing it."

A player in the NFL can have a long life living by that special-teamer's credo, especially in the nineties, in the era of the ultra-close games.

The Punt Team
Punter: Sean Landeta, New York Giants
Gunner: Reyna Thompson, New England Patriots

Scarnecchia on punters: "The most important thing for a punter is hangtime. A guy who can hang the ball in the air takes so much pressure off the coverage. That translates into a better net average, which is what everyone wants. And like kickers, these guys need to have confidence in themselves, because things can go wrong, and they can't afford to blow up."

Scarnecchia on gunners: "Boy, are they rare. To do this job, you've got to beat two or three people at the line of scrimmage at one time. The talent here is to be able to have enough strength and quickness to beat two people, then have the raw speed to run forty yards in time to force a fair catch."

At 212 pounds, Landeta probably carries a good fifteen pounds more than he should. He is not ruggedly handsome. He has a puffy face, a black mustache, and black straight hair that peeks out from the back of his helmet. But at the Giants' Super

Bowl party in 1987 in Pasadena, his date was Donna Rice. Yes, that Donna Rice. A couple of years later, he went out in New York with Marla Maples. Yes, that Marla Maples. His teammates couldn't believe the women he walked around with.

Landeta could. He leads the NFL in confidence. If you believe in yourself, you succeed in life. If you believe you're handsome, women will flock to you. Landeta's married now—to one of the prettiest women in recent history—so those playboy days are over. But those were the truths he lived by.

In high school, Landeta would go to football games at Memorial Stadium in Baltimore, his hometown, and look at the punters and kickers. As a high school senior, he watched Tony Linhart. "I can do that," he thought, watching Linhart kick in the pregame. "I could go out there and do it just like that." And he did, once he became a punter. On his first punt at Towson (Maryland) State in 1980, he boomed it forty-three yards to the Morgan State three. His first punt in the United States Football League, in 1983 for the Philadelphia Stars, was for forty-five yards, to the opponents' nine. And his first punt for the Giants, in 1985, went sixty-eight yards.

God, was he confident in himself. Still is.

He might have saved his career because of his healthy ego. That's what helped him survive his Soldier Field fiasco. "I'd punted forty-five games in fifty weeks because the USFL and the NFL were back to back, and we made the playoffs in both seasons," Landeta says. "So by the end of the year, my back was hurting. But I still felt good. There was a real strong wind at Soldier Field that day. I went to put the ball out to punt, and I probably should have had a better grip on it. I kind of lost control of it. Instead of falling straight to the ground, it almost did an end over end, and as I went to kick it, it wasn't there. I tried to chase it, and it grazed the end of my foot and dribbled off to the side."

It was like Fred Couples missing a tee shot, Michael Jordan airballing a dunk, Tony Gwynn whiffing in slow-pitch softball.

"I just wondered, after punting thousands and thousands of balls in my life and this never happening, how it could happen there, in a playoff game," Landeta said.

Here's the truly amazing part: Landeta, twenty-three then, hit his next punt sixty-four yards, and the one after that fifty-two. After the game, he didn't talk like it was the end of the world. He seemed concerned, but hardly disconsolate. The next day, as the Giants packed their belongings for the season, it was like, hey, I missed a punt. Life goes on. Big deal.

That's why he's a great punter.

"The mental game," Landeta said, in front of a VCR at the Giants' summer camp site in 1992, "has more to do with success or failure than anything physical. There's too many guys, hundreds of guys, who can punt the ball today in the United States. Why do some succeed? I'm convinced it's mental. I'm just glad that, for whatever reason, the nightmare of that punt in Chicago hasn't hurt me. I still go out, just this past offseason, and people still say, 'Jeez, how'd you whiff on that punt?' If I'd have let it, it would have killed me. I wouldn't let it. The next year, I go to the Pro Bowl and I have the highest one-year average, 44.8 yards, in the history of the NFC."

Landeta says a great punter must have a strong leg from years of work as a kid and young adult; he played soccer, ice-skated constantly, practiced karate, and got hand-eye-coordination work from baseball while growing up. He says a great punter must have no fear. "All I think on every punt is, catch the ball, kick the perfect ball for the conditions, and don't let a single outside force influence the punt: the weather, the crowd, the pressure—all meaningless. Basically, I think I'm going to make the perfect punt every time I go out there."

He made quite a few more, especially after Reyna Thompson arrived in 1989 as a Plan B free agent from Miami. In Landeta's first four Giants seasons, pre-Thompson, Landeta had a net punting average (yards punting minus the opponents' return) of 35.2 yards per punt. In 1989 and 1990, Landeta's net punting increased to 37.5 yards per punt. "Since football is basically a game of field position, you can see how important it is to give your team extra yards every time you punt," Landeta said. "The reason we were able to do that in 1989 and 1990 was largely due to Reyna."

The next time you watch a punt situation, look at the two

players on the punting team lined up as wide receivers. Across from them, often times, you'll see two defenders wedged in on this player. When the play starts, they'll slap and push and block and pinch in the punt-team guy, who has to be a bullet to beat the double-coverage. The best gunners in football right now are Tasker, Thompson, Bennie Thompson of the Saints, and Elvis Patterson of the Raiders. "What a job," Tasker says. "You have to be smart, and you have to think on your feet with two guys beating on you, and you've got to beat them and run downfield in four seconds, and you've got to have the presence of mind to know exactly where you are. You might have to run a tightrope on the goal line and be ready to bat the ball out."

Most special-teams coaches think the punt team is the most important single special team. "Marv Levy gave us the stat that eighty percent of the time that a team scores off a blocked punt, that team wins the game," Tasker says. "What happens on a blocked punt is that your offense has just been defeated by the defense, and it goes to the sidelines to regroup, and then, bang, the offense is back out there, and the defense is all fired up because they've just scored an easy seven points. We've haven't had a punt blocked here since '89, but the punt team is the first team we work on every year in camp. It's crucial to our success."

No team has gotten more from its punt team in recent NFL history, arguably, than the 1990 Giants. And no player keyed a punt team like Thompson.

"I want to tell you what Reyna Thompson meant to our team," Bill Parcells says. He was in Manny's, his favorite restaurant, in Moonachie, New Jersey, a few football fields from his former office at Giants Stadium. Parcells picked up his plate with the tuna on rye toast and pulled out the paper placemat. He started doodling.

He wrote:

490

49

3

And he talked as he wrote.

"We get Reyna Thompson on Plan B before the 1989 season, and we figured we were 490 yards better in the punting game in

1989 than we were in 1988. That's 49 first downs. That's three first downs a game. It doesn't matter how you advance the ball, whether it's on the ground or through the air or from an exchange of punts. The important thing is advancing it."

"How'd you arrive at 490?" he is asked.

"Our net punting went from about 33.7 to 37.8 per punt [the *exact* numbers, by the way] with Reyna. That's four yards a punt, and we punted the ball seventy times." There're 280 yards (287, actually). The rest comes from five more punts being downed inside the 20 and a huge difference in the Giants' punt-return game, with the addition of Thompson and returner Dave Meggett.

Thompson's influence can be seen in the two-year figures before and after his arrival. In 1987–88, the Giants punted 172 times; eighty-nine were returned for a 12.5 yard average. In Thompson's first two years with the team, they punted 155 times, and seventy were returned for a 7.5-yard average—a five-yard edge on every punt return, and that's putting aside the fact that punts were being returned less often. They also downed the ball inside the 20 fifteen more times in '89–90, despite having seventeen fewer punts. That's a huge territorial advantage. And football is a land war. Yards are yards. Thompson became an impact player for the Giants, probably the biggest impact player in the early history of Plan B free agency.

Parcells just nodded when it was suggested to him that probably four of his six most valuable players in 1990, the Super Bowl season, were specialists. Quarterback Phil Simms and linebacker Pepper Johnson were superb for the Giants that season. Return specialist Meggett, punter Landeta, kicker Matt Bahr, and Thompson were four other of the most valuable. In game one, Meggett returned a second-half punt sixty-eight yards for a touchdown; Giants 27, Eagles 20. In game six, Bahr hit a forty-yard field goal as time expired; Giants 20, Cards 19. In game nine, Landeta put down three second-half punts at the Ram three, with excellent coverage from Thompson; Giants 31, Rams 7, despite the fact that the Giants outgained the Rams by a measly thirty-three yards. The Giants played eight quarters against the 49ers in 1990 and scored no touchdowns. But they won the NFC Championship on five Bahr field goals, including a forty-one-yarder as time expired.

Now, a couple of years later, here was Parcells talking about how important his specialists were. He said when he took over the Giants, he wanted two things—a quarterback with toughness and ability, and a great punter. He inherited Simms. And the Giants signed Landeta out of the USFL in time for the 1985 season. As he grew with the job, Parcells saw more and more how much special teams meant. So when pro personnel director Tim Rooney asked Parcells in February 1989 to watch some film on a Miami defensive back named Reyna Thompson, who was a free agent on Miami's Plan B list, Parcells went into Rooney's office. For about ninety seconds.

They watched three plays of Thompson chasing punt-returners down on special teams. "Sign him," Parcells said.

Thompson, who wants to enter the field of national educational reform when he leaves football, was in college in south Florida at the time. He told the Giants he wasn't going to make a decision until late in March, when the Plan B period was winding down. In an extraordinarily bold move for the solid Giants, general manager George Young flew to Fort Lauderdale with a prepared contract the day Thompson said he would begin his football negotiating. They met at the Fort Lauderdale airport, Thompson and Young did, and they talked for several hours. Thompson signed, and Young flew home that night.

Landeta came in '85, Thompson and Meggett in '89, Bahr in '90. Bahr's kickoffs stunk, but he was one of the most confident and self-assured yet modest guys the Giants had on their team. The Giants entered the nineties with three cornerstone special-team guys under thirty, and old-guy Bahr, who would do quite nicely for a few years. Parcells, in the season he had these four guys together, became an absolute special-teams devotee. When CBS's John Madden would come in to do Giants games, Parcells would tell him Reyna Thompson stories, and they'd watch some film, and they'd both shake their heads about how incredible it was that Thompson could get off the line of scrimmage—against double- and triple-team blocks—and foil the opposing return game. "Reyna Thompson is the best special-teams player in history," Madden said in 1990.

"That really threw me for a loop," Thompson said. "His word is truth. What an incredible thing for him to say. What an honor."

Parcells brought Thompson with him to New England in 1993. Thompson's job is harder now than it once was because of the attention he's paid. He broke his shoulder blade early in 1991 and was relatively ineffective. He broke his hand and strained knee ligaments in 1992 and wasn't the player he was in 1990 either. At six feet and 193 pounds, tremendously quick and fast, he finds his natural tools are no longer enough to make him the best player in the NFL at chasing down a punt and pinning the opposition back deep in their own territory. He has to be more of a student now than he ever was. He spends his first night of film study each week soaking in the habits of the players he'll see Sunday. Almost always he will face two men. Are they fast? Are they strong? Do they hit you? Do they grab you? The second night he'll focus on their play together. Do they play in tandem, one quick and one strong, to try to knock you off your game? Do they have a game plan against the gunner? The third night, he tries to put himself in their shoes, figuring out what they'll do to him. Will they give him the outside? Will they give him a gap between them he can shoot through? It's not till the fourth night that Thompson even looks at the return man.

He plays a different game than Tasker, in some ways. With Thompson, it's not much of a pregame chess match. There are no Iocane-powder games. He learns as much as he can about his opposition, then, when head-up on the guys, uses what he's learned all week. He tries not to think, Well, if they do this, then I'm going to do this, and then they're going to do this. He just does it, and his brain instinctively tells him what to do, split-second by split-second.

Maybe Thompson's secret is this: He looks for mental weakness in the guys across the line from him. "Say there's two guys right across the line from me," he said. "I'm not much on talking out there, even though lots of times I can hear the taunts from the sidelines. Take him out! Kill him! Things like that. I want to look these guys right in the eye and see the tremble. I want to see who can meet my gaze and who looks away. It's like the ref bringing two boxers to the middle of the ring before a fight. You have to look the other guy right in the eyes. Don't back down. When I see the guy who looks away or who won't look at me right in the eye for a long time, that's the guy I'm focusing on. That's the guy I want to kill."

Every other special-teamer in the league probably would like to get into the game as a regular, because you don't grow up saying you want to play special teams. But not Thompson. "If I had my choice, if I had to give up one special-teams play to be a regular player, I wouldn't do it," he says.

Now, a week before Christmas in 1991, Thompson steps into his office. The office is one hundred yards long, fifty-three yards wide, with a hard plastic carpet and no ceiling. It's dusk in East Rutherford, New Jersey, twenty-three degrees, and the wind is whipping the visor of Thompson's floppy black hat up and down. He's a former high-hurdles champion, both in high school and in college at Baylor. His favorite thing about football, he says, is making the killer hit on a big play. What more could you ask for in the position of gunner? Great student, great burst off the line, great power, great speed, great explosion into the ballcarrier.

"When I come out here," Thompson says, walking to midfield of Giants Stadium, the frigid day enveloping him, "I'm just thinking of one thing: big plays, big, big plays. It doesn't matter what obstacle's put in front of me. That's meaningless. I've got to make a play. I take advantage of whatever I can. I try to find somebody's weakness, because I don't feel like I'm invincible. The way I think of it is I'm invincible if I can find every player's weakness. Whatever team I'm playing—kickoff, kickoff coverage, punt, punt coverage, whatever—I try to make the guy I'm going to be playing make a mistake."

He walks to his left end position, the left gunner.

"The ball's in the middle of the field, and I line up at the top inside edge of the numbers. I don't want to be too close to the pile because then one of the guys across from me can roll off me and rush the punter and have a decent chance of blocking a punt. And I don't want to go much past the outside of the numbers, because if I do, I'm close to the sidelines, and they have a chance to push me out of bounds. Right now, at the numbers, Carl Lewis couldn't block this punt. The main thing with me, because Sean's such an outstanding punter, is I can't get pushed out of bounds, because the rules say if you step out of bounds, you can't be the first one to down the ball. So I've got to stay inside.

"Across from me, the two guys'll generally line up toe to toe, their hands at the ready. They play me a little bit more to the inside, so I can't get a free inside release. Now, just this year I've started to see a different formation against me. We call it the stack. One guy's in front of me, the other guy ready to hit me after the first guy. Perhaps they do it because they don't want to risk me getting away from both of them with one move. What I try to concentrate on when they're both playing me straight up is to find the little gap they give me and take advantage of that."

Now he shoots off the line, showing the type of quick juke he hopes to give the defenders during the game. "I call it a freeze move. I hope to make them both move and then get confused about what I'm going to do. Then I've got the separation. I've split them."

He's winded now. "The big key . . ." deep breath . . . "is making sure" . . . deep breath . . . "both of them don't get their hands on you" . . . deep breath . . . "at the same time." . . . Deep breath . . . "That's when they both pretty much can kill you."

Deep, deep breath. Now he shouts, because his office is in the flight pattern of Newark International Airport, and a descending 747 is directly over his head right now. "As long as one of them's hitting me and I'm free of the other one, I pretty much don't mind it! Because I have a track background, hurdling, which is an aggressive running style, which is great training for playing this position, so I can pretty much just keep my balance and take a licking and keep my shoulders to where I'm going forward!"

Sometimes, Thompson says, you can have all the ideas in the world about what you plan to do entering a game, and the opposition will totally frustrate you. "Washington did the greatest thing that's ever been done to me before," he says. "Their returner, Brian Mitchell, is a good inside runner, and they line up one guy slightly inside, and another guy more inside off me. And then, there's this big old fifty guy (fifty on the Redskins is linebacker Ravin Caldwell) waiting for me about seven yards off the line to kill me if I get free of these two guys. That's one I couldn't solve. That's one where I'll take home the film and try to figure something out before our next game. But three guys? That'll be tough."

"Why," he is asked, "wouldn't it be good defense to, once the ball's snapped to the punter, immediately swarm all over you and smother you, so you couldn't get downfield?"

"The thing you've got to keep in mind," Thompson says, "is these two guys have to watch me. They can't watch the ball. I watch the ball, and I get the initial split-second jump. I'd love it if both guys jumped at me, trying to kill me. I'd just jump back, like this." He jumps back like he has foot springs. "If they come at me, I have 'em."

My other question: "Why is it that people know you're good, can watch you on film for two years, can study everything you do, and when you play them, you still are down there, forcing fair catches and downing punts inside the ten?"

"See, in my mind, I play them. I play Dallas, and they have James Washington on the outside and Robert Williams [both defensive backs] on the inside, and I know Washington's more physical than Williams. So I'm going to play that matchup a little different. When I play Williams and he's the only guy hitting me, I may play more physical. The way I view it, I take one on at a time. I work him first, and then go after the other. And I try never to do the exact same thing twice in a game. See, they have to be smart to know what I'm going to do too. The next week, I could be completely different. I basically change my style week to week. They're making me change. I'd be stupid not to change."

The wind blows up. It's almost dark, and it's freezing out here. But Thompson is wound up now, and he's showing the swim move, and the power move, and how he eludes guys. "With the attention that's come my way, and making the Pro

Bowl, and what John Madden said about me, I feel like I'm being attacked more every week. It's more of a challenge to succeed. Guys come up to me after games now and say things like, 'Man, our jobs were on the line today. We had to hold you down.'

"Special teams, like football, is a game of intimidation. Different guys interpret intimidation differently. Some intimidate by going down and pushing guys with cheap shots. My way to intimidate is to make big plays, to run through blockers, to do what I have to to make the play. So I'm not going to try to be the toughest guy on the field. I'm going to try to be the guy who makes the play on the field. See, I'm not interested in being the tough guy. I might have to just pop the guy if I can't get him out of the way, but I don't let emotion decide that. I do what's best for each guy on each play.

"Now, getting to the ballcarrier, that's different. When I do that, I'm thinking total destruction. I have a small target I put on the ballcarrier as I get closer to him, and when I get near him, I line up that target and as I'm about to hit him, I tense up and I explode, baby, I explode."

He smiles.

"There's nothing greater, nothing, than when you hit somebody and you hear that wind go out of him—uhhhhhhhhhhhhh-hhhh—and he just crumbles! Oh man, you just swell up! You know you've made a play. You know you've fired up your team. Within the rules of the game, I want to hit the return man as hard as I can and get as big an impact as I can."

Landeta and Thompson would usually meet on the Giants' sidelines on all second-and-longs. And they'd plot.

Thompson might say, "What are you thinking here?"

Landeta, bouncing a ball off his right shoe, a half-inch to the right of the center of his laces, just to get the rhythm of the punt he's about to make, might reply, "I feel good going to the right. It'll be a little short but high. What are you thinking?"

Thompson: "Sean, I have to release outside. The inside guy's too tough. I can't shake him."

Landeta: "Okay, I'll give you plenty of hangtime."

179

Thompson: "I'll be there. Big play now."

Over the years, they'd developed a chemistry. When they jog onto the field—punt teams don't huddle, they simply go straight to their positions—Landeta first looks to see if the punt-return team across the line is overloaded to one side or the other, and whether the opposition has a rush called. If he thinks he's going to be pressured heavily from one side, he'll stare at Thompson and give him a facial sign where he's going to punt. "Most ends don't give a shit where I'm going to put it," Landeta says. "Reyna does."

Landeta and Thompson would watch the opposition's punt-return team together for thirty minutes on Wednesday and another thirty minutes on Friday. From that they'd make a best guess where the rush will come from and who will line up on Thompson. "I always figure Reyna is going to get off the line somehow, and if I can put the ball in the air for 4.5 seconds—that's my ideal time—then Reyna will somehow get down and be able to make a play. Sometimes, we'll just get a gut feeling that I'm going to punt better to the right, and we'll have Reyna switch over to the right side from the left. It's just a feel you get, or a favorable wind. Like this year [1992], in Los Angeles against the Raiders, I had a good feeling about punting right, and we decided he'd switch to the right. Now he still had two guys on him, but he released outside, sprinted down the sidelines, got down really quick, and waited near the goal line for the punt to bounce. It bounced around the five, right near the sideline, and Reyna jumped up and tipped it like a basketball player, tipping it out of bounds at the three.

"When I run out, I make sure I'm lined up fifteen yards behind the line, and then I take a look at the opposition. Are they going to try for a block? You can tell that if they've got eight guys up on the line, all in a sprinter's stance. I take a glance at the ends to see if they're coming hard, or if they're setting up for a return. Then I think about the weather, and how it's going to affect the punt. If there's a strong headwind, I probably want to hit a low liner to fight through the wind.

"Lots of times I can't hear the signals being called because of crowd noise. So I just have to stare at the center. When he snaps, everything else goes away, and I'm thinking only about catching the ball, taking my proper two steps, and hitting the ball just slightly to the right of my laces, right in the middle of the foot.

"From the time the ball's snapped until I punt, that get-off time has to be 2.0 seconds or less. Then my goal when I punt is to have hangtime of 4.3 seconds, so my coverage can have time to get down and cover."

Thompson takes it from there. "When the ball comes down, I immediately focus all my energy on the return man if he's going to catch it or on getting into good position to down it if he's not. Assume the return man's going to catch it. Then I'm going for the kill shot, if I'm not blocked. Then the important thing to me isn't making the tackle; it's don't blink. If you blink, you're clinching up, stiffening up. And then you have a better chance of getting hurt. You just zero in on the spot, and explode into the guy, and he's going to go down."

He is asked about the plays so close to the end zone, about how he knows where he is and when to stop and how much room he has before one of Landeta's punts booms over his head into the end zone.

He laughs. Special-teams players have to have quirks. They have to be different.

"I have a rule," Reyna Thompson says. "It's kind of—what would you call it?—a voodoo tradition. Before every game, I scrape the toe of my shoes on the paint in the end zone. So when I'm running down there during the game, and I don't have time to be as careful about stepping into the end zone, my shoes will know. My shoes will know the color of the end zone, and they will know: Hey, we don't want to go in there. We've got to stay out of that end zone."

Long-Snapper
Sam Anno, San Diego Chargers

Scarnecchia: "There are a lot of guys in the league who can snap well. They've found it prolongs their career or gives them a career in the first place. The biggest thing is accuracy. They take so much pressure off everybody if they're accurate. The two other big things they need to do: One, they've got to put the ball on a punter's thigh, on a line, and right in the holder's hands, on a line. Two, when they snap for a field goal or PAT, they've got to have the laces forward when the ball hits the holder's hands. They have to be precise."

Sam Anno was eleven when he first long-snapped. He did it for his Pop Warner team in Santa Monica, California, for a coach named Mr. Perry. He'll never forget walking off the practice field in Santa Monica after long-snapping one day when this Mr. Perry put his arm around young Sam's shoulder and said: "Sam, someday this could make you a lot of money." He did it in high school, and at USC. It was his ticket to a free-agent spin with the Rams in 1987, then with the Vikings later in 1987 and 1988, then with Tampa Bay in 1989 through 1991, then with San Diego, on Plan B, in 1992.

Like all snappers—all special-teamers, really—he struggles with his identity. Here he was, a college linebacker at USC, a six-two, 235-pound strapping guy, getting scouted to be a real player on a real NFL team, getting all the girls with his blond good looks and bright white teeth, calling the signals for the USC defense, and bam, he blows out a knee. There went his pro prospects. But former Trojan coach John Robinson knew Anno could snap, and Robinson, coaching the Rams, picked up Anno when he needed a snapper in 1987.

And Anno has flourished. Twice a week during the offseason, he goes somewhere—to a school, a gym, with friends, with no one—and snaps thirty to fifty balls to an imagined punter fifteen yards behind or an imagined holder seven yards behind. In season, he does it every day but Saturday. He's proudest of the fact that he's never had a bad pro snap at a crucial time.

"It's a valuable thing, and I know it, but I still have trouble with it from an identity standpoint," he says. "I mean, how am I going to be remembered in life? As a snapper? That's my fate? Then I realize what the reality of my job is: If I get hurt, we're dead. I have a lot of games in my hands."

It happened three straight times in 1989. On November 19 in Chicago, he snapped for the game-winning field goal as time expired; Bucs 32, Bears 31. On November 26 in Phoenix, with five seconds left, he snapped for the winning extra point; Bucs 14,

Cards 13. On December 3 in Tampa, he snapped for the go-ahead field goal with 1:35 left against Green Bay; the Bucs went up 16-14 but lost 17-16.

"The Chicago game will tell you what you need to know about snapping," Anno says. "The game's a shootout, back and forth. It's a cold day in Chicago, getting colder by the series, and we're a Florida team. We're feeling it. Near the end, we're down by two, and we're in our two-minute offense, trying to get into field goal position.

"Now this is an important time for a snapper, because your job is always to be ready. You never know when you're going to be needed. So I pace. I go to the heater. I stretch. I snap a few into the net. I grab a ball. I squeeze it, getting my hand used to it in the cold. I'm trying to calm my nervousness, but there's no getting around it, and I don't care what anybody says: You get nervous in a big spot of a game. Every snap's not exactly the same, so I'm thinking about this one: which way the wind's blowing, whether it'll be easy to hear the snap count, who'll be on the other side of the line. And these Bears, they're big. They put a thousand pounds in front of you, and they yell all kinds of crazy things at you and the kicker. I try to visualize it while we're going downfield. I lean over the ball and try to visualize a successful snap—a line drive into the holder's hands—and a good kick and everybody congratulating each other.

"I get some water, just for something to do. It's amazing what the human mind will think of. I think: If it's fourth down and we go for it, I'm off the hook. Phew! Because if we try it and I screw up the snap, we lose and we fly home and everybody's gonna hate me for a week. But the other feeling in my brain is stronger: I want to be out there with the game on the line. You go through the cooker the whole day, and you want to be the guy everybody on your team rallies around, and you want to be part of the unit that wins the game.

"So we get one play away, and we pretty much know it's going to be up to us. The mouth gets dry. There's stuff flying around my stomach. I gotta tell you, I'm nervous as hell."

Just then, coach Ray Perkins spins around and yells: "Field goal team!"

183

And voices all over the bench at Soldier Field yell, "Field-goal teamgoalteam!FieldgoalteamteamGetoutthere!!" That's the cacophony of sound and confusion as the members of the field-goal team sprint to the eighteen-yard line. The line of scrimmage is the Chicago 11. It will be a twenty-eight-yard attempt by kicker Donald Igwebuike.

"As I run out, I see the big guys of the Bears coming out. There's going to be four monsters, butt cheek to butt cheek, right over me, pressing on me as soon as the ball's snapped, trying to block it. They're going to have William Perry, Dan Hampton, Steve McMichael, Keith Van Horne. That's more than a thousand pounds, right in my face. I go to the line for the snap, and I see them, and they look at me, grim. They call time, which pisses me off. I want to get going. Now I gotta think about it for ninety more seconds. And they're yelling at Iggy, teasing him, making fun of him because he's Nigerian. It's still cold. One of our linemen, Randy Grimes, says to me, 'Just another day at the office, Sam.' I appreciate that. I want to feel normal.

"The ninety seconds are up. I take a quick look back at the sidelines, and everybody's gathered there about the thirty-five. Some guys are holding hands. The call in the huddle is simple: "Field goal snap, ready, break!" I run out to the line, get in my stance, and look at the Bears. They're huge, right across from me. Their fingers are going to be inches from mine on the ball.

"I hear somebody on their team say, 'We got a light guy here,' trying to intimidate me. Talk is cheap. That's what I'm thinking. I don't care if I'm 240 pounds. My adrenaline's pumping so fast, I can block anybody right now. I lean over the ball, and God damn it! Those guys hocked a huge loogie, a big green loogie, right there on the football! I'm not trying to gross you out, but I mean, here's a gigantic loogie, like three inches by three inches, like some big honker somebody saved up for three weeks, just to spit it on the ball and screw up some team trying to beat them with a game-winning field goal. And it's right where I'm gonna have to put my right hand to snap the ball!

"We got the time clock running down, and I rise up, and I'm screaming for the ref. 'CLEAN OFF THE BALL! CLEAN OFF THE BALL!' And the crowd's so loud he can hardly hear me. Finally he comes over and I say, 'You gotta dry this ball off,' and the ref gets a new ball.

"Now, across the line, I can hear them. They're saying, 'Damn, he saw it! Fuck! Shit! I can't believe it!' All that stuff. So we get a fresh ball, and the game's in my hands. Do or die. Your mind starts to play tricks on you, but I'm strong enough here to focus in on what's important: putting my hands on the ball, aiming for [holder] Chris Mohr's hands, making the ball rotate properly so Chris gets the ball with the laces straight ahead. My hands are on the ball, and I shut everything out. I pray a little bit. I say to myself, 'Let me snap it good, God.' That's it. And then, all I'm thinking to myself is, Perfect snap perfect snap perfect snap perfect snap perfect snap perfect snap, over and over again.

"When the ball leaves my hands, I can just feel it. It's perfect. It spirals right back to Chris, and in less than a second, I get big to wall off the rushers trying to overpower me and our line. I mean, I stand up and try to make my body as big and wide and forceful as possible, and I wall them off. And I hear the ball being kicked, and the ball sails right through, and the emotions shoot off like a skyrocket. We're so fired up, jumping and yelling and screaming. We beat the Bears at Soldier Field! And they're so dejected, heads down.

"And that's what it's like to be a long-snapper in the NFL."

Holder
Rohn Stark, Indianapolis Colts

Scarnecchia: "A holder's got to have quick hands, soft hands, good hands. Not only does he have to get the ball right on the spot, but he has to rotate the ball so the laces face forward. The ball has to be kicked in 1.35 seconds or less. The snap is .4 seconds. So he's got to catch, rotate, and spot the ball in less than a second."

This is like riding a bicycle. Once you learn, and you practice periodically, you never forget. Rohn Stark has fallen off the bike just once. In 1984, against Dallas, he misjudged a snap and fumbled it, and the Colts didn't get a field goal off. That's it. In twelve NFL seasons, he hasn't mishandled another snap from center. He takes about a hundred snaps a year. Over his career, it's taken about twenty-seven minutes for him to take snaps, rotate the laces, spot the ball, and have it boomed from his index-fingertip.

This is an easy job, once you've perfected it.

"For a punter who's a good athlete with good hands, it's a natural thing," Stark says. "You have a lot of time when you can work with a kicker because the punter and kicker are together so much. My very first year, 1982, I started holding, basically because I had good hands and I had the time to do it."

Stark's routine: "Once our offense gets to midfield, the kicker, Dean Biasucci, and I go to the net and we practice some field goals. When we're called on the field, I try to get out as quickly as possible, because I've got to set the spot and I've got to make sure everybody's in position to play, and the time clock is running. When the clock runs down to about ten seconds, if there's a couple of guys standing at the line or with their hands on their knees, I have to start screaming: 'GET ON THE LINE! GET ON THE LINE!' Then I get down. I look up at Dean and say a couple of things to try to relax him. 'Head down, follow through now,' or 'Stay down,' or 'Relax; just kick it down the middle.' He nods at me to tell me he's ready. Then I'm staring at the point of the ball between the snapper's legs. That's all I watch. I say, 'SET!' There's no cadence. When the center's ready, he snaps it. Usually, about ninety percent of the time, the laces come back to me fine and I just put the ball down. But if the laces aren't right, I feel it right away and spin the ball around. Then it's down, and it's kicked."

Stark says he's fielded snaps that bounced back to him, and he's had to jump in the air to fetch a couple. None of that matters. "In my job as holder, it's a given," he says. "Things can only go wrong."

Kicker
Gary Anderson, Pittsburgh Steelers

Scarnecchia: "Demeanor is really important. Obviously, we'd like a guy with a great leg. But after that, the mental part of it is huge. How does he respond to misses? The perfect guy is one where he can walk off the field and you never know if he made

186

it or missed it, because he's such an even guy. How tough is he? When you miss a kick in the pros, you can really let down your teammates, and you can feel there's an avalanche coming down on you. Your teammates can have absolute venom in their hearts for you. The fans can be merciless. This one area, evaluating kickers, is probably the biggest single failing in the history of the draft."

In the first two years of the nineties, kickers made 73.9 percent of their field-goal attempts. That's up about five percent from 1986, when kickers made 68.6 percent. Field-goal kickers are getting almost a percentage point better a year, and while it has to stop somewhere, the fact is that kicking is much more of a science than it once was.

It's also maddening.

First of all, when you talk about kickers, forget extra points. Everybody makes them. And though kickers who put two unreturnable ones in the end zone every week can be tremendous weapons, great special teams can make up for a kicker who plops his kickoffs consistently at the eight. When you talk about kickers, you're talking about field goals.

George Blanda made 52 percent of his field goals, Jan Stenerud 67 percent, and they're the only kickers in the Pro Football Hall of Fame. The top three kickers by percentage in history, entering 1992, were:

1. Nick Lowery, Kansas City, 79.33
2. Morten Andersen, New Orleans, 77.22
3. Gary Anderson, Pittsburgh, 76.33.

They're all active players. Twelve times between 1978 and 1980, teams told Lowery to get lost, either waiving him or flunking him in a tryout or not even allowing him to suit up for one. In 1979, Lowery walked into Veterans Stadium in Philadelphia when the Eagles were having kicking troubles. He took the elevator up to the team offices, where the special-teams coach asked him why he was there. Lowery said he was there for a kicking tryout, even though no one had invited him. The coach told him to scram. When Lowery pressed the issue, the coach threatened to have him ejected from the premises. His thirteenth attempt at the NFL was the charm, with Kansas City in

1980. He's been there ever since. Morten Andersen was a fourth-round pick of the Saints in 1984 who's been a godsend, a perfect dome kicker, a guy who'll kick the ball consistently as far as any kicker who ever played. Gary Anderson, Buffalo's seventh-round pick in 1982, was released there and latched on with the Steelers, where he's lived happily ever after. The three most accurate kickers ever mirror perfectly the unpredictable state of the kicking game.

"I think it's one of the hardest things to figure in football, who will be a successful kicker and who won't," Dallas kicking coach Steve Hoffman says.

Take Gary Anderson and John Lee. Anderson is five-eleven and 179 pounds, Lee five-eleven and 180. Anderson played soccer in South Africa, moved to the United States as a youth, tried and succeeded at kicking a football well enough to earn a college scholarship at Syracuse, and was drafted by the NFL. Lee played soccer and baseball in South Korea, moved to the United States as a youth, tried and succeeded at kicking a football well enough to earn a college scholarship at UCLA, and was drafted by the NFL. Anderson kicks for Pittsburgh, where, until 1992, his coach was Chuck Noll, who was not at all sympathetic to the problems of kickers. Lee kicked for the Cardinals in 1986 and 1987, and the coach there, Gene Stallings, was not at all sympathetic to the problems of kickers.

Lee and Anderson differed only in draft round, Lee going in the second in 1986 and Anderson in the seventh in 1982.

But there's one other thing.

"The difference between Gary Anderson and John Lee is almost nothing," said Cleveland special-teamer Ron Wolfley, the former Cardinal. "So why is Anderson one of the greatest of all time, and why was Lee a bust? Mental toughness. It's a cliché, but it's the absolute truth. The kicker is all alone. You miss it, you blew it. It might not be true, but that's what everybody thinks. It's all on you. John just wasn't tough enough."

"I've wondered about that a lot, about the mental part," Hoffman said. Entering the 1992 season, he was the only kicking coach in the NFL. He also broke down films for Jimmy Johnson and the Cowboy staff, but his primary job was to be talent

188

scout, mental headkeeper, and mother hen to the Dallas kicker or kickers. "The bottom line is, the mental part is a huge factor in determining whether a kicker's going to succeed or fail. I go out every spring and look at the top five or so kickers I think will be available to us, either when we want to pick one in the draft or take one as a free agent. And when I work them out, I try to get into their heads, because I think ultimately that's what's going to determine whether they succeed. I'll go out and work a guy out, and I'll want him to miss so I can see his reaction. If he gets a little panicky and says, 'Oh, I know what I did wrong on that one. Don't worry. I'll fix it,' I know this guy might get too tight in an NFL game.

"Before we signed Ken Willis out of Kentucky as a free agent, I remember working him out on a real windy day, with a crosswind blowing right across the field. Sometimes I start talking to guys when they're about to kick, because I want to see what kind of concentration they have, and when I did this to Kenny, he looked me right in the eye and said, 'Can't we talk about this later? I've got to kick.' That impressed me. And he never said a word about the wind, which was brutal. Last spring, I went to work out another kid, Lin Elliott, at Texas Tech, and I'm trying to distract him by saying some really stupid things while he's trying to kick. And he's looking at me and saying things like, 'What are you talking about?' He was a rock. He kicked it great, too. I happened to be working out another kid named Secrist there at the same time, and so Secrist came out and went through the same workout, only he wanted to make one from farther than Elliott. He banged one in from fifty-eight yards, and suddenly Elliott comes down from the stands and says, 'Hey, you didn't let me try one from that far.' I told him he wasn't warmed up, but he didn't care. He kicked one from sixty-one." Lin Elliott now wears a Super Bowl ring he earned kicking under Hoffman.

The college game and the pro game are very different. In the Southwest Conference, for instance, kickers can bring their own balls onto the field for field-goal attempts. In the NFL, the officials get twenty-five brand-new balls before every game, and those are the ones they use. The sweet spot is small, the leather is hard. Ask any kicker. They all want the old balls.

They also have to want the pressure. Atlanta coach Jerry Glanville said, "I never want the rookie kicker. They're too close to college. In college, you miss a kick for the game and you're disappointed, but everybody goes back to the frat house to get loaded after the game, win or lose. In the NFL, you're messing with people's jobs and their lives."

Glanville cut a rookie in 1991, Brad Daliuso, after three games and brought in veteran Norm Johnson, who'd failed and almost lost his mind during tough times in Seattle. "It gets to the point, when you miss a couple, where you feel like the salaries of your teammates are on your back, and your back's right square against the wall," Johnson said. "Anybody kicking in this league better be tough mentally because you just can't think negatively. It'll kill you. It got to the point in Seattle where my wife was so nervous she'd drop me off at the stadium and couldn't go in. She'd pick me up and ask me how I did. It ate at her."

The batty part about kickers—all but the absolute best ones, like Nick Lowery and Morten Andersen, and the absolute cool ones, like Matt Bahr and Jim Breech—is the uncertainty. The steadiest feet can suddenly turn shaky. Dennis Eckersley can turn into Mitch Williams overnight. In the four seasons from 1986 to 1989, Norm Johnson missed a total of seven field goals between thirty and thirty-nine yards. In 1990, he missed six of them. In 1991, cut by Seattle and picked up by Atlanta, he was perfect again from between thirty and thirty-nine, hitting four of four. In other words, Johnson moved from the weatherless Kingdome to Atlanta, who played fifteen of their sixteen regular-season games outside in 1991, under Glanville, who puts a tremendous emphasis, perhaps a mentally straining one, on special teams. And Johnson was perfect—thirteen of thirteen, in fact—inside the 45. He had his best percentage kicking season (nineteen of twenty-three, 83 percent) in seven years.

Johnson's theory: Once a situation starts going bad, the negative feedback will start steamrolling, a kicker will hear it all, the mental game will start playing in his head, and he'll have to change teams.

Gary Anderson is lucky. Nothing fazes him. In 1991, when

Chuck Noll refused to make a change in his long-snapper, the Steelers struggled with unfit Dermonti Dawson fluttering balls back to the holder. "The tough thing as a kicker is not having control over your own destiny," Anderson said one day late in 1991. "When you strive for perfection and you get bad snaps and bad holds . . . Dermonti just shouldn't be out there. He has no business snapping for kicks. It's like sending a kicker out there who doesn't know how to kick."

On Saturday, before the Steelers played their final game of the season in 1991 (Noll's final game, too), Anderson stood on the sidelines at Three Rivers Stadium, waiting to practice field goals. He was talking about the "science" of kicking—which, he insisted, was a misnomer.

"I'm probably going to shock you with this," he said. "But I don't think a kicker can afford to be overanalytical. You ask me what I do on every kick. The thought process is very simple. It's not like I have a one-two-three-four approach to kicking. I just kick. Kicking gets to be a problem when you start to think too much.

"Now, you have to know the conditions. Here, for instance, today. Look up at the flags over there. The stadium flags are always blowing opposite up there than they are in the stadium. It's actually a diagonal wind. When you're going into it, to make a fifty-yard field goal, it's actually like making one from sixty. Today, we're fortunate. The wind's not too bad. And it's thirty-five, forty degrees. That's balmy for this time of year. It could be zero. And that makes the ball you're hitting feel like a rock."

He went to kick. After the workout, he toured me around his field. "Here's a big problem," he said. "A lot of AstroTurf fields have this problem. It's the pitcher's mound and second base. There's quite a few ridges around that. You have to deal with the mound. It goes up and down a little bit in there. Of course, it's better than Cleveland. That's the worst field in the league, with the awful grass and the wind off the lake and the mud you have to kick in. In Cleveland, your accuracy suffers by I'd say ten percentage points. You almost have to tiptoe up to the ball in Cleveland or you'll slide and fall. Here, all you worry about is the wind and the uneven turf around the mound and second base."

He asked me to hold for him, from thirty-five yards.

"Watch what happens," he said. There was a slight cross-wind, from our left to our right. I held the ball with the laces forward, toward the goalpost, slightly bent in toward Anderson, who would be coming soccer-style from my left. He took four steps and BOOM! It was like my right hand getting sucked forward into a vacuum.

The kick started out straight, then faded to the right.

"You missed," I said.

"See, I kicked that ball right down the middle. You see what happens when you have just a little wind and you don't account for it? Now watch. Line it up again."

I did. He kicked it. WHOOSH! Again, my hand got sucked forward. This time the kick started to the left and split the uprights.

Walking off the field, Anderson said, "You've got to be able to account for weather to kick in this town. In this league, really, because you never know when weather's going to come. I like that part of it.

"I like the thinking part. You know, when I watch golf, I love to watch Jack Nicklaus. I love to watch his face—the concentration, the ferocious mentality. I look at him and I think how he must love to be playing the game when the match is on the line. That's a part of the game I love, too."

As it happens, one of Jack Nicklaus's loves is place-kicking. It figures: The kicker is icy in the midst of a furnace, with victory or defeat riding on his individual effort. Jack and Gary would understand each other very well.

The Head Coach
WINNING *IS* EVERYTHING

As the Dallas Cowboys' charter made its final descent into DFW Airport, Jimmy Johnson glared back from his seat—first class, 1A, as it is on every trip—into the main cabin. The plane got lower, and Johnson glared over his right shoulder again. The Cowboys were returning from a poorly played October 1991 loss in Detroit, and there was some commotion back in coach. The World Series game between Atlanta and Minnesota faded in and out of one of those little Watchman TVs, and some of the media members on the charter were getting a bit raucous over the tightly contested game. They had a pool going: What inning would the game be in when the charter touched down? And the inning was about to change as the plane descended lower and lower.

Understand a few things about Jimmy Johnson. Many but certainly not all NFL teams have a head coach who is a commanding presence. Johnson is certainly that. At six feet tall and a tad-chunky 190 pounds, with his signature plastered black-with-a-touch-of-gray hair, he doesn't exactly cut a Shulaesque figure. (Looking imposing is nice but not crucial; when Bill Parcells came out of his postgame shower to break up a shouting match between Carl Banks and a radio reporter in 1985, he cut quite a lardy figure, dripping in a towel. But a path was made, quickly, when people in the crowded room saw Parcells coming. End of rhubarb.) But hang around the Cowboys long enough and you'll see who's unquestionably in charge.

It's been this way since the first season, 1989, when owner Jerry Jones deposed longtime Cowboy monarch Tom Landry and installed the every-hair-in-place Johnson. At the University of Miami, Jimmy had a reputation for being the big boss, but also for letting the talent be talented and getting the hell out of their way. "He'd always tell us, 'You guys just win, and I'll take care of all the other bullshit,'" recalled wide receiver Michael Irvin, who was with Johnson then and now. But in Dallas, he had to get his points across right quick. So during his first training camp as Dallas coach Johnson established his presence, flitting and screaming from practice group to practice group. He offered this little first-year message to his offensive line one morning during practice: "YOU GOTTA POUND THE LIVIN' SHIT OUT OF 'EM! QUIT LOOKIN' FOR A PLACE TO FALL DOWN! DAMMIT, RUN THROUGH THERE! C'MON!!"

And while he can be funny, he spends most of his time around his team being very, very serious. After the 1991 draft, when the full squad of Cowboy rookies and veterans gathered in the team's large meeting room, he told every player in the room, one by one, to rise, state his name and college and position, and then sit. After seventy or so guys did this, Johnson was walking back to the podium to resume the meeting when a well-hidden voice from the back of the room called out, "And who are *you?*" Laughter. Much laughter. "I'm the guy," Johnson said, spinning around, "who decides whether anyone in this room makes any money this year!"

Control. Obsessive control. Always, always in control.

And so, back on the plane, Johnson was getting annoyed at the media noise. A few minutes earlier, he'd heard defensive assistant Ron Meeks chattering about the baseball game, and he just couldn't stand the thought that someone on his staff, a couple of hours after a 34-10 loss to a team everyone thought they'd beat, would actually think to talk about baseball.

"Hey, Ron," Johnson said acidly, turning to Meeks. "Nobody gives a fuck about the baseball game."

Silence in first class.

After the two glares back to coach, Johnson could take it no more. With the plane a thousand feet off the ground and descending rapidly and the flight attendants already buckled in, Johnson whirled out of his seat and stalked back to the media seats.

"Jimmy, leave it alone!" said Bob Ackles, then the Cowboys' personnel director, sitting next to Johnson.

Defensive coordinator Dave Wannstedt, in the row behind them, tried to grab him. "Jimmy, no!" Wannstedt said, grabbing air but no part of the quick-moving Johnson.

Fifteen feet later, Johnson faced the offending media, steam coming from his ears. "Will you guys PUHLEEZE keep it down!" Every head on the plane turned. Johnson stalked back to his seat.

Silence in coach.

After the plane landed, Johnson cooled off and thought about the week ahead. Dallas, 5-3, would play the mediocre Cardinals, 4-5, at Texas Stadium on Sunday. The Cowboys were halfway through their season now, a bit disappointed. That's the way Johnson wanted it. He wanted his players to feel a sense of accomplishment at having come from 1-15 in 1989 to 7-9 in 1990 to 5-3 now, but he wanted them to be hungry, and he wanted them to want to be better. His message for the week would be continued improvement, continued hard work, a continued doing-the-little-things-right attitude. Nothing big, nothing major—just keep doing what we're doing, because it's the right way to do things, and we'll improve.

Johnson, at heart, is a little-things guy. He sees the big picture as a collection of tens of little pictures, like one of those electronics-store TV walls; a hundred TVs, tuned to six or eight different channels. If he had his way, Johnson would storm into the store, find the remote control, and flip every channel to the same one.

His mantra came bubbling out late one night in Hawaii at the annual NFL winter meetings a couple of years ago. We were at a lagoon bar at the obscenely luxurious Hyatt on the Big Island. The place had ten or twelve tables—one with a honeymooning couple, three with what appeared to be a Japanese tourist group, and a couple more with vacationing Americans. Johnson chose a corner table, and his trademark Heineken over ice. The weather was calm, idyllic. A Hyatt-made waterfall whooshed behind us. But there's one thing about Johnson, and about most head coaches in the NFL: They don't stop to stare at many waterfalls. They won't win many Trivial Pursuit games. They think about football. They're focused. They're obsessed.

"I know it's not a popular thing to say these days," Johnson said that night. "You're not supposed to say that you're obsessed with your job. But I am. My work's an obsession. I am absolutely obsessed with winning football games for the Dallas Cowboys."

For six months a year, a coach can't be a husband or a father, and he has to accept all this or get out. This is part of what Bill Parcells was thinking in his last year or so with the Giants. It was the in-season routine (up at 5:15 A.M., at the office at 6:30, work till 8:30 P.M., home by 9, asleep by 10) that finally helped put Parcells over the edge into semiretirement at fifty. One early morning in his office before his final season, 1991, he said with some desperation, "Do you have any idea how isolated we are? I have no idea what's going on out there in the world. I have no hobbies. I have no other life. This job . . . It just consumes you."

Often, when a coach gets out, he wants back in, quickly. Parcells, who likes money, was making $400,000 as a network analyst for NBC. When he took the New England coaching job in 1993, he got an $800,000 annual raise. Plus, he wanted to prove that, unlike in New Jersey with the Giants, he could run a successful football operation as coach and personnel chief.

Some coaches can accept this as their lives. Gibbs, for instance. He's very intelligent, but in many ways he's just a big kid who loves to play games. "I've never seen anyone who loves to compete the way he does," says friend Dan Henning, the Redskins' former offensive coordinator. As a young assistant coach, Gibbs was still barnstorming around the country playing in age-group racquetball tournaments. Once, at age thirty, he found himself in a Milwaukee motel, playing cards late at night with kids ten years younger, wondering what in the world he was doing with his life. "It seems like I was always in search of the next game," he once said. Was? Is, even though he surprisingly left the Redskins last March. His friends expect him to coach again.

"There are tremendous positives to being an NFL coach," Gibbs said, "but there are also tremendous negatives. For six months a year, even if someone in the family gets sick, you can't take time off. Even when my dad got sick, I couldn't take two days off to go see him in California. [Gibbs' dad died during the 1989 season.] You have to give your life to football for six months. I mean, I love what I'm doing, but for six months, coaching is like an emotional marathon. You've got to be ready every year. You've got to have your jaw set, because the game is going to wear you down at some point during the season. I think guys who do what I do are very competitive, and when things don't go well, people start to say things behind your back. You want to fight back. You want to punch somebody when you hear things like this or when you start losing. But you can't. You've got to keep it all inside you. This is what happens to coaches: When things don't go well, you don't have an outlet. You're kind of trapped."

There are several key attributes for NFL head coaches. One is the ability to jettison all the influences and experiences that have nothing to do with winning. Johnson divorced his wife, Linda Kay, after taking the Cowboy's job, because they'd grown apart and because he didn't want any family concerns getting in the way of the biggest job of his life, his dream job. "My nightmare, and something I absolutely refuse to do, is to sit at some three-hour dinner party between a couple of coaches' wives, making small talk," he said. His ideal dinner: Heineken on ice, nachos, salsa. Period. He doesn't remember birthdays, not even those of his two sons, and he doesn't do Christmas. And he's stern about it: Don't tell me how to live my life, his glare tells you, and I won't tell you how to live yours.

Attribute number two is having total power over whether you win or lose. Johnson, hired by old Arkansas college teammate Jerry Jones as coach in 1989, has final power over trades, draft choices, roster moves, and the coaching staff. He and Don Shula are probably the two coaches in pro football with the most control over their own fates.

Three is having a solid base of knowledge about football, knowing players. You'd figure he has both, if college proficiency is a good indicator. In five years recruiting players and coaching the University of Miami, he finished first or second in the country three times, and his teams were 52-9.

Four is ruthlessness when necessary. It's a pretty cold thing (or, at least, very questionable timing) to split with your wife when you hit the very big time. On the other hand, it's honest. The number of phony marriages among NFL coaches is huge. If he can cut ties thusly with his wife, he can cut ties with players. In 1992, the back who some said would succeed Emmitt Smith someday, Curvin Richards, fumbled twice in one game. Johnson cut him the next day.

Five is the ability to obsess. When you obsess and have total power and know football and know football players and can be ruthless, then you will have control over whether you succeed or fail as an NFL coach.

The Dallas Way of Acquiring Players

The week of the Dallas–Phoenix game at home in 1991 was a good week to be around the team, because four rookies—first-round picks Russell Maryland and Alvin Harper, second-round linebacker Dixon Edwards, and third-round tackle Erik Williams—were about to prove whether the Cowboys' unusual scouting methods really could pick players. The world would soon see if the Johnson way was a winning way in the NFL.

Every NFL team has scouts who write reports on the best college talent in the country. Every NFL team has personnel people who take another look at the college players and line them up, in order, for the college draft. In the summertime, coaches use the same drills and tests and scrimmages and preseason games to decide who stays and who goes and then who plays among those who've stayed. A couple of teams think they've found an edge in all of this: Cincinnati and Dallas, especially, use their entire coaching staffs for two or three months each offseason to scout and choose the players they'll be trying to teach.

The Dallas way, though, is unique. Because Johnson's staff is almost exclusively composed of veteran college coaches who've worked from coast to coast they know coaches everywhere. Johnson, after his battles royale with Notre Dame while at the University of Miami, walked into the Notre Dame staff offices in 1989 and heard a secretary shriek in mock horror, "Oooooh, the devil!" But she still ushered him into Lou Holtz's office, which he used to interview Notre Dame players and to watch films. At Colorado in 1991, coach Bill McCartney likewise handed Johnson his office for the afternoon to do his interviews.

At every stop on the scouting trail, the assistants fan out to talk with trusted assistants whom they've known or worked with at other college jobs. Here's why it's so valuable: Before the draft, when most scouts and some pro coaches visit campuses, they're ushered into a meeting room or film room, where a graduate assistant or perhaps an assistant coach will sell the player's strong points—usually downplaying the weak points—while showing film clips of him on a large screen. Then the scouts will work the prospect or prospects out and interview them. Usually they'll also speak with an assistant coach and perhaps a trainer. Unless the pro people know them exceedingly well, the coaches or trainers aren't likely to tell them a player's dark side, if there is one.

The Dallas staff, en masse, went out for two weeks in March 1991 to scout the top prospects for the 1991 draft. It was a glorified recruiting trip, with a couple of exceptions. One, they flew in Jerry Jones's private plane, with the Cowboy star on the tail. Two, they were going to visit old college cronies and many players they'd once recruited; they weren't going cold to remote high schools and into the living rooms of kids they'd never met, as they might have at the University of Miami. Most of these kids they already knew, and many they'd lost in college recruiting wars.

Johnson thinks pro scouting is more like college recruiting than you'd think. "This is kind of touchy," Johnson said, "but do you think one of my friends in college coaching will sit down with a lot of these other NFL guys and tell them if a guy's had drug problems some time in his career? You might eliminate one mistake if you're out [on the road] two weeks. But if you do, then you've saved your club a lot of money and a draft choice. The athletic ability you can see on film. The skeletons in their closet are going to have to come from a coach or trainer or teammate."

The coaches call it "grinding," as in: "Hey, when we go to Tennessee, we've really got to start grinding the staff about Alvin Harper." Or, "When we get to Notre Dame, let's grind real hard about Chris Zorich." Which they did. Grinding is, well, a grind.

"We've got to be investigative reporters sometimes," Cowboys defensive line coach Butch Davis said. This happened, on this trip, at North Carolina State with a defensive end prospect named Mike Jones. The Cowboys liked his athleticism, but they were puzzled in their film study on campus because he didn't play every play. They asked six Wolfpack staff members, and the answer was the same: Three defensive linemen alternated, and Jones was one of those. Davis thought this odd, that a top prospect would alternate plays. And when Davis saw the Auburn film, with Jones on the bench for the end of the game, he thought something was very, very strange. About ten minutes before the Dallas staff left Raleigh that day, Davis found one last Wolfpack staffer. The guy told Davis, "I don't know if he's tough enough. I question whether he wants to hit anybody."

There it was, the chink in Jones's armor they'd been looking for all day. But the Phoenix Cardinals didn't know this; they saw the athletic ability, found out what a nice kid he was, and picked him in the second round, the thirty-second pick in the draft. The Cardinals paid him $661,000 in his rookie season, 1991, and for this they got no sacks, no starts. He's the kind of player who, if he hadn't been a second-round draft choice, might well have been cut late in the season. He did, however, rebound to start in 1992 and get six sacks.

Sometimes they find nothing out of the ordinary. Take Eric Swann, the defensive lineman who came into the NFL out of semipro football because he'd never been able to get a high enough SAT score in eight tries to enter his intended North Carolina State. Dallas sent a club envoy, undercover, to his hometown and high school in rural North Carolina. The guy went to the library and scanned three years of back copies of the local paper to check out Swann, athletically and personally. He ducked into the high school and interviewed some of Swann's former teachers. He asked around town about Swann. He wrote a report for the Cowboys that said, in effect, that Swann was a good kid from a nice family who didn't test well. The Cowboys won't talk about the other nuances from the investigation, but they didn't end up drafting him, and they weren't very excited about him entering the draft.

One of the scouting weeks began on a seasonably cold Monday morning in Knoxville. It was a perfect place for the Cowboys, for this draft. The University of Tennessee had three players—tackles Charles McRae and Antone Davis and wide receiver Alvin Harper—likely to go in the first half of the first round of the draft, along with three other legitimate prospects (wide receiver Anthony Morgan, cornerback Harlan Davis, and running back Chuck Webb). And the Cowboys were very close to this staff. Head coach Johnny Majors, one of college football's elder statesmen, had coached Johnson as a player at Arkansas and hired Johnson as a coordinator at Iowa State. Majors also once hired Wannstedt (at Pitt) and special-teams coach Joe Avezzano (at Tennessee). The Tennessee defensive coordinator, Larry Lacewell, coached in three cities with Johnson and probably was his best friend in college coaching. The trainer and strength coach, Tim Kerin, had applied for a job with the Cowboys the previous year, and the staff knew him well. The defensive line coach, Rex Norris, succeeded Johnson as Oklahoma's defensive line coach in 1972; Johnson left him the Selmon brothers, and he and Norris became good friends over the years. The veteran receivers coach, Charley Cole, used to recruit head-to-head with Dallas's receiver coach, Ax Alexander.

That morning, six Cowboys' coaches and player personnel director Bob Ackles ducked out of the snow flurries into Tennessee's football building and went right into a big meeting room to watch the prospects on tape. This was a designated pro scouting day at Tennessee, and thirty-two NFL folks (scouts, mostly, with some assistant coaches) were here to see the cream of the Vols. Scouting heads Tom Modrak, Tom Donohoe, and Dick Haley came from Pittsburgh. Wideout coach Fred Biletnikoff came from the Raiders. They sat in the 112-seat auditorium as a graduate assistant coach ran tapes of McRae, Antone Davis (with one of the widest rear ends in football history, which every scout kept marveling at), Harper, Morgan, Webb, and Harlan Davis. Johnson loved Harper, who looked just like Al Toon, long and lean and fast, beating corner after corner. "This guy could be real special," Johnson whispered while the grad assistant droned on about Harper's strengths and his good collegiate games. Webb looked good too. But the scouts and coaches assembled on this day kept questioning Webb's desire to play hurt. The scouts didn't think he was reliable. That was one of today's jobs—to find out what the deal was with Webb.

Johnson sat off to the right, watching the tapes and commenting on each player in a whisper, not wanting to alert the rest of the scouts, who were jotting down notes and forty-yard dash times in their notebooks. "Crucial time for us," he said softly. "Gotta see a lot of players in these two weeks . . . Texas and Colorado last week, Tennessee, N.C. State, Notre Dame, Michigan State, and Nebraska this week . . . This might be the most important stop. I don't know that I've seen this much pro talent on one side of the ball in one year."

After the tapes, Avezzano went to grind on his friend Tim Kerin. Wise went to watch tapes with Phil Fullmer, the offensive coordinator, and McRae. Alexander and Norv Turner, offensive coordinator, went to see Cole. Johnson went on the prowl. He found and cornered Lacewell in a secretary's office.

"There's something I need," Johnson said softly, motioning Lacewell to the corner of the office.

"What's that Jimmy?" Lacewell said.

"Tell me about Webb. What's the deal with him?"

"Jimmy," Lacewell said, earnestly, "he's the real deal. You know all those great offensive players we had at Oklahoma? Well, this guy is one of 'em. And he's a tough son of a bitch. Don't listen to what you might hear about him. He's a hell of a player. Somebody's gonna get a steal with him."

(Bad report. It happens. Webb quit the Packers a year later, just vanishing. Johnson still liked Lacewell enough in 1992 to steal him; Dallas hired Lacewell as the club's director of college scouting.)

Down the hall, McRae was wowing offensive line coach Tony Wise, who kept up a running commentary while they watched tapes together. "Nice job, Charles, real nice job," Wise said. "Nice job getting your hands out on the defender."

Johnson had some private time with Majors and a long chat with Lacewell and hung out in the afternoon with Morgan and Harper. He'd recruited both while at Miami and lost Harper, a Florida native, in an intense battle with Tennessee. That night, a Tennessee booster hosted a catered southern barbeque for the Cowboys clan. Off to the side, while Johnson and Lacewell discussed Harper's work habits, Butch Davis talked about his boss. He's worked for Johnson since 1979, at Oklahoma. "Jimmy's got a great feel for football players," Davis said, picking at his dinner. "For thirteen years, I've watched him reshuffle guys, putting 'em in position to make plays and putting his teams in position to win. It's just a feel you have to have for the game and for your opponent, and Jimmy has it so well. And this is a big part of it. Jimmy feels like if we're going to be coaching these players, we damn well better like them and have a feel for them before they get to Dallas. What I've learned out here on the road scouting players is if you talk to enough people and watch enough film, you'll find out the truth. What baffles me is how some scouts feel they can know a kid by coming in, watching one can of film, talking to the position coach, and blowing out."

For four hours, bourbon and beer flowed, and plates of barbequed chicken came off the grill. By about eleven, with common sense sufficiently impaired, a guitar came out, and everyone sang along to "Rocky Top Tennessee," and Johnson broke out his best off-color coaching stories. Quite a raconteur, this Jimmy. If you ever see him in a bar, ask him about the time he and Lacewell and Barry Switzer were holed up in a fleabag Oklahoma hotel on the way to a coaching clinic, and ask him what Switzer did to Lacewell's shoe.

(The Dallas staff went through the same drill, basically, in South Bend, taking the coaching staff out for a feast/grinding session at an Italian restaurant, and in East Lansing with George Perles's staff, grinding and eating and drinking in Perles's basement.)

The morning after Knoxville, Johnson leaned back in the rear seat of the plane with the Cowboys star on the tail. It rose steadily through the morning overcast, the coaches reading their *USA Today*s and Johnson trying to get some rest. Suddenly remembering something, Johnson's head snapped forward, and he fumbled through his leather briefcase, looking for his schedule. Finally, under the Paul Mitchell Freeze and Spray Shine, he found it. Six of Johnson's assistant coaches were on board, and Jimmy wanted to make sure where everyone was going when this trip ended.

"Hey, Ax," Johnson called to Alexander. "When's Herman Moore's workout?"

"Thursday," Ax called from a front seat, above the loud engine hum.

"Gotta take a good look at him now, Ax," Johnson said. "Gotta grind on some people there now."

Ax nodded. Moore, the wide receiver from Virginia, would be working out for pro scouts on Thursday, and Alexander would splinter off from the Dallas group to go to Charlottesville, Virginia, for the workout.

"Hey, Tony," Johnson said to Wise. "You got the Donnalley kid today?"

"Yup," Wise said. He was headed to see North Carolina offensive lineman Rich Donnalley when the plane landed in Raleigh, splitting off from the Dallas group going to N.C. State.

Then Johnson summed up the first leg of the week-long trip. "We confirmed what we already knew about the Tennessee players, for the most part. But two things really helped us: We were really impressed with the personalities of McRae and Harper, and now we know they'd fit in with our team, and we really hadn't given much thought to Morgan before this trip. But he was so impressive on film and in the drills that now we will. Basically, the pictures on these guys were all a little fuzzy when we got here. We weren't sure about any one of them, because we hadn't seen them or talked to them in a setting like this. But now we've found out they don't have any skeletons in the closet, and they've come into focus."

Wannstedt, sitting nearby, being in Miami so long, chimed in with memories of Don Shula. Wannstedt actually was on Shula's Dolphin staff for three weeks before Johnson got the Cowboys' job and hired him. "Shula always used to say the biggest thing to winning is building a winning edge. Do what you do well, and build a winning edge over the other teams. Well, we feel this is our winning edge."

This, plus the Herschel Walker trade, which allowed the Cowboys to make trips like these fruitful. The 1989 trade netted them seven high draft choices, including first- and second-round choices in this draft. Later on this day, with the trip to North Carolina State behind them and the Cowboys' plane airborne over southwestern Virginia, Johnson popped open a Heineken and poured it into a glass filled with ice. As he poured, he said, "Thank you, Herschel Walker."

The Dallas Way on Draft Day

There is no textbook to study to prepare for a draft. You have to know what you want, and you go about getting it. That's it. You enter a draft with a couple of objectives: You want to get the players you really want, and you want them to be in training camp on time.

The Cowboys, three days before the 1991 draft held on a Sunday, had the eleventh, twelfth, and fourteenth picks in the first round. On Friday, they traded first- and second-round picks, with three players, to New England for the overall first pick in the draft. They knew who they wanted. If Rocket Ismail, the Notre Dame receiver/returner, had wanted a regular NFL contract, Dallas might have wanted him. But his agents faxed the Cowboys a fourteen-page contract proposal, calling it "non-negotiable" and asking for an average salary of $3.36 million over four years. That alone would have made him the highest-paid player in NFL history, in terms of average salary. But the incentives Ismail wanted were head-spinning. Here's one: If the Cowboys made the Super Bowl in Ismail's four seasons, they'd have to pay him an additional $750,000 per Super Bowl appearance. The Cowboys didn't even fax back a counteroffer.

Now they held the first, twelfth, and fourteenth picks. They wanted Miami defensive tackle Russell Maryland and Tennessee players Alvin Harper and Charles McRae and Michigan State linebacker Dixon Edwards. They also wanted to be sure they could sign these players. So, on the weekend of the draft, Johnson and Jones agreed who the target players of the first two rounds were, and they set about getting in position to sign them. Why? Because rookies who hold out can destroy their first seasons, and the Cowboys were tired of paying lots of money to rookies who are unable to contribute their first year because they don't know the pro system and the pro game well enough by the time the season starts. In the days before the draft, the Cowboys felt out the agents of these players and tried to assess their signability on draft day. Dallas put out the word that it wouldn't take a player high in the draft unless he agreed to contract terms during the time alotted to make the draft choice. It was a brilliant stroke by Jones, and Johnson appreciated it.

So, on the night before the draft, six friends of the Cowboys—nonemployees, among them a lawyer from Arkansas and a retired businessman from Bozeman, Montana—fanned out across the country to perch on the doorsteps of prospective high draftees. The businessmen went with cellular phones to the homes or draft-day sites of Maryland in Newport Beach, California; of McRae in Tennessee; of Harper in Frostproof, Florida; of USC tackle Pat Harlow in southern California; to Edwards in Cincinnati; and to one other player's place. On the day of the draft, these friends were asked to sit in cars outside the homes of prospective high draftees so they'd be able to swoop in and get contracts signed.

Johnson had decided on Friday he definitely wanted Maryland and he wanted Harper. He thought he could wait until the twelfth pick and get Harper. He wanted McRae too, but knew he'd have to move up in the first round to get him. After they took Maryland—they'd agreed on the basics of the deal the night before with agent Leigh Steinberg—they tried to work a deal with Tampa Bay, which held the seventh pick in the round, hoping to improve their chances of landing McRae, but the Bucs wouldn't budge. Dallas lost him. Next, they picked Harper at number twelve, Jones's people working the cellular-phone contact in Frostproof to get a verbal agreement over the phone before announcing the pick.

The next guy they wanted was Edwards, but this was too high to take him, at number fourteen. None of Johnson's moles around the league expected Edwards to go in the first round, so he looked to trade down. Why risk this? Why not just take the guy you want right here, with all the picks you still have on the board? "Never reach. Never. You'll kill yourself reaching," Johnson said. Taking Edwards, an undersized playmaker many thought was too light at 221 pounds to be an NFL starter, would be a big reach in the first round. Besides, if someone shocked the Cowboys and picked Edwards before Dallas in the second round, they could turn to another lightish linebacker, Roman Phifer (230) of USC. Here's where the Cowboys did things only a few other NFL teams did: They started wheeling and dealing their picks.

To Johnson it was simple: If you can get a guy with a second-round pick, you're wasting value by using a higher choice on him. Even if you know he's the player you want, you're wasting strength by not dealing that too-high pick to someone who wants it. The trick is finding that person.

This is no mystic art, believe me. I watched it happen. I watched the Cowboys phone most of the league and get phoned back over a forty-five-minute period. It's hustle. If the New York Jets, for example, had moved down in the 1989 draft's first round, they'd certainly still have gotten their man, defensive end Jeff Lageman, plus they would have picked up an extra high draft choice for nothing, just for moving down a few spots. But they played it safe. They stayed right where they were midway through the first round and picked Lageman. You can't always play it safe, or you'll be playing meaningless football in December every year—like the Jets.

From fourteen to seventeen Dallas went, picking up an extra fourth-rounder from the Patriots; and then they went from seventeen to twenty, picking up a fifth-rounder from Washington. And there the Cowboys sat at twenty—waiting. Still too soon to take Edwards.

"We don't want to use it," Johnson said in the draft room. "We've got to come up with a deal."

Although Jones was in the room, as were sixteen other Cowboys personnel people and executives, the boss was Johnson—controlling his fate. The phone rang in the draft room eighty-three times in the first round, and eighty-three times player personnel director Ackles or scouting guys Dick Mansberger or John Wooten looked to Johnson for an answer. As during this four-minute sequence, with the twentieth pick on the clock:

It's 2:41 P.M. A minute earlier, club vice president Mike McCoy had snapped at a secretary, "I can't talk to anyone! We're in the middle of the draft. Take a number." Now, seven men sit around a ten-foot-by-ten-foot table. Four minutes remain before Johnson has to tell the Dallas choice for the pick into a speakerphone in the middle of the table connected with draft headquarters in New York. Ackles speed-dials teams trying to get somebody to take his twentieth pick. But no one seems to want it, and Johnson is getting very, very nervous.

At 2:42, Atlanta general manager Ken Herock calls Johnson, and they dicker. Ackles gets San Diego GM Bobby Beathard on the line; the Chargers have two picks in the second round, and Ackles wants one, plus lower choices. San Diego makes a lukewarm offer. It might be Dallas's only option.

At 2:43, Herock offers Johnson picks in the second, fourth and seventh rounds for Dallas's first-round pick. "Is this a firm deal, the two, four, and the seven for our one right now?" Johnson asks Herock. Herock says yes. Johnson pauses, happy. In five seconds, he was going to agree to the deal. In three seconds, another phone rings. "One minute," the voice from New York says over the speakerphone.

At 2:44, McCoy picks up the one ringing phone and says hello to Detroit director of college scouting Kevin Colbert. The Lions want the pick. "Hold it, Jimmy!" McCoy says, cupping the phone. Johnson puts Herock on hold. Colbert offers second-, third- and fourth-round picks for Dallas's first-rounder. Johnson and owner Jerry Jones look at each other and nod. "Let's do it," Johnson says, and he picks Herock up again. "Got a better deal, Kenny. Sorry." Thirty seconds. Starting to get dangerous now, because if the Cowboys don't choose on time or trade on time, the next team in the draft order, Kansas City, can jump ahead of them. Dallas and Detroit won't get the language worked out in time, so Johnson tells McCoy to find out who Detroit wants, and they'll take the guy for the Lions and then make the swap official. It's Ole Miss defensive end Kelvin Pritchett. "Kelvin Pritchett, defensive end, Mississippi. P-R-I-T-C-H-E-T-T!" Johnson says with urgency into the phone, when the name is misunderstood.

At 2:45, "Time!" is yelled in New York, as the Cowboys rush the pick to the NFL draft table. "Done deal," Jones says with emotion. And the Dallas room erupts. With this trade plus the two earlier deals, Dallas has turned what was originally the four-teenth pick in the first round into five choices between the sec-ond and fifth rounds. Fists pump the air. Grown men shouted. "WHOA BOY!" Johnson whoops, and he high-fives the owner's son, Stephen Jones. "Now we can pick our guys!"

"HEY, JIMMY!" a voice yells over the speakerphone. It is De-troit coach Wayne Fontes. "You screwed us! You took our guy! I thought we had a deal, dammit!"

Fontes hasn't heard that the Cowboys were picking Pritchett only to trade him. All he heard on the ESPN feed into the De-troit draft room is commissioner Paul Tagliabue at the podium saying, "With the twentieth selection, Dallas picks Kelvin Pritchett, defensive end, Mississippi." And Fontes is livid.

"Take it easy, Wayne," Johnson says, after the whooping dies down. "We just picked him for you, and now we'll do the deal."

Crisis solved.

At 2:46, McCoy walks from the room, calling out, "Oxygen! I'm about to have a heart attack."

"In my six drafts here," Ackles says, "I've never seen action like this."

Dallas got Dixon Edwards with the thirty-seventh overall pick of the draft, in the second round. In the third round, with the Cowboys scheduled to make a pick, Johnson calls in offensive line and special-teams coaches Wise and Avezzano, who were standing outside the room with the rest of the scouts. When Johnson calls, they come, lickety-split. And here they are, with ninety seconds left on the clock before they have to make a choice.

"Okay, both of you, right now: Who do you like better, Curvin Richards or Sammy Walker?" Johnson asks. Richards, a running back from Pitt, and Walker, a cornerback from Texas Tech, were third- or fourth-round prospects. Two seconds ticked by.

"Richards," Wise says.

"Richards," Avezzano says.

Johnson makes a couple of third-round picks, then rushes into the scouting office to call the Texas Tech defensive coordinator. He is concerned about Walker's sight. He is blind in one eye.

"Just between coaches," Johnson says softly over the phone, "how's Sammy?"

A few minutes later, this becomes moot. Pittsburgh picks Walker early in the fourth round. Johnson got Richards.

When the day is over and the battles finished, Johnson relaxes for a while. He sits back, pulls on a Heineken, and looks at the clock. It is 1:56 in the morning. He'll have to be back by 7:00, ready for day two of the draft. But he has one final thing to say.

"We'll be good, big-time good," he says. "There's no doubt in anybody's mind here. I just want to get our guys together and play the type of aggressive football we're used to playing. I could care less what the people out there think of us."

One last fact: Of the eight total draft choices the Cowboys got in the Herschel Walker trade, they traded eight.

The Dallas Way of Working a Week

On Monday, Johnson's staff began putting the game plan together for the Phoenix game. At 7:00 that morning, he poked his head into defensive coordinator Wannstedt's office with his ideas for the week. Each Monday, Johnson gave Wannstedt and offensive coordinator Turner his nickel's worth, his advice for that week's opponent. It might take two minutes. It might take ten. He always has final authority on what's put into each game plan, but he trusts them enough to let them plot their own plans and make their own decisions.

"Let's move Russell up this week," Johnson said to Wannstedt.

Wannstedt had a feeling Johnson might be ready to do this. Russell Maryland, the first pick in the draft, had been playing twenty plays or so a game in an uneven rotation with fellow former Hurricane Jimmie Jones. Johnson wanted Wannstedt to start Maryland now, because his play was so impressive in his spot duty. Wannstedt agreed. They decided that Maryland and Jones would play in a fairly equal rotation from here on out, with Maryland starting.

Then he ducked in on Turner, and then on special-teams coach Joe Avezzano. The game-planning week was underway. Actually, this process had already begun. For the previous two weeks, assistant coaches watched tapes of Cardinal games and began to track the Phoenix tendencies—what the Cards would do offensively, for instance, every time they had a third-and-five situation—and now they'd just update the Cards' tendencies through their ninth game. On Mondays, Johnson reviews the previous game with the players, puts them through a limbering-up practice, meets with his staff to outline plans for the next game, jogs, eats dinner and goes home.

Some coaches—Sam Wyche in Tampa, Mike Holmgren in Green Bay, and the New York Jets' Bruce Coslet offensively; Cleveland's Bill Belichick and San Francisco's George Seifert defensively—still roll up their sleeves and take charge of making half of their teams' strategic plans for each game. But Johnson, like most other prominent coaches, leaves it to his coordinators and assistants to figure out what offenses and defenses they'll throw against the opponent in every situation. "The way it worked for us," Parcells said, "is [defensive coordinator] Bill Belichick would pretty much organize the game plan each week, knowing what I'd like to run. A lot of times he'd have too much in there, and on Tuesday I'd have to go in and tell him to take this out or take that out, it's too complicated. But he was with me for so long he usually knew what I wanted." Which is exactly how Johnson felt with Wannstedt, who'd been with him for fourteen years, and with Turner. The head coach has to be able to delegate, because he has so many other things to do.

Tuesday was an important day. At a 7:00 A.M. staff meeting, he reviewed some of the fine points he expected to be installed for the Phoenix game by the offensive and defensive coordinators. Then he watched films in between flitting in and out of his office to take calls from anyone he thought could help give him a clue or two about how the Cardinals are playing. By the time he met the press at 11:00 in the morning, he had an excellent idea of how the Cowboys would attack and defense the Cardinals.

That afternoon, he and Wannstedt spent a good chunk of time talking about blitzing Phoenix quarterback Tom Tupa. Wannstedt wanted to throw the kitchen sink at Tupa. Johnson thought a faucet and a couple of spigots would do.

"I'm all for the blitz," he told Wannstedt, sitting in Wannstedt's office. "But let's not totally press 'em. Let's blitz 'em kind of soft."

In other words, blitz linebackers almost every third down—more than they had at any point during the season—and blitz on obvious passing second downs. But when blitzing, play soft coverage on the Cardinals' wide receivers, making it impossible for them to beat the Cowboys deep. Say it's third-and-nine, and the two outside linebackers blitz Tupa. Let the Phoenix receivers have the quick five-yard catches, but make sure to smother them right at the catch. And don't get beat deep, above all. Don't give Tupa the chance to throw a rainbow the wideouts can run under. Why the soft blitz? The Cowboys saw the vulnerability of the thirty-one- and thirty-three-year-old Card tackles, Tootie Robbins and Luis Sharpe, and the inexperienced-under-pressure Tupa. They knew pressure could fluster Phoenix.

"Okay," Wannstedt said. "No problem. We'll blitz 'em soft."

It was quite a significant week, actually, because Johnson, who'd been thinking of making some lineup changes for some time, now had the ammunition to do it. The 34-10 a couple of days earlier jostled Johnson into realizing there was no time like the present to make the changes. He decided to bench the underachieving Alexander Wright at wide receiver and replace him with first-round rookie Alvin Harper. He made Maryland the starter at defensive tackle and put him in a rotation system with Jones, who would understand the need to get the big stud draft choice in the starting lineup. And he put third-round draft choice Erik Williams at left tackle for the injured Mark Tuinei.

So Johnson was just bursting with news. But he couldn't stride into the press conference and tell the writers something the players didn't know yet. "One of the quickest ways to lose a player," he said privately, "is to have them read about something big involving them in the paper before you've had a chance to talk to them." Instead, Johnson delivered a message he wanted the players to hear on TV that night and read in the papers the next day, if they were so inclined. At the podium in the Cowboys' large meeting room where the players, in about twenty-five hours, would hear the same message, he met about thirty members of the local media. For the press, he was in a dark suit, the type of suit some men wear when they get married. So formal. Johnson thinks it lends an air of importance to the press gathering, and he wants it that way. He likes to do important things.

"I like where we are," he said. "I see us getting nothing but better. On the other hand, we're not at all satisfied. A year ago we were 3-5 and I think everybody was disappointed. This year, we're 5-3, and I think ninety-nine percent of the people around here are disappointed. We know we can be better."

And who's the one percent?

"Somebody who doesn't know football."

Johnson also used the briefing to tell the media folk about motivation. He likes to get across little lessons lots of times with the press, feeling that it gets him their respect. "When you're dealing with fewer players, like you are here compared to college ball, and when the difference between the bottom and top teams is so much smaller than it is in college ball, I really think the attitude of the team in preparing themselves for Sunday and in playing the game is more important here than in college," he said. "When you're dealing with 120, 130 players, and you can replace a slightly injured one or one who's not playing quite up to par, and you can replace him just by snapping your

213

fingers, well, those players are going to have a great attitude. And you're going to be able to win week after week after week. But the swings in momentum and the swings in attitude in pro football can make a team a playoff team one year and a team that has a difficult time winning the next year. A lot of people have a misconception about motivation in pro football. It's not a lot of rah-rah, clap-your-hands, always-positive stuff. Motivation has to be an individual touch with individual players. It might be a slap on the back to one player and some positive counseling to another player, off to the side. Professional players don't need whooping and hollering. But they all need something. It's up to the coach to find out what that something is for each player."

Head coaches have to believe they can find out what buttons to push on each player. Bill Parcells always thought he was the only guy to run Lawrence Taylor's football life. How presumptuous. Taylor was always one of those I'm-bigger-than-the-program guys, and Parcells gave him a ton of breaks. But Parcells—through embarrassment, semihumiliation, personal challenges—could set Taylor's mind to the right pitch before big games, and no one else could. Johnson didn't have any such stars. Quarterback Troy Aikman was still an unassuming person with a terrific work ethic. There was friction between him and Johnson dating back to the Cowboys' first-round pick of quarterback Steve Walsh in Aikman's second year, but Aikman was a team guy and didn't need to be big man on campus. Wideout Michael Irvin needed some stroking, but Irvin and Johnson went way back—Johnson coached him for four years in college at Miami—and Irvin bought into the coach's program. The other premier players—running back Emmitt Smith, defensive tackle Russell Maryland—were still young enough that Johnson didn't have to worry about occasionally ruffling their feathers. They didn't have enough pelts on the wall to challenge the coach yet. Actually, no one on the team did. But in building the kind of team Johnson thought he could in Dallas, it was just a matter of time before some problems with players would surface.

Johnson had prepared for this. That became apparent as Johnson told his life story late that day in his office at the Cowboys' practice facility and offices in suburban Irving. A sprawling office, with a big wooden desk and stuffed black chair for him, with game plans, newspaper clips, and a pile of phone messages in front of him.

As a kid, growing up on the gritty side of Port Arthur, Texas, on the Gulf Coast, Johnson played pickup football games—whites versus blacks—on grassy medians between main avenues. "They kicked our ass, but it was was very, very competitive, and very fun," Johnson said.

Big key number one. At Arkansas, he enrolled in the College of Arts and Sciences, majoring in psychology (and graduating on time) while playing a defensive line position, despite being somewhat small, in the early sixties. "Introduction to psychology, abnormal psychology, psychology of learning, psychology of anything—I took it all," he said. "No PE stuff. To me, that was the easy way out. I enjoyed physics, English, psychology. I had to enjoy it, because if they weren't going to make it interesting, I wasn't going. So as my college football career ended, I in no way was preparing to go into football or coaching. I thought what I'd probably do is go back and get my master's or my Ph.D. in psychology and go around to different companies and help them motivate their employees or deal with problems with their employees."

Johnson was married then, to Linda Kay, with one son, and he figured he'd survive by taking a grad assistant's coaching job on the Arkansas staff while going to class there. "Right now, I'd probably be working nine to five, weigh about 350, and watch football games on TV all weekend," he said. But the coaching grapevine snagged him. The defensive coordinator at Louisiana Tech had a heart attack just before the season, and the school went looking for a one-year assistant—at the princely salary of $1,000 per month—while the coordinator recovered. And someone at Louisiana Tech knew someone at Arkansas, who said the Razorbacks had a smart-as-a-whip grad assistant who might be right for the job. "That was a fortune, $1,000 a month," Johnson said. "I had to take it. And I enjoyed it. So I figured I'd stick with it for a while." A while weaved through Picayune (Mississippi) High, Wichita State, Iowa State, Oklahoma, Arkansas,

Pittsburgh, Oklahoma State (in 1979, as a head coach), and then Miami, in 1984.

"Jimmy was always known as a guy who'd try to get an edge on you," said Johnny Majors, the man who brought Johnson to Iowa State as a twenty-five-year-old defensive coordinator. "We got a cold snap once at Iowa State, and they flooded the tennis courts there to make a skating rink. So we planned an outing with the wives to go out ice skating. None of us knew how to skate well. Everybody's kidding Jimmy, because he can't skate at all. Well, nobody knows this at the time, but Jimmy gets a pair of skates and spends night after night practicing. And by the time we go, he's better than anybody else, and he's skating around us, all happy and proud. He'd beaten us all. The next day, there's more coaches in the trainer's room than players. We're all hurt. I've got a huge egg on my forehead from a fall, and everybody's got sore knees or something else. But Jimmy's fine."

Along the way, he started getting the idea he wanted to be a head coach. And then he got the idea he wanted to be the best head coach there was. So he started gathering assistant coaches as he went, guys he trusted, guys he knew could beat anybody given the right players. He found that the key to winning in college football was recruiting your ass off, and so he gathered assistants under him at Pitt, Oklahoma State, and Miami who had no concept of what a clock—and in some instances, a family— was. He formed almost intimate bonds with some of his players. Black, white, whatever. "When I hear the word 'nigger,'" he said, "it truly makes me cringe. Always has. I've heard the comments from people that if it comes down to the white or black guy, I'll always favor the black guy, but that's bullshit. I help whoever helps me win." At Pitt, defensive end and Heisman Trophy candidate Hugh Green lived with the Johnson family in the summer before his sophomore year; Green would bring his girlfriend over to formal dinners at the Johnson house. When Johnson took over at Oklahoma State, the most difficult thing he faced was forcing Green to stay at Pitt and not transfer with him to Stillwater. Green didn't care that he'd be moving from a national championship team to an annual loser. But Johnson told him it wouldn't be right for the best player in the program to transfer when the program was on the brink of greatness. Green stayed.

"Wherever I've been, I've taken the attitude, 'It's our team. It's our company,'" Johnson said. "Most successful coaches aren't working for the dollar. They're working for the wins. Those are the coaches I want, and I'm going to do anything I can to make them successful. You have to be a driven, ambitious guy to coach on my staff. The first step in getting the right kind of relationship with your players is to establish respect, and you establish respect by you personally having a great relationship with your staff. Because players will deal with the assistants ten times more than they'll deal with the head coach—in meetings, in coaching at practice, in coaching during games, in just talking to them constantly—and assistants have to be branches of the head coach. You want the players getting the same message from the head coach and the assistants. You know things are working out okay when I say something to the assistants one day, and two or three days later in the paper I see the players saying it."

The Johnson blueprint for assistant coaches:

1. Loyalty to Johnson and the organization. "I've got to know they're behind what we're doing."
2. Chemistry. "They have to fit in. We spend so much time with each other we can't afford to have an asshole coming in and spoiling our chemistry. This, and loyalty, are important above and beyond anything."
3. X and O expertise.
4. Teaching excellence.

"When I've looked for assistants, I've made it clear that any decision made will be made for us to win ballgames. Whatever we do today has to help us win tomorrow. That's one of the reasons it was very foreign for me my first year here. I couldn't get close to any of the players. I didn't want to. I couldn't feel comfortable and sincere—and this was hard on the assistants—talking about the team, because we had no team. We just had a bunch of players wearing the Dallas uniform. If you were around here in 1989, you saw a different coach and a different degree of involvement."

But now, at 5-3, with seventy or so percent of the real, long-term team in place, the Johnson way was firm.

On Wednesday, bounding from office to office at the Cowboys complex, Johnson tried to have a little bit to do with everything, all the while formulating in his mind his first speech of the new week to the players, which he'd give at 9:30. (Bounding: the perfect way to describe Johnson. When he moves from room to room or practice group to practice group, he strides determinedly, on the balls of his feet, in a hurry to get to the next thing, like he's on a constant coffee buzz.) He looked over the game plan and made a few calls from 7:00 to 8:00, then met with Bob Ackles to discuss Phoenix's activation of returner Larry Centers and cornerback Robert Massey from injured-reserve. "Who do you think they'll have inactive for Sunday?" Johnson asked, and he and Ackles discussed the possibilities for a few minutes. Then, with the heavy rain in the area, he told the staff they'll be practicing at Texas Stadium instead of their regular grass practice fields both today and Thursday. Then he finalized the Thanksgiving week schedule with head trainer Kevin O'Neill and operations director Bruce Mays. Then he coordinated the Thanksgiving-week hospital visitation in Dallas and Fort Worth by the players; this is an annual thing, in which the squad is split and half go to visit sick kids in each city.

Then it was time for Johnson's message to his team. "Nothing profound, usually," he said. "But important. I want them to feel the importance of the week, and I want to set the tone for the kind of week I expect."

Johnson, in a shiny blue sweatsuit, waited for the fifty-four players to settle into their seats in the large meeting room. Everywhere on the walls were signs, motivational signs and statistical-goal signs to the team, like:

Protect the Ball

ZERO

Turnovers

The players sat and shut up. Johnson, in his very slight Texas twang, gave his four-minute tone-setter with a little bit of emotion but no histrionics. This was the troop leader telling his scouts the schedule for the hike, the platoon sergeant telling the privates where the march would take them and how they'd be expected to behave, the mom telling the kids the day's schedule over breakfast.

"This week we're going to change practice a little bit because of the rain and the fields," he began. "Tentatively for tomorrow and for sure today we'll practice at Texas Stadium. What we'll do is have our eleven o'clock walk-through, offense in the locker room, defense in the dance studio, kicking game in the locker room. One o'clock sharp, buses will head to Texas Stadium. We'll go straight from the buses to flex-and-stretch. We will do the exact practice we do out here. And as soon as the practice is over with, no interviews, media et cetera, we'll load up the buses and come back here. Everything else will be a regular routine, like we normally do.

"Just a couple of things starting out the week. Yesterday we had the press conference and a couple of the reporters said, well, at the halfway point, how do you feel about the progress, and are you satisfied? I said, well, number one, no. We're not satisfied. I don't think you're ever satisfied until you get to where you want to go. It's the same thing we always talk about: You get better or you get worse. And in our situation, as good as we feel about ourselves, you know, I think we need to make a push to get better, and we will. We'll be a hell of a lot better football team the second half of the season than we were the first.

"It all comes down to attitude. A lot of people think it's attitude on game day . . ."

Pause for effect.

"THE HELL . . ." in a booming voice, breaking the monotone.

Pause for effect.

". . . with attitude on game day. Shit, everybody's excited on game day. It's the attitude of preparing for game day. That's when you need the attitude. So right now, the second half of the season, there's a hell of a lot of teams close to our situation. They have four wins, five wins, they may have six wins. And so we're in good position. What's going to make a difference is what we do from here on out. Do we, in our minds, try to stay the same? Or do we do some things to make ourselves better? And do we have the kind of push where we get some momentum, we get on a roll, we get some good things to start happening for us? And all of a sudden, shit, do we get where we want to be, or do we just kind of hang loose and let teams pass us by?

"You say, well, that's easy to say in this meeting. But how do you do it? How do you make that big push? Well, the way we make the big push is to concentrate on fundamentals. Concentrate on the little things. If scheme-wise—and you know, shit, we've got a hell of a scheme—we're going to do the right things, the scheme is fine. How we get better is concentrate on the little things. You know, last week, we did the little things. Every day in practice we tackled, right? Every day we're in pads—TACKLING! I mean, you guys have been tackling ever since you've been playing football. But we concentrated on tackling. And we go up against one of the best backs in football [Barry Sanders of Detroit] last week, and we had fewer missed tackles than we've had all year long. We had three missed tackles in the entire ballgame, because we concentrated on the little things.

"Let's continue to do that. Let's bear down when we're simulating the opponent, scout-team-wise. Defensive backs, let's bear down on your footwork, your alignment. Bear down on the little things. Big thing this week, Steve [Beuerlein], help us with cadence, because [Phoenix quarterback Tom] Tupa, he's good. Look at every one of these films. He does a hell of a job with cadence. The last time we played Phoenix, cadence would have helped us. We jump offsides because of cadence, and we get an interception, and it doesn't count because we're offsides. Bear down on the little things. We do that, and we will get on a roll. We will get momentum. We will make a push. Take care of the little things, and we're going to end up having a hell of a football team. Okay?

"Let's have a hell of a week of practice, starting at Texas Stadium today. Let's concentrate on what we have to do. Let's get better."

He sat with Wannstedt in Wannstedt's office for twenty minutes, and they finalized the Sunday game plan. Then he stopped by special-teams coach Joe Avezzano's office for ten minutes to go over a couple of fine points about kickoff coverage, which the Cowboys had screwed up in Detroit. He got an updated area weather report from equipment manager Buck Buchanan, and worked out with Buchanan how much and what exact type of cold-weather gear Johnson wanted brought to New Jersey, Washington, and Philadelphia, all road trips set for the coming weeks. Then he poked his head into offensive line coach Tony Wise's office to ask about the health of Mark Tuinei, bothered by a groin pull. "We'll try to get him going," Wise said, "but I think he's pretty doubtful for Sunday." Mentally now, Johnson knew he'd have to plug the crucial left-tackle hole with a rookie from a small college (Williams of Central State of Ohio) in his first NFL start, which made him increasingly uneasy about the game because he had three regular linemen missing or badly bruised.

That was all before lunch.

"Why," Johnson was asked later, "do you worry about who visits what hospital or what parka goes to East Rutherford?"

"Look," Johnson said, his eyes pointing lasers to the stupidest question he's heard in the last decade. His answer seemed almost too practiced, too perfect, until you saw the emotion in his eyes when he answered. "I've prepared my entire life—forty-eight years, twenty-four hours a day, 365 days a year—for sixteen Sundays. Everybody out there in the world judges whether I'm a successful human being based on how I do on those Sundays. If we lose, I'm a complete bum, a worthless human being. If we win, I'm a success. That's the way this business is. I will not be a loser. And so that's why I'm so concerned with every detail affecting even slightly the lives of my players."

A football practice can fool you. It can start out all raggedy, with players limbering up in uneven lines, and in two minutes players can be in precise lines, running by rote the patterns and drills the assistant coaches run them through every day for twenty-six weeks. Wow, you say. How'd everything get so organized all of a sudden? But it does, and that's how the Dallas practice happens. Johnson, this day, walked through the lines of players during the calisthenics, hands clasped behind his back, heavy blue jacket protecting him from the occasional mist and constant dreariness of a central Texas fall day. He strode purposefully everywhere.

He went to the field-goal team, watching a couple of plays and then, on a poor snap to the holder, barking out, "This is the play that cost us the ballgame last week!"

He went to Alexander Wright, in the receiver group. Wright had a feeling he was going to be demoted, and so he was wary when Johnson approached. "We're going to make a change," Johnson said. "We're going to give Alvin Harper a chance to start. But I don't want you to get down over this. You're still a great talent, and you're still going to be a great player here."

He went to linebacker Reggie Cooper. Cooper was healthy and ready to play, but the Cowboys had him on the developmental squad because they didn't have a roster spot for him. Johnson liked him. He was a bright, six-two, 230-pound outside linebacker, converted from strong safety, which he played at Nebraska. Probably half a step slow, an inch short, ten pounds light, but Johnson loves great college players, and he loves playmakers. Cooper was both at Nebraska, a big-time school, and Johnson wanted to keep him around to see how he'd develop. "Reggie," Johnson said, "you're doing a great job. I don't know if we'll be able to activate you [this year] but I want to get you signed for next year. You're in our plans." Cooper seemed pleased.

He went over to backup tight end Alfredo Roberts. "Alfredo," he said, "with all the injuries we've got on the line, you're going to have to be ready to play guard or tackle in a disaster."

Then he chatted with Aikman and Irvin and with mega-guard Nate Newton, the 330-pounder, and with a couple of assistant coaches, and then he just watched for a while. Back at the complex, he announced the lineup changes to the press—Harper for Alexander Wright, Maryland for Jones, Williams for Tuinei. Johnson knew he had to be careful talking about the moves, especially the benching of Wright (since traded to the Raiders). Wright's a sensitive guy. The Cowboys drafted him as a long-term project out of Clemson in 1990 because he had the best speed of any receiver coming out of college football in recent years. In fact, when the Cowboys ran forty-yard sprints on an electronically timed track in 1991 mini-camp, Wright had the fastest time in Dallas history, and perhaps in recorded NFL history, running the forty in 4.07 seconds. The man generally considered the fastest player in the NFL, Washington cornerback Darrell Green, runs about a 4.25 forty. But Wright was not a disciplined route-runner, and the quarterbacks didn't have faith in him to get open consistently, despite his speed. He needed more practice.

Johnson went to receivers coach Ax Alexander after practice to see how Wright was taking the demotion. "If he goes into the tank, I've got something to deal with," Johnson said. Alexander thought Wright was okay. Johnson told the press, "There's been a lot expected out of Alexander Wright, too much too soon, I think. Let me tell you, he's come a million miles in the last year, and I think he's going to improve even more. We'd like for his progress to be at a faster pace, but in no way have we lost sight of the fact that he's a player with great promise for our future."

Blah, blah, blah. Johnson didn't really know if he felt this way anymore about a player for whom he had truly stuck his neck out. But he knew he had to say it. He had to make Wright believe that he believed he was the same hot prospect the Cowboys plucked out of Clemson eighteen months earlier. This, of course, was the danger with every player the Cowboys' coaches and scouts fell in love with every spring, fanning out across America to scout the best the colleges had to offer. Now Wright was demoted, and Jimmie Jones pushed aside, and Tuinei was down.

On Thursday, the first thing Johnson did in the office at about 7:00 A.M. was to listen to what Phoenix coach Joe Bugel said on the previous day's conference call with the Dallas writers. Johnson heard everything, and he read everything—or so he'd have you believe. He picked up this little habit one year at Miami. Before playing Florida State to open a season, he arranged to get a tape of Seminole coach Bobby Bowden's coach's show. Deion Sanders and some FSU players recorded a rap song talking about how great they were, and there were some negative comments about Miami on the show. Johnson showed his players. His players got mad and then beat Florida State. Did the show help? Who knows? But they won, and Johnson had a new tool.

"And you use every tool, no matter how insignificant it might seem, to get an edge," he said. "Even if you're not sure you can get an edge using it."

Bugel's conference call was such a tool. Bugel said two things that pricked Johnson's ears.

"He called Randal Hill 'the young kid,' " Johnson said, referring to the rookie Card wide receiver. "If I'm a coach, and I'm talking about a 'young kid,' I'm not thinking of him as a starter. So I'm assuming that, although Phoenix hasn't said who's starting at wide receiver, Hill probably won't start and won't be much more than a third receiver and not featured much in the game."

He turned out to be right.

What else?

"Well," Johnson said, "he gave me a feel of their defensive approach to the game, I think. He talked about having to play a good, solid fundamental defense to have a chance to beat us. Now, I hear that and I think he's either just not saying anything to the writers and doesn't want to give anything away, or he's telling them they're going to play a conservative game. I believe he's telling us not to expect a lot of blitzing."

That turned out to be right, too.

"Hey, I'll cover every base there is. It's my job. Will any of this help us win? I don't know. All I know is that I have to go into a game knowing I've done everything possible to help us win."

He ducked into a few coaching offices, and then, about 9:40, trainer Kevin O'Neill ducked into his. The results on weakened linebacker Vinson Smith's blood work were in, O'Neill told him. Smith had hepatitis. For about three seconds, Johnson was angry. For a second, he felt a tinge of sadness for Smith. Then he marched over to Wannstedt's office. "Smith's got hepatitis," he told Wannstedt. "Get Dixon Edwards ready. He's starting."

He pulled Smith out of a linebackers' meeting and broke the news to him. He was careful to tell Smith that his life wasn't in danger, that hepatitis was very curable, that he'd been put on injured reserve for four weeks, and he should be able to come back to play in a month—and that he'd get his job back when he returned. "Hey, it's no different from somebody spraining an ankle," Johnson told him. "It's nothing serious." Reassured, Smith left the team immediately. And Johnson started lining up hepatitis shots for the players with O'Neill.

At 10:40, he had to tape his Sunday morning radio show with Cowboys play-by-play voice Brad Sham, in a radio studio at the Cowboys complex. He had to tell Sham about Smith off the record; he'd announce it to the press after practice. But Sham needed to know, because they'd be taping a show to be heard just before Sunday's game, so obviously Sham needed to mention Smith's absence along with the other lineup changes.

"It's time some of the rookies started stepping up anyway," Johnson said when the red light went on. "Now we're going to find out about a few of them."

After the taping, Sham and Johnson talked for ten minutes about some inside stuff. Sham told him he thought he knew what the Cowboys would do in the draft six months hence, and Johnson warmed to the topic. "Next year, we'll have fifteen picks," Johnson told Sham. "Betcha right now seven will be defensive backs. Betcha this too: Of our top six picks, two will be offensive linemen and four will be DBs."

(Dallas did have fifteen picks on draft day 1992; they took seven defensive backs—five safeties and two cornerbacks. Of the top eight picks, two were offensive linemen and four were defensive backs. Johnson's prediction might have been perfect if two things happened differently: One, the Cowboys lost free agent middle linebackers Jack Del Rio and Darrick Brownlow in Plan B free agency after the season, forcing middle linebacker to be a high priority in the draft; they picked East Carolina linebacker Robert Jones in the first round. Two, they missed out on safety Darryl Williams from the University of Miami by eight picks and thus chose wide receiver Jimmy Smith in the second round instead of Williams.)

Why'd he give Brad Sham so much? That was a pretty good gut-spilling—or so it seemed. But think like a coach for a minute. You want your players to be playing in a positive environment. You want to foster a sense of team, not a sense of self-ishness. And so you want the media on your side, because if the media's on your side, they're writing and talking—for the most part—the way you'd hope they would write and talk, and the players are reading in the papers and hearing on the radio just what you're telling them. You can promote this sense of team, or for that matter, you can get most any message out that you want. (This also is a way of showing your power to the players. If you tell them, "Now this is what you'll be reading in the papers this week . . ." and then it comes true, they'll know what a powerful guy they're dealing with in the locker room.) One of the ways you get the media on your side is to tell the trusted ones a few trade secrets off the record, knowing they won't spill the beans to anyone else or their pipeline will dry up. Plus, knowledge is power. Giving newsy nuggets to the select few in the media allows them to sound very authoritative, very in-the-know. If a talk-show caller calls Brad Sham and says, "Brad, what do you look for the Cowboys to do in the draft next year?" Sham can be ready.

"They'll go heavy on defensive backs early, and then fill a couple of holes on the offensive line, I think," Sham can say, without giving away his little secret. "The Cowboys know it'll be a good draft for defensive backs, and anyone who looks at their secondary right now knows they need big-time help back there. They might go for—heck, I don't know—three or four DBs on the first day of the draft."

And Sham can say the same kind of thing to his 104-station Cowboys Radio Network during the season. If the Dallas secondary is getting burned some Sunday late in the season, Sham can say on the air, "Well, the Cowboys won't have to wait long to address that need. They've got fifteen picks in the draft, thanks to the Herschel Walker trade, and there's little doubt they'll be going for major secondary help early in the draft next April . . ." And so the folks in Alpine and Eagle Pass and Texarkana and Big Spring and Sweetwater who turn down the TV sound and listen to the Cowboys on radio can start to build their expectations about better pass coverage, and then, when the draft comes and the Cowboys fulfill the promise and take four defensive backs in the first five rounds, they can sit back on the porch and say, "Boy, those Cowboys had a helluva draft, didn't they?"

Positive, positive, positive. Team, team, team.

It's like this all over the league. Not often to this extent, though. Why does Sam Wyche seem to be such a likeable guy? Well, for one thing, he is a likeable guy. But he'll occasionally take the newspaper beat guys aside and tell them his first offensive play-call of the next game. And, more than that, he'll take the network TV crew incredibly into his confidence. He'll tell them what plays to look for right off the bat, and he helps the producer by telling him graphically which players will play in certain formations and which players are likely to be featured so the crew can isolate cameras on certain players and get some story angles ready as the game proceeds. In exchange, TV people treat Wyche well. When he does something wacky, they don't make much fun of him—at least compared to the newspaper guys.

After practice, Johnson dressed in a suit to tape his TV show at a station downtown. He should have put his fireman's suit on. There was one more little brushfire to put out, it turned out.

As Johnson walked from the coaches' locker room back past the players' locker room, he had to pass the offices where assistant coaches show tapes and meet with their players daily. The minute he walked past Tony Wise's office, his face turned from bright and cheerful to somber. He stopped fixing the left cuff on his pressed white shirt, and he stopped bounding past the locker room. He stopped, period.

"FUCK . . . DUMB SON OF A BITCH . . . SICK OF THIS FUCKIN' SHIT!" were some of the intelligible words floating out of Wise's office, through a thick metal door.

Johnson immediately turned toward the fire. Some of the players got up on their chairs and tried to peer over the lockers to see what the fuss was all about. "Oh good! A fight!" Michael Irvin chuckled.

Johnson walked into the room.

"Jimmy, I can handle this!" Wise yelled.

"Settle down, settle down!" Johnson said, closing the door,

and from there it was muffled for fifteen or twenty minutes.

When the door opened up, lineman Mark Stepnoski emerged, sullenly. He wouldn't talk to anyone. Nor would Wise, nor Johnson. The players were dying to find out what happened. For now, no one would know.

Already today, Johnson had studied the words of an opposing coach to get an edge. He parried with the play-by-play guy to gain an edge for the future. He shattered a kid's dreams with the hepatitis news and tried to make the kid feel good about it. He ran practice. He was positive with the press about his four rookies starting in an important game Sunday, hoping the media would paint the picture for this game as an opportunity for youth, not as a panic situation. He stepped into his mediation costume and stopped a fight or some conflagration like that between his starting center and line coach. And now, looking all Paul Mitchell-freeze-and-spray-shined, was on the set of his TV show, happy-talking with host Ted Dawson.

Later, he had a dinner of nachos and salsa with his girlfriend, Rhonda, and talked about his day.

"The Stepnoski thing, I definitely wanted to handle it," he said, without being specific. The players said the next day that Stepnoski was pissed off about being criticized for being a lousy practice player sometimes, and for being an unwilling special-teams player. "You don't shy away from confrontations in this job, or the players will walk all over you. He could bully his way with Tony a little bit because Tony loves all his guys so much. I'm the one who needed to confront the issue."

"Do you enjoy it?" he was asked.

"I do. I enjoy the confrontation, because I enjoy solving problems, in whatever form they come. I want to jump in, because I want to be in control. I want to be in control because I want to win, and in order to win, you've got to have a guy solidly in control of the team. That's the one thing about the NFL you've got to realize. I may be an asshole. People may hate me. Some of my players may hate my guts. But either way, I'll be in control. And we will win. The players understand that, and that's the main thing.

"Like today, I have to deal very closely with two players. I've got to be kind of fatherly with Vinson Smith. But he knows I'll bring him back to play, because he knows all I care about is winning, and he knows he can help us win. Same with Stepnoski. I've got to be stern with him, but he knows I'll be the guy around here to take responsibility."

Johnson's an interesting person in private, like here at the On The Border Cantina, munching nachos. He won't throw meaningless and insincere praise on coaches or teams, like he has to do on Sundays and during the week. He'll stare through you and tell you what's up, for the most part.

"I'm a selfish person, very selfish," he said. "But I admit it. People know who I am. I have to do this to satisfy myself. I wouldn't be happy doing anything else, and I have to do it my way, all the way. Sometimes it hits me. I'll say to myself, 'Why am I like this? Why am I not doing a normal job and going home to the wife and kids every night for dinner at six?' I don't know exactly why. I do know this: I have to do it. Deep down, I know it, and I know I'd be bad at living any other way, because my heart would be into this. Fortunately, my two sons understand me.

"Winning has become so important to me, obviously in this business. And over the years you program yourself to do whatever it takes to win. I don't say, 'I've got to break the news to Vinson Smith, damn,' or 'I've got to be careful talking to the Phoenix media.' You always remember where you are, who you're with, and what you should be doing, and you always remember you're trying to get your team in the best position possible to win. One of the reasons I got the divorce is I didn't want to have to go to the cocktail parties and the social events you go to as a coach. Everything I do now—I mean, everything—winning has to come first."

These are the kinds of days in which a head coach wins or loses games. On Sunday, Wannstedt will make all the defensive play calls, and Turner will pretty much decide what runs and passes to call, with some unspecific input from Johnson. At halftime, Johnson often lets the coordinators talk the entire nine or ten minutes in the locker room. He's not alone; the head coach's job throughout the league is most often done by Thursday or Friday. He can have major input on Sunday if he wants, but many don't choose to take it. They've put the plans in place, and now it's up to the players to carry out the plans. But that doesn't stop the networks from wasting a camera following the head coach's every move. On Sunday, the head coach is a supporting actor. The real stars are the coordinators and the players.

Friday and Saturday are dress-rehearsal days. Johnson had the CBS crew doing Sunday's game, Dan Fouts and Verne Lundquist, in his office for a very official visit Saturday. Fouts is good, and he tried to pry some stuff out of Johnson. Nothing doing.

Fouts: "They handled Novacek pretty well last time."

Johnson: "Well . . ."

He pauses to think about how unspecifically he can put the answer.

Johnson: ". . . we've got a few things planned . . ."

Pause.

Johnson: "We'll use some three-tight-end stuff with Rob Awalt and Alfredo Roberts . . ."

Fouts: "How much?"

Johnson: "Some."

Strange how he pours his guts out to Sham and he treats Fouts, a future Hall-of-Famer, like he'd treat a social visit from Joe Bugel right about then. Always remember where you are; that's what Johnson had said two nights before. He didn't want Fouts spilling something on TV that some future opponent could hear and learn from.

After the CBS session, Johnson puts the team through its weekly walk-through practice, a twenty-minute quickie just to get the guys limbered up and remembering their assignments for the game. Then he goes home to his modest bachelor pad, a new home two miles from the Cowboys' complex in the middle of suburban Dallas Yuppieville.

He loves Saturday afternoons before home games. Johnson puts some chili on the stove, eats chili and chips, and holds the remote for the forty-nine-inch screen connected to his satellite dish. He sits there for four hours, vegging out. Kids go zombielike watching *Mister Ed* and *Gilligan's Island* reruns on Nickelodeon; Johnson goes trancelike on this day, switching between

Michigan–Purdue ("They're giving Desmond Howard that interference call? Oh, puhleeze!") and Texas–Texas Tech, and paus-
ing for snippets of Columbia–Princeton, Cornell–Brown, North
Carolina–Maryland, Youngstown State–Georgia Southern, West
Virginia–Rutgers, and BC–Pitt.

And what's this?

"Looks like the New Hampshire Democratic Party Conven-
tion," Johnson said, proud of the fact that he could figure that
out.

Can't have reality interrupting Saturday at Johnson's College
Football Central.

And what's this?

Johnson found the live feed of Florida State quarterback
Casey Weldon waiting to be interviewed at halftime of the
Michigan game from his hotel in Louisville, where the Semi-
noles would play that night. Weldon sat in front of a camera, not
on live TV, but just waiting to be interviewed. It's like Johnson
had a one-way mirror and could watch Weldon for ten minutes
and maybe get some clues about him. Now, the Cowboys
weren't in the market for a quarterback, but you never know
what you might learn about a kid that might be useful someday.

He paused, slouched way down in his couch.

"Let's watch him," Johnson said. "Let's see what kind of kid
he is."

And so we watched. Weldon commented on the last couple of
minutes before the half, calmly dissecting a few plays. Johnson
liked him. "He's a thoughtful kid," Johnson said. "Hell, we
don't need a quarterback, but at least I have a feel for the kid
that I didn't have before."

On to Alabama–Mississippi State, and the Texas game, and Oklahoma State–Iowa, and Auburn–Florida, and Marshall–Somebody.

And what's this?

Montana–Montana State. It's snowing in Missoula. The
field's half-white, and Johnson is clucking.

"Great!" he said. "Now this is football."

On and on it goes.

• • •

Dallas won the game with Phoenix, 27-7, rebounding from a sluggish first half to dominate the Cardinals and their woeful offense in the second half. Except for Williams, who almost got Aikman killed by allowing three first-half sacks, the rookies did nicely. Harper caught three balls for sixty-seven yards, Maryland batted down a pass at the line and clogged the middle effectively in the second half, and Edwards was all over the field. Dallas had no sacks, which might indicate the blitzes didn't work out well. But Card quarterback Tom Tupa threw for just eighty-nine yards and spent most of the day running from someone.

At halftime, Wannstedt and Turner yelled mightily at their players, broken up by unit into halves of the locker room. Johnson stayed out of it. "We're not playing physical football!" Wannstedt said, lighting into his guys. "We're not playing WORTH A SHIT!" Johnson looked on, inwardly happy. Wannstedt was Jimmy Junior, and in the second half the players responded.

Afterward, Johnson and his staff, and their families, and his sons, met for a few cold ones in a Texas Stadium lounge, the last relaxing evening before preparing for the next game, against Houston. "You've just seen an extremely typical week in the life of a coach," he tells me, and then he spots Wannstedt.

Johnson put his arm around Wannstedt.

"Well, that's a one-week reprieve from Death Row," Johnson said. "Lose and the warden turns the juice on you. You're dead. You're fired. If you win, the governor yells, 'You got one more week!' Your head's shaved, you've had the last meal, and you're ready to die, but you're saved to coach one more week."

Everybody laughed, because it was a good speech. But this is how Jimmy Johnson feels. You cross him, you pose any threat to him winning, you crush his dream? "I'll crush you like a squirrel in the road," he said. "People don't realize what they're dealing with here. This is my life. A lot of people might say, 'This is a bunch of bullshit, the life you're leading.' Hey, I'm not typical. This is what I am. Fortunately my boys understand. Chad understands. Brent understands. If they didn't, I couldn't handle it. I'd spin out. If they said to me, 'This is bullshit, Dad! Why don't you ever have time for me? Why don't we have a real father?' I couldn't handle it. But they understand that nobody's going to throw a brick in my way, and if anybody tries to, I'll kick their ass."

I mentioned to him how he must feel bad for poor Ricky Blake. Blake, a backup running back, was helping the Cowboys run out the clock on the last play of the game when, in a freak accident, he sheared the leg bone from his hip socket, ending his season and possibly endangering his career. Bad enough for the team, but they'd probably also have to use a valuable roster move to bring rookie Curvin Richards onto the roster unless they wanted to risk putting him on waivers and exposing him to the league. But Ricky. Poor Ricky. Hard worker, great kid, really wanted to play in the NFL. Tough break.

"Well," Johnson said, shooting right back, and here came the truth, "as bad as it is for Ricky, all I'm thinking about is: Can I get Curvin through waivers without losing him? And how are we gonna beat Houston?"

He saw the look of disbelief in his questioner's eyes. Some kid is downstairs lying in the trainer's room or on his way to the hospital right now, his career may be over, and this guy, his coach, can't spare a few minutes of melancholy for what might have been.

"Hey, the crisis is not the issue. The issue is how you handle the crisis. Is feeling sorry for Ricky gonna help us win? No. And remember something: My whole life revolves around us winning."

Understood.

Index

Index

Index

Index

237

Index

Index

Index

DATE		
AUG 0 1 1995		
OCT 0 9 1996		
10/20/97		

DATE DUE		
DEC 1 1 1997		

GAYLORD No. 2333   PRINTED IN U.S.A.

BAKER & TAYLOR BOOKS